TOLLESHUNT KNIGHTS
Salcott
Tolleshunt D'Arcy
Tolleshunt Major
Tollesbury
Goldhanger
Goldhanger Creek
Osea Island
RIVER BLACKWATER
Bradwell Waterside
Bradwell-on-Sea
St Lawrence Bay
Bradwell Marshes
Tillingham
Tillingham Marshes
Steeple
Maylandsea
Lower Mayland
Asheldham
Dengie
Dengie Marshes
Southminster
Althorne
ALTHORNE STA
BURNHAM-ON-CROUCH
RIVER CROUCH
Canewdon
Paglesham
Wallasea Island
Churchend
FOULNESS ISLAND

My life is here, where soon the larks
will sing again, and there is a hawk above.

J. A. BAKER, *The Hill of Summer*

PUBLISHED BY LITTLE TOLLER BOOKS in 2017
Lower Dairy, Toller Fratrum, Dorset

Typeset by Little Toller Books

Printed in England by TJ International, Cornwall, Padstow

All papers used by Little Toller Books are natural, recyclable products made from wood grown in sustainable, well-managed forests

A catalogue record for this book is available from the British Library

ISBN 978-1-908213-49-5

MY HOUSE OF SKY

The life and work of J. A. Baker

HETTY SAUNDERS

LITTLE TOLLER BOOKS

CONTENTS

J. A. Baker photographed by Doreen Coe in the 1950s.

Robert Macfarlane
FOREWORD

'I looked into the wood', wrote J. A. Baker in a journal entry. 'In a lair of shadow the peregrine was crouching, watching me.' For decades, Baker occupied his own 'lair of shadow': a private man who lived a largely unreported life. That shadow was cast in part by his disinterest in celebrity as conventionally understood, even after the success of *The Peregrine*. It was cast also by the fierce light of his style, which possesses – as one of Baker's earliest and best reviewers, Kenneth Allsop, put it – a 'magnesium-flare' intensity. When I first read *The Peregrine* as a teenager it did not occur to me to wish to know anything of its author, for the prose itself was so forceful that it fully exhausted my attention.

But as Baker's work has lived on – it is fifty years this year since *The Peregrine*'s publication – so an interest has built among its hundreds of thousands of readers as to the life of its maker. Like many of those readers I cannot imagine being innocent of *The Peregrine*. It has shaped my writing, walking, teaching and dreaming for twenty years now. Baker's prose reaches into the body as well as the mind. I hear *The Peregrine* as crack of ice and Geiger clicks, billhook blade-thuds, signal and chatter, the mew of raptor. I see it as blast-walls, silver light on metal casings, landscape X-ray, mudflat and a swarm of golden beetles. I feel it as a cold east wind brittling my bones, a mask of green ice pressed hard to the face. And I wonder: who was the man who could write a work of such visionary power and such suppressed violence? What does it cost a person to compress a book of this condensed energy?

My House of Sky is Baker's first book-length biography, and it will be his last. There is no need for another. Hetty Saunders has written a superb, subtle account of his life and work. This is a book distinguished not only by the calm clarity of its prose and the quiet cleverness with which it tells its story, but also by its tact. As a biographer, Hetty has practised a kind of careful tracing, a building-up of a picture of Baker's behaviour from the marks he has left behind. In this respect, of course, Hetty's method echoes Baker's own pursuit of the peregrines. Confronted with the mystery of their wildness, Baker learned to deduce aspects of their existence from displaced signs of their presence: bloodied corpses found in wood and saltmarsh, or the way a falcon sets prey-species moving long before it comes into human sight. Confronted with the mystery of Baker's life, Hetty learned to deduce aspects of his existence from displaced signs of his presence: letters in the archive, jottings in the margins of books, torn-out journal pages, scribbled codes on maps.

The frontispiece of *My House of Sky* is a startling image by the artist Jo Sweeting. As with Wittgenstein's duck-rabbit, so with Jo's falcon-man. The image flickers unstably between its poles – collapses the space that divides them. Baker and peregrine inhabit one another, blown through by the same wind that bends the trees. It is clear here, as throughout, that this is a special book, beautifully published: committed to honouring the strangeness of Baker's vision and the force of his achievement. It carries an important afterword by John Fanshawe, who has done so much work over the years gathering and making available the documents that comprise the archive.

That archive itself is also present in photographs of Baker's maps, optics, proofs and manuscripts, taken by Christopher Matthews. And at the book's heart is Hetty's biography: a brilliant work of tracking and of seeing. Hetty has 'looked into the wood' of Baker's world, and lit up his 'lair of shadow' to just the extent that it needs illuminating.

Robert Macfarlane
CAMBRIDGE, SEPTEMBER, 2017

ROBERT MACFARLANE is the author of a number of award-winning and bestselling books about landscape and nature, including *The Wild Places*, *The Old Ways* and *Landmarks*. His work has been widely adapted for film and television, and translated into many languages. He is a Fellow of Emmanuel College, Cambridge.

The photograph of a peregrine falcon by Frank Lane featured on the cover of The Peregrine *first edition, placed on the inside flap, where you might expect the author's portrait to be.*

Chapter One
THE MYSTERY OF J. A. BAKER

> But who knows the fate of his bones, or how often
> he is to be buried?
>
> SIR THOMAS BROWNE, *Hydriotaphia, Urn Burial* (1658)

ON A SPRING MORNING in 1945, John Alec Baker and his friend Ted Dennis set out on a walk from their home town of Chelmsford. The young men were aiming for Danbury village, which was then a cluster of small shops and red-tiled houses around a church with a spire like an upturned golf tee. From Danbury - perched on its hill overlooking the wide, flat Essex coast – could be seen what Baker thought of then as 'the loveliest country of all'.

The day was fine. A strong wind blew behind them from the west, where showers had washed clean the orchards and stands of elm, and, more distantly, the glittering factory windows of Chelmsford. That glitter was matched to the east as the land drew down to the silty waters of the Blackwater Estuary, populated with rusty-sailed barges, cockleboats and wide saltings veined by creeks and eelgrass. The Estuary itself wound out beyond the horizon, leaving the reach of the hog's-rump bulge of land that makes up the witch-astride-a-pig shape of mainland Britain, to join the steel line of the North Sea, all that lies between East Anglia and the Low Countries.

The pair walked along in good spirits, enjoying both the freshness of the new season and the pleasure of each other's company. Baker and Dennis had known each other as boys at the local grammar school, and now, aged almost nineteen, were making their first forays into adulthood. Dennis was on leave from his National Service army training; Baker (disqualified from the Armed Forces because of poor health) was living with his parents and working for a local packaging manufacturer. A year earlier, Baker had been bedridden by a bout of painful illness – what would turn out to be the onset of ankylosing spondylitis, a chronic arthritic disease that inflamed his joints and laid him low for weeks at a time. A period of rehabilitation had followed, during which his friends had graduated from the sixth form and received their call-up papers. Baker had taken up employment instead; but the work bored him to tears and he soon felt stifled and miserable, emotions exacerbated by a sometimes melancholic disposition. The company of his friend Dennis was a welcome relief.

Something happened, though, as Baker would later recount, to mar the day's enjoyment. The two men were cutting through a wood when they found a rabbit caught in a poacher's snare. The creature was still alive and began kicking frantically in its struggle to escape. Taking pity on it, Dennis held it in his arms while Baker tried to untangle its legs from the snare. But it was no good. They couldn't undo the mess of wire, and Dennis, trying to keep the frantic rabbit still, said to Baker that the kindest thing would be to strangle it. Later in a letter, Baker wrote of watching the creature's terrified reaction:

> A rabbit struggles unremittingly in the snare with an energy born of desperation and, I should imagine is affected by a similar sensation at being so pinioned as humans suffering from claustrophobia would experience when locked in a cupboard. When taken up by Dennis the rabbit commenced to writhe agitatedly but as soon as the hand touched the neck it seemed that the wretched creature resigned itself to death and was paralysed by fear of that event. Its eyes were bolting and abnormally bright and so poignant in their utter terror that I could not watch the deed and turned away.

The death of a rabbit would have seemed inconsequential to most people in 1945 compared to the losses of human life in wartime. Baker, however, was beginning to understand that his experience

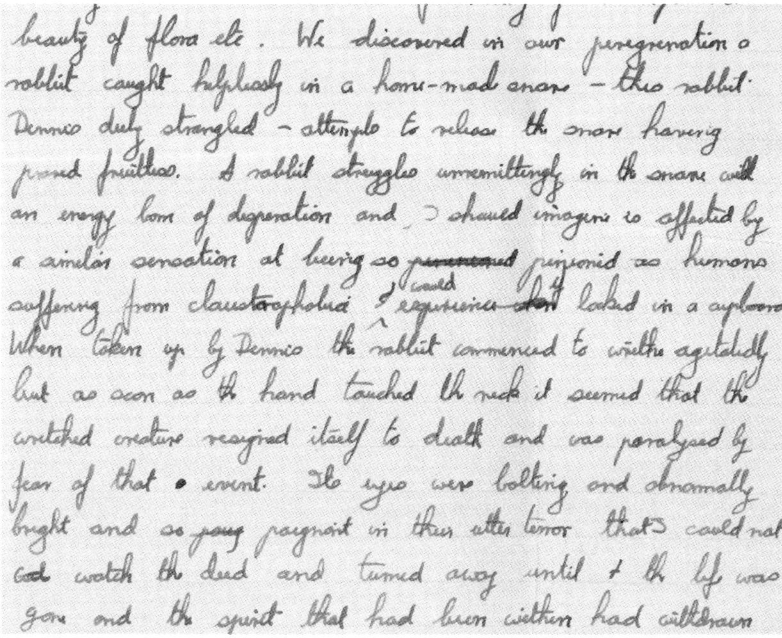
beauty of flora etc. We discovered in our peregrination a
rabbit caught helplessly in a home-made snare – this rabbit
Dennis duly strangled – attempts to release the snare having
proved fruitless. A rabbit struggles unremittingly in the snare with
an energy born of desperation and I should imagine is affected by
a similar sensation at being so ~~pinned~~ pinioned as humans
suffering from claustrophobia would experience ~~when~~ if locked in a cupboard
When taken up by Dennis the rabbit commenced to writhe agitatedly
but as soon as the hand touched the neck it seemed that the
wretched creature resigned itself to death and was paralysed by
fear of that event. Its eyes were bulging and abnormally
bright and so ~~poig~~ poignant in their utter terror that I could not
~~could~~ watch the deed and turned away until the life was
gone and the spirit that had been within had withdrawn

Detail of the letter to John Thurmer from J. A. Baker in 1945, recalling the walk with Ted Dennis and the encounter with a snared rabbit.

of the world was not like other people's. The skill of the writer rests in his power to reveal that which the rest of us cannot or will not see, and Baker's ability to do this, particularly when it came to understanding the lives of non-human animals, would make him one of the most influential nature writers of the twentieth century.

In 1967, twenty-two years after this encounter in Danbury woods, Baker would publish the work for which he is now best known: *The Peregrine*. This book, a journal written in vivid, poetic prose, records a single winter during which its narrator tracks migrant peregrine falcons along a desolate section of the East Anglian coast. He follows one bird in particular, a tiercel (the male of the species) a year or two old, and between them there begins to grow a sort of bond. When he was writing *The Peregrine* in the early 1960s, Baker came face-to-face once again with wild animals threatened by humans; though, due to the ravaging effects of the myxomatosis virus and toxic levels of organochlorine pesticides, animals faced more horrible ends than a poacher's snare. By the time he came to write *The Peregrine*, Baker was older and less squeamish about the realities of death than he had been in Danbury woods. And he was angrier: 'No pain,' he wrote, 'no death, is more terrible to a wild creature than its fear of man.'

Now, fifty years on from the first publication of *The Peregrine*, Baker's vision of what he called 'the bloodiness of killing' remains troubling. This bloodiness belonged, Baker reminded the reader, not just to the peregrine falcon, a bird vilified by one gamekeeper as 'a meaningless murderer, shedding blood from mere wantonness,' but to his human persecutors as well. 'Man,' Baker wrote, 'is in no way superior.' Today this rings true more than ever as ecologists report that we are entering into the planet's sixth mass extinction period. As we learn more about our role in this time of the Anthropocene, it's hard to ignore the fact that Baker's insistent warning in *The Peregrine* remains relevant: 'we are the killers. We stink of death. We carry it with us. It sticks to us like frost. We cannot tear it away.'

If anything, fifty years has served to emphasise Baker's prescience of thought on the topic of ecological crisis. Nowadays his book is used in schools and university campuses to teach students about the beginnings of the modern environmental movement, but it was in many ways ahead of its time: in an early draft of *The Peregrine,* Baker wrote that 'science can never be enough; emotion and sentiment will always rule.' I have yet to read a better summation of the strength and weakness of the environmental movement, both today and historically.

Baker's writing might seem to be specific to the environmental concerns of his lifetime: the use of hydrogen bombs at the end of the Second World War and the Cold War terror of nuclear apocalypse that followed, are expressed in his descriptions of sunlight bright as a 'magnesium flare', or birds that are 'withered and burnt away' by the 'pollen' of agricultural chemicals. But there's much in *The Peregrine* that sets it apart from the years in which it was written. It's not a typical 'green' book, emerging from the hippie counterculture of the 1960s, and Baker doesn't seem to have been a typical 'green' writer.

Until recently it has been hard to imagine what sort of person Baker was at all. He was always the observer and never the observed in his own writing. He gave little away about the personal details of his life. For much of *The Peregrine*'s publication history its author has remained as enigmatic as the birds in its pages.

Perhaps, then, it's not surprising that the obsessiveness with which Baker hunted down his falcons has been passed onto his readers. Many have become as obsessive in their following of the cult of Baker. His work has influenced some of our best-known contemporary chroniclers of nature in film, literature and natural history. *The Peregrine* in particular has been cited as an inspiration by the naturalists Chris Packham and Simon King, as well as writers like Mark Cocker, Tim Dee and Helen Macdonald. It's hard to read any account of birds of prey from recent years that doesn't hold within it glimmers of Baker's own adamantine style, so recognisable, breaking now and then through the prose like flints in a ploughed field. Werner Herzog, the award-winning German film director, admires Baker's work so much that he encourages his students to 'learn it, learn the whole book by heart.' There's something about *The Peregrine* that has made its readers respond as if the words were a source of mysterious power. Reading the book, Herzog said, is like reading an account of a religious experience – but religion of an ancient stripe, full of incantation, blood and bone – 'the kind that you find in the writing of late medieval mystics.'

Baker received sheaves of letters from fans of *The Peregrine*. One admirer, writing in December 1983, told Baker that he was planning a walking trip to Maldon, on the Blackwater Estuary. 'Maybe your peregrine might appear', he wrote, as if Baker could draw one down from the sky, like a shaman's familiar, despite the fact that 'his' peregrines, seen in the fifties and sixties, would have been long dead. Another wrote to say that, although he wasn't 'by nature' one for writing to authors, Baker's book had 'so filled [his] mind' that he should 'have no peace' until he had done so. Early reviews of the *The Peregrine* also remarked on the magical relationship that Baker had with the birds he followed, saying it was as if he could conjure the falcon at will, as those who wrote letters to him wished.

An event early on in the writing of this biography brought home to me the uncanny connection that seems to persist between Baker and 'his' peregrines. I had spent a morning in Cambridge with conservationist John Fanshawe and the author Robert Macfarlane. J. A. Baker was the focus of our meeting, or more specifically, the collection of papers, letters and objects that John had gathered after the death of Baker's wife Doreen. This archive had been donated to the University of Essex, where I had been working on a catalogue of the material. Our meeting that day had been to discuss how to reconstruct the story of Baker's life using the archive. We wanted to answer the question of how it was that this most mysterious of authors had come to write something as monumental as *The Peregrine*, a work that has been called 'the gold standard for all nature writing.' Despite the book's success – it won Baker several prizes – very little was known about how he came to write it. John, Robert and I hoped that the treasures contained in the archive could help change that.

Our talk of Baker naturally led to talk of falcons. John mentioned that the city's nesting pair of peregrines, absent until recently, had been spotted that morning returning to breed, an event that had sent Cambridge's resident birders scrambling for their binoculars. We joked about how uncannily serendipitous it was that the peregrines' reappearance should coincide with our discussions on Baker. It felt fitting that birds that Baker had followed for more than forty years should be in such close proximity, among the spires of the city's skyline.

They were, in fact, far closer than we thought. For as we left, Robert found, not much more than thirty yards away from the café in which we had been sitting, visceral evidence of their presence: a white dove beside the road, headless, wings opened sacrificially either side of its gored breast, and with its entrails bared to any passing haruspex's eye. It lay stark as paint on the wet pavement.

I had never seen a kill made by a peregrine. I had, however, read and re-read Baker's descriptions of them many times, so the sight of the dove came with a strange jolt of recognition. Fifty years ago, not so far away in the Essex saltings, Baker had found a feathery body, the 'wings, breast-bone, legs and pelvis [that] lay at the centre of a widely scattered circle of blowing feathers', 'raw bones [that] stood to the sky, like the ribs of a wrecked ship.' It was as if J. A. Baker's ghost had left us his bloody blessing.

Even before his death, Baker had all the makings of a successful ghost. His has been a figure like the birds he wrote about: fleeting, hard to make out, always disappearing into the distance.

If there's one thing that the enthusiastic amateur naturalist cannot resist, it's the challenge of a rare or elusive species – and sightings of Baker have been as rare and elusive as they come. The nature writer Mark Cocker, watching a vast mass of crows heading to roost at dusk, remarked that 'matters are at their most compelling at the point when they're virtually invisible.' The harder things are to make out, the more interesting they become; much the same could be said about writers.

Most of what has been known about Baker comes from his two published books: *The Peregrine*, and the less recognised *Hill of Summer*, published two years later in 1969. During the story of *The Peregrine* the writer grows more hawk-like: he avoids other human beings, never speaks aloud, and haunts the same paths and fields, hunting for the tiercel. The town where he comes from and returns to each day isn't named, nor is it clear who he is or why he began his quest. His own strangeness is part of the book's otherworldly feel – the author's own revenant-like state becomes a mirror for a species that was facing chemical extinction. The figure of the writer in *The Hill of Summer* is similarly indistinct.

Thus, since *The Peregrine* first appeared in print, the life of its writer has been the subject of rumour. The book received rave reviews, and, when it won the 1967 Duff Cooper Memorial Prize and *Yorkshire Post*'s Book of the Year, readers clamoured to know more about its author. Reviewers speculated on his occupation: he was a clerk, librarian, a groundskeeper – or he was none of those, and lived on the dole? Journalists caught the scent of a good mystery. They dubbed him 'the man who thinks like a hawk' and hailed his book as a visionary masterpiece, quite probably a work of genius.

The acid test for genius, as everyone knows, is eccentricity. As far as the papers could find out, this oddball author – one of the new, angry tribe of environmentalists, a man who spent his spare time crawling around in marshes seeking transformative encounters with a grey-brown bird not much bigger than a chicken – was the real deal. Baker was a recluse, the reviewers claimed. *The Sunday Times* ran the only column on *The Peregrine* that offered any clues as to its author, and even these were just tantalising hints about the man whose peregrine 'obsession had taken over his life':

> John Baker is forty and lives in a council flat in Essex. He doesn't want it known which town. He doesn't want his neighbours to know what he does. He hasn't got a TV or a phone. He never goes anywhere socially and the last time he went out to be entertained was twelve years ago when he went to the pictures to see *Shane* … As he's at home all day now, his neighbours are even more puzzled about him. "They probably think I'm a burglar, but I don't care."

This curious information (or lack of it) came presumably from Baker himself; though, as he had a dry sense of humour, it's hard to know how much of it was true. After getting to know him through the private writings and other odds and ends that he left behind, I suspect that, as well as being guarded by nature, Baker was amused by the image of himself that he could create – the solitary writer removed by choice from society.

Over the rest of his lifetime little more information was

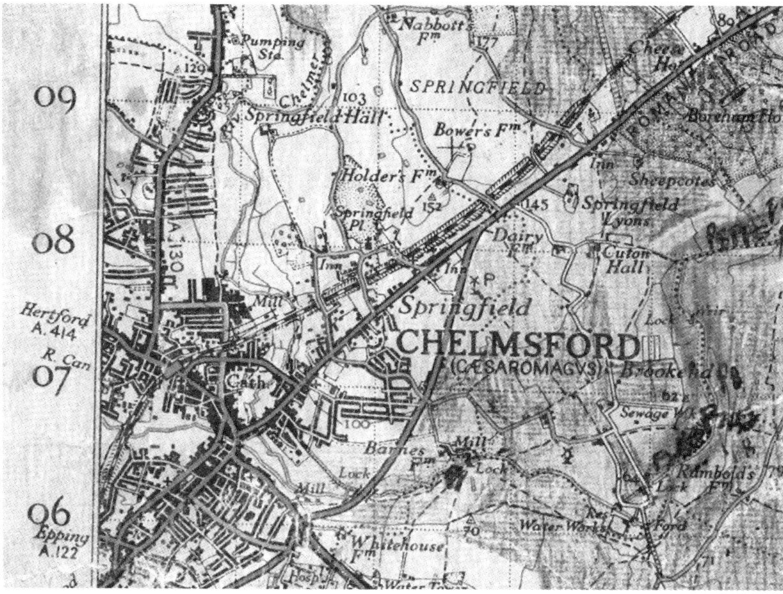

Detail from one of Baker's many Ordnance Survey maps, this one a stained and well-thumbed copy of 'Southend-on-Sea: Sheet 162.' Baker used coloured pencils to annotate areas east of Chelmsford and along the River Chelmer.

forthcoming. His death from cancer in 1987 went unpublicised, and when his widow Doreen died in 2006 many believed that with her, too, passed away any hope of knowing more of Baker's story. Everything else had gone to the grave, to sift down into the Essex gravel alongside the bones of untold generations of the falcons about which he had written with such passion.

If it hadn't been for the work of dedicated people like John Fanshawe, Baker's story might well have ended there. The archive assembled includes the paraphernalia of Baker's writing and birding life. From a few dusty boxes kept by Doreen, and recovered by her brother Bernard Coe, there appeared Baker's weather-battered maps, and the binoculars and scopes that had accompanied him on peregrine-hunting expeditions; as well as an assortment of his diaries, notebooks, letters, contracts, and the manuscripts of *The Peregrine* and *The Hill of Summer*, all laid out in his cramped, careful handwriting. There were packets of photographs, his baptismal certificate, the order of service for his and Doreen's wedding, newspaper cuttings, and a small sheaf of poems. Later additions included a series of letters written to close friends, and the unfilmed screenplay of *The Peregrine* written by David Cobham, whose 1979 film adaptation of *Tarka the Otter* is one of the best-loved family films of all time. With the help of this collection, brought together over the past ten years, the story of Baker's life has returned from obscurity.

This story has not been without its controversies. The main one of these is: did Baker really see what he claimed to have seen? When Baker wrote *The Peregrine*, he made clear in his introduction that the life of the falcon couldn't always be separated from that of its observer: 'I do not believe that honest observation is enough,' he wrote. 'The emotions and behaviour of the watcher are also facts, and they must be truthfully recorded.' Such a combination of objective and subjective truths has created no end of friction among Baker's readers.

From the time of its publication, the accuracy of *The Peregrine* has been under fire. Early in the book, Baker claimed to have found and identified 619 peregrine kills. Most bird-of-prey specialists will tell you that it's hard enough to find a single kill made by a bird, especially when it's made among the dense scrub of fields and hedgerows. Harder still would be to say for certain what sort of raptor had made it. Could Baker really have found all those falcon kills, as he claimed he did? At least one reviewer in 1967, rather unfairly, questioned whether Baker could even tell the difference between a peregrine falcon and a kestrel – and ever since, the book's readers have been trying to tease out the fact from the fiction. Were the birds that he reported seeing actually peregrines? Did the book's close encounters between man and falcon really happen?

It's not clear that such questions ever bothered Baker unduly. He maintained that his accounts were accurate as far as he had experienced them. On the one hand, when *The Peregrine* won the Duff Cooper Memorial Prize the judges made clear in their awarding letter that it did so 'squarely and incontestably' under the category of 'poetry' rather than natural history. On the other, the scientist Derek Ratcliffe, a leading scientific authority on peregrines, cited Baker in his 1980 guide to *The Peregrine Falcon* along with other qualified ornithologists. Ratcliffe and Baker had exchanged a number of letters, and Baker had assured him that *The Peregrine*'s information was accurate, if made more lyrical. That was enough for Ratcliffe, who had seen for himself that what scientists knew about animals by no means accounted for the often eccentric behaviour of individual creatures, any more than it could for humans.

Now, with the benefit of hindsight, it's possible to bring more information to this debate. There's a lot of evidence that during the years in which Baker was following the peregrines, the birds were suffering from serious pesticide poisoning. Baker knew this. He knew that agricultural chemicals were destroying the lives of the birds he was watching, like a 'burrowing fuse'. 'Many die on their backs,' he wrote, 'clutching insanely at the sky in their last convulsions'; when a peregrine's code of behaviour is 'persistently broken, it is probably sick or insane.' If these comments were taken from first-hand observation, it's possible that Baker's birds could have been behaving abnormally – as though suffering sickness or insanity – because of the effects of these pesticides. They would have been more sluggish, less naturally wary of man, and thus perhaps easier for Baker to find and follow. I'll come to more on this later, but such an argument would satisfy both sides: to support the idea that what Baker wrote was true and that his observational skills were not superhuman.

Baker's papers can only partially put these debates to rest. Though a great deal of his life is revealed in them, there are still gaps – some accidental, others deliberate. For instance, as I was reading through one of his earliest field notebooks – a faded, roughly A4-sized diary from Boots the chemist – I found that he had made an index at the back of every bird sighting from that year. I knew that this diary must contain some of those early, rapturous encounters with peregrines that Baker mentioned at the start of his book. With some excitement I scanned down the list. 'Peregrine,' it read, 'p. 99, p. 105.' I flicked back through the chalky pages, tracking page 97, 98, then 101. Puzzled, I flipped forward: 103, 104, 107. Both pages 99 and 105 were missing, cut out with the same economical violence characteristic of Baker's bird. Precisely why he excised those entries in the diary (as he did in the many of the diaries that followed) isn't clear; but of those first peregrines there's almost no trace, and it's likely we'll never know the truth of them.

If Baker's papers haven't cleared up all the mysteries, they have at least cast light on others, particularly those around the man himself. From them, here are a few general observations about J. A. Baker.

His wife Doreen, whom he met when she was just sixteen, maintained that he was not particularly political: he voted Conservative and had strong opinions on environmental issues, but that was all. His parents were Congregationalists, but his childhood was not one marked by strict religious practice: 'I was not brought up in a well-defined and implicit faith,' he said, but rather, 'from the first, I was free from all dogma or persistent church attendance.' His own faith remained loosely within the confines of Christianity throughout much of his adult life.

He was a grammar school boy – well-read, loquacious and aware of his own intelligence. As a child he was serious and often isolated by his obsessions. As he grew up, this tendency towards introversion would contribute to bouts of depression that often coincided with periods of physical illness. Though he was friendly and amenable company, he retained a guardedness that led others to label him as a 'loner'.

At school, Baker struggled between his sensitivity and his longing to please. He was on the edge of groups more often than not, something that drew him to develop a clownish persona. He loved the comic writing of G. K. Chesterton, and quoted passages at length in his letters. He often signed them 'Your faithful jester,' betraying his wry sense of humour.

One of his enjoyments was in writing amusing character sketches. In one letter Baker described the owner of a bookshop, at which he was interviewed for a job in 1945, as walking 'like a fish wearing secondhand clothes ... the sort of miserable drainpipe that would have delighted Chekov.' In another letter, he described a statue of William Wilberforce in Westminster Abbey as having 'an abominable squint ... the expression was reminiscent of a small child being dosed with Castor oil.'

Through these years, he began to develop an eye for the sort of observation and imagery that would later come to be his mainstay as an author. After a visit to London in 1944, for example, he remarked upon the damage that bombs had done to the city, and his shock at seeing it:

> The ravages of modern warfare have destroyed the soul of the city ... St. Paul's was remarkably ugly seen in the fog-laden air of the late morning and the vast dome was like a gigantic humpty-dumpty leering goblin-wise on the broken walls of the city. Strangely unreal are the weed-covered ruins.

Letters such as these show Baker developing his authorial voice – at turns whimsical, sensitive and poetic. His correspondence was at all times extraordinarily honest, something that would become the touchstone style of his books.

Baker's playful humour with his friends served as a distraction for some of the difficulties in his life. He developed a chronic arthritic condition as a teenager, and there were points over the rest of his life that were spent dealing with the effects of this disease, which slowly attacked his joints and seized up his back, hips, hands and feet. Though he rarely mentioned his condition to others, and strived to remain active even late into his life, illness and pain led him to withdraw as an adult and exacerbated his obsessive and depressive tendencies.

Far more significant in his life than his arthritis was a deep and burning desire, harboured since childhood, to become a great writer. From his late teens this passion became all-consuming, his anguish intensified by repeated (and failed) attempts to come up with what he hoped would become his masterpiece. In a letter to a friend, he called this 'my "house of sky" ... my novel, or whatever shape it may ultimately assume,' a name that would prove prophetic of the world of the peregrines he came to discover.

Like many a lonely child, Baker had been drawn to books from a young age, and they came to dominate his life. He was very much a writer first and a birdwatcher second; the sort of person who could produce *The Peregrine* was one obsessed not just with raptors but also with literature. Before birds, books were his passion.

One of the archive's most interesting treasures is a series of photographs of Baker's personal library: the shelves of his books that Doreen had kept after his death. You can tell a lot about a man by the books he keeps, as the philosopher Walter Benjamin said; if Baker's books are a clue to the sort of reader he was, they also indicate the kind of writer he was to become.

On his shelves were, predictably, countryside and coastline guides, atlases, and encyclopedias of birds. There were as many books on mammals, trees, mythology, ancient peoples, geology and mountains. Baker was mad about cricket, and one whole section was devoted to it. Another was filled with books about opera. He favoured the music of Verdi in particular – as a young man he would carry copies of Verdi's operas stuffed into his coat pockets to read while drinking tea in cafés or when waiting for a train.

But the most striking component of Baker's library was its collection of literary works. Novels crowded out the nature guides – works by J. G. Ballard, T. H. White, Kipling, Hemingway. Dickens' *Pickwick Papers* was a lifelong favourite, as was Melville's *Moby-Dick*. Above all else was poetry. Volume after volume lined his bookshelves: works by Keats, Shelley, Wordsworth, Housman, Edward Thomas, Dylan Thomas, T. S. Eliot, Philip Larkin, Ted Hughes and Seamus Heaney. He kept many anthologies: rural verse, seasonal verse, American verse, Shakespearian verse; old

Detail of J. A. Baker's library, taken by his brother-in-law Bernard Coe.

poetry, war poetry, modernist poetry.

All of these books (and many more – as almost all of his letters included lengthy reading lists) Baker studied with an intensity that rivalled the hawk-eyed attention of his beloved peregrines. He understood the maxim that great writers start off as great readers, and consumed poems and novels with an insatiable appetite. He began by absorbing literary techniques by rote, and went about this with a fanatic energy. In the spring of 1946, for example, at the age of nineteen, he wrote to an old school friend Donald Samuel to say:

> I have managed to fill up sixty pages of a new exercise book. I now have, in my personal anthology – over 600 poems by some 300 poets. 802 written pages so far. I think that this proves, if proof were needed, that I do not take my vocation lightly.

Even at this young age Baker knew for certain that his 'vocation' was to be an author. Several of these exercise books have survived:

hundreds of verses in his neat, round, schoolboy-hand. Models, or inspiration, perhaps for his own writing – though the real focus of his attention, his local over-wintering peregrines, wouldn't come until many years later.

Along with his passion for literature, Baker cultivated a deep 'love of nature which poetry developed and defined.' From his teens he knew somehow that being out of doors in fields and woods was crucial to fulfilling his writerly ambitions. Every spare minute was spent walking or cycling the countryside around Chelmsford. In 1946, for example, Baker wrote to Donald Samuel (or 'Sam'), extolling the benefits of these outings:

> I may say, Sam, that – on your return – I shall use every means in my power to get you to see Purleigh, and Danbury, and many other beautiful parts that I have discovered. I think you will agree that such experiences are far more valuable to the fulfillment of our common ambition [of being writers] than any amount of book-learning.

Such experiences worked their way into his writing early on. As poetry was Baker's first love, it was also the site for his first steps into authorship, and many of his first subjects were natural ones. As a young man he wrote with the same compulsive, fixated energy that came to epitomise his approach to every literary project he undertook during the rest of his life. He would often exhaust himself drafting half-a-dozen poems at the same time, before copying them out to post to friends. He would write asking in urgent tones for criticism and encouragement: 'I occasionally despair of my capacity as a poet,' he confessed in 1946, 'solely because I have so few people whose opinion I can obtain.' Support from his own home was in short supply: his father, Wilfred Baker, thought little of his son's literary pursuits, and when he was young the pair had frequent and violent disagreements about his career prospects.

A number of these early poems of Baker's are included in this biography. Most are not very good – but they are important because they show his development as a writer. His flair for metaphor, acute observation, and a telling preoccupation with nature can be found in their first stages in these poems.

In one, for example, titled 'The Lost Kingdom', he describes how the rural landscape of his childhood has been colonised by urbanisation: 'tall, intrusive pylons / [Lurch] across my sight / Like slender giants in armour'. 'Now – all this is changed', he says of the countryside he had known: 'Across the green fields lie long rows / Of the sharp red roofs'. Twenty years later, John Betjeman's lines from his 1966 poem 'Inexpensive Progress' echo Baker's lament: 'Encase your legs in nylons, / Bestride your hills with pylons / O age without a soul'.

Similar feelings of loss pervade *The Peregrine* and *The Hill of Summer*. By the time he came to write them, Baker had moved on from his imitations of the Romantic poets of which he had been so fond. When he claimed in *The Peregrine* that he had come 'late to the love of birds', he must have meant this only in the sense of observing them in the field, because he had, from a young age, enjoyed regular encounters with birds on the page. Many of their Romantic incarnations can be found perched among the lines of his early letters: Keats' nightingale, Tennyson's thrushes, Newbolt's nightjar whose loveliness is 'Far deeper than the optic nerve.' Baker transformed this lyricism into something new and raw – and relevant to the nature of his own century. The stance he took in his writing has much in common with what literary scholars might now call the 'post-pastoral': literature that pushes back against idealised rural scenes of natural harmony, and recognises mankind's impacts on nature for bad as well as good. In *The Peregrine*, the man-made is always muddled into the natural: 'Spring, the air mild, without edges, smelling of damp grass, fresh soil, and farm chemicals.'

Baker's birds are, then, something unusual. He had an intense interest in avifauna, despite wanting 'to be a great writer, not a bird nerd', as his editor at Collins, Michael Walter, said. He owned as many books on ornithology as on poetry. And, in his later life particularly, Baker collected material about all sorts of birds of prey, not just peregrines, to an extent that would have qualified him as a bird 'nerd' to most people's minds.

But for Baker peregrines were special. He was, in his own words, 'possessed' by them. In one of his undated poems he referred to a 'winter madness' – a phrase that could easily have described what gripped him during the months of each year in which his life was fixed to the rhythms of the migrating birds of the Blackwater Estuary: the wild, cold months of the peregrine's hunting season. He gave this poem the title 'Pilgrimage', a word that, as he would surely have known, hails from the same Latin root as 'peregrine': 'This staff I carry is winter madness, / I have stripped it of seasons, / Down to the livid bone', he wrote, 'With it I will cut the shapes of birds upon the air'.

After Baker's death, a journalist contacted Michael Walter, asking him what sort of person Baker had been. There had been rumours that Baker had been a hard man to work with – was he charming or difficult? Walter replied tersely that, as far as he had known Baker, he had been 'not either at all', and that he was instead 'ordinary but nice'.

'Ordinary' is perhaps both the best and the worst term to describe Baker. In many ways his character and achievements were not 'ordinary' at all, if we take that to mean 'average' or 'commonplace' – that he wrote *The Peregrine* is testament to that. Yet before he wrote *The Peregrine* J. A. Baker seemed wholly unremarkable. He had few qualifications to speak of. Though he had scraped a pass on his School Certificate (the equivalent of GCSEs), his exam marks were not good enough to let him either stay on into sixth form or apply to university. He lived in the same town in which he had been born and had never been abroad. For most of his adult life he had cycled each day to and from the office in which he worked, keeping very much to himself; many of his colleagues had little idea of what he did in his spare time, or even if he was married. And he *looked* ordinary – tall, but not unusually so; thickset, but not so much that you would remark on it; with soft features and a face that was pleasant but not handsome. Heavy-framed spectacles aside, he would have been hard to pick out from a crowd.

Some have questioned how it was, then, that this man, whose life appeared so banal – who worked for the Automobile Association in the uninspiring urban overspill of Essex – came to produce works of such poetic violence and vision.

If Baker's real life appears meek, his inner life was anything but. His writing burns with outrage against the carelessness of mankind towards the environment, and it's this that makes *The Peregrine* one of the most enduring pieces of nature writing from the last century, rather than the obscure account of an eccentric. In both *The Peregrine* and *The Hill of Summer* there's a sense of a world in which humans have become lost, literally and figuratively. Sightings of people are scarce and disturbing, warnings perhaps of a future in which man's position at the top of the foodchain is as precarious as that of the peregrines Baker tracked.

We are used to thinking about nature as 'wild' – removed from our normal lives, the prerogative of explorers and mountaineers in exotic locations. Perhaps that is why it's disappointing to find out that Baker lived an 'ordinary' life. One of Baker's motivations for writing, however, was to prove that it's both possible and necessary to slough off the misconception that we are separate (and separated) from nature, and to rediscover wildness even in that most familiar of landscapes: the English countryside.

'Wild' is a relative term, as the philosopher David Abram has pointed out. There are no places that are truly beyond or without wildness. If, for example, you mix flour and water in a bowl and leave it covered over on your kitchen table, in a matter of days the mixture will start to froth and thicken. Feed it a little more flour and you'll have accomplished the oldest known way of making leavened bread, thanks to a swarming mass of tiny organisms: the floating spores of wild yeast that roam the air, ravenous predators of starch. Wildness can be found on the small scale as well as the large. Baker knew this – exotic drama to him was not confined to the African savannahs or South Sea Islands, places marvelled at by the British public on their television sets in the 1950s and 1960s in programmes like the BBC's *Zoo Quest*. Baker's own quest was to his mind no less intrepid: the world of East Anglia was as compelling, he said, as that of Mars.

Baker had the extraordinary ability to make everyday things appear remarkable. *The Peregrine*'s imagery stays in our memory because of its incongruity: ducks that look like bobbing kettles; a dead porpoise whose beak is likened to the open zip of a valise; or a heron whose legs upon landing 'reached down with a slow pedalling movement, like a man descending through the trapdoor of a loft and feeling for a ladder with his feet.'

Baker's work might today be set as a 'gold standard for all nature writing', as Mark Cocker has suggested, but when it first appeared in 1967 it was strange and extraordinary: no one had written in quite the same way before. Since the mid-1940s Collins had been publishing the *New Naturalist* series of books on natural history. Each was written by an expert (which meant, usually, someone with at least one university degree), and used academic language accompanied by technical illustrations. One set of *New Naturalist* monographs was dedicated to different species, and included titles like *The Badger*, *The Wren*, *The Greenshank*, and *The Heron*. At first glance, Baker's own work for Collins, *The Peregrine*, would have appeared very like others in the series.

But once past the title page, Baker's book was a very different beast to the ornithological monograph that its covers might have suggested. It contained no Latin names; no analysis of the contents of the crop; no tables reckoning geographical distribution to two decimal places; no history of the evolution of the family *Falconidae*; not an index nor a footnote in sight. Readers who picked up *The Peregrine* expecting to open a field guide would find, instead, something that was part journal, part prose poem, and nearly all surprise.

The point that I am trying to make here is that it was Baker's 'ordinariness', perhaps, that allowed him to write something that was in itself so out of the ordinary, and which has sustained such a powerful influence over the past half-century. Would the continuing power of *The Peregrine* be greater or lesser if Baker had been like those other 'experts' of his time – an accomplished research scientist, or a wealthy celebrity campaigner, or an upper-middle-class intellectual? Would it, or could it, have been written as it was?

I suspect not. In 1967, the peregrine, an endangered animal, needed the support of the general public. It needed a messenger to tell its story, someone who could be understood: someone, perhaps, who had been made sensitive to the violence that man is heir to; who could sympathise with the birds' suffering because of his own mental and physical ills; but also someone who was familiar with the world of his readers, who worked in an office, lived in a council house, and who had struggled in school exams. Someone whose life was, indeed, 'ordinary' – but who longed secretly (as so many of us do) to be, in his words, 'out there on the edge of things'.

'An escape' was how Doreen Baker described what writing *The Peregrine* meant to her husband. What follows is the story of that escape.

'Trinity Rd., Boys' School', June 1936, with the young Baker looking out from the top row. At a later date, Baker annotated the photograph with the names of some of the children and a pencil line pointing to himself.

Chapter Two
EARLY YEARS

> We all grow up the same way, more or less.
>
> W. H. AUDEN, 'Letter to Lord Byron' (1937)

> I don't grumble, for poets are shaped by circumstance and, ultimately, I may be thankful for my childhood.
>
> J. A. BAKER, letter to Donald Samuel (April 23, 1946)

THERE'S A TENDENCY when looking at a writer's life to overdramatise childhood events for the sake of satisfying hindsight – to source their artistry in some youthful trauma, or to endow the child in retrospect with precocious gifts, the root from which would later flourish genius. It pays to be aware of the limits of this sort of biographical fallacy. No doubt much of Baker's journey through childhood was as unremarkable as that of countless other schoolboys of the time, and no doubt like them he too, as Auden wrote, lost his 'taste for sweets, / Discovered sunsets, passion, God, and Keats'.

That said, there were certain childhood experiences that Baker himself would point to as significant – or at least so he thought – because of their influence on him as a writer.

These concerned his family relationships, his early illness, and his love of the countryside around Chelmsford. What is known about Baker's early years comes mostly from the accounts he gave as a young man to his friends, and a number of notebooks he produced much later in his adult life. He was an only child, so with few surviving relatives we must take his version, framed by what other facts can be found – and moderated with the pinch of salt that should be taken with any child's description of his family.

Baker's family is perhaps the best place to start. As far back as his great-grandparents on both sides, Baker's family lived in a handful of parishes clustered around central and eastern Essex, not far from Chelmsford – the very same landscape that he would use as the backdrop to his writing.

Baker's paternal great-grandfather was an agricultural labourer. His son, Alexander (J. A.'s grandfather), worked as a draper before opening a grocer's shop in the village of Sisted, where he lived with his wife Edith. In the back of this shop (called The Supply Stores), Wilfred Samuel Baker, J. A.'s father, was born in 1899, the youngest of six siblings.

J. A. Baker, as Wilfred's only son, was to be the last in the immediate line of Bakers. Wilfred's only brother, Arthur, died unmarried at the age of twenty-one, a private in the 2nd Battalion, Essex Regiment. After surviving action at the Second Battle of Ypres and the Somme, Arthur was killed at Arras on May 3, 1917 during the disastrous Third Battle of the Scarpe.

Baker's mother, Pansy, was four years older than Wilfred. She was born in Chelmsford to Walter Collis, a grocer's assistant, and his wife Alice. Like Wilfred, she, too, was the youngest of eight children. From the age of fourteen or fifteen she worked as a milliner's assistant, until 1925 when she and Wilfred married in Chelmsford.

Just over a year later John Alec was born. His memories of his maternal grandparents were vague. Though his mother's parents lived only a ten-minute walk from his home, both of them had died by the mid-1930s when he was still a small child, along with at least three of Pansy's siblings.

In a cracked and peeled black and white photograph of the boys of Trinity Road Primary School, taken in the mid-1930s, the tow-headed boy peering from the back row from behind large, round spectacles is unmistakably Baker. He must be about nine or ten. A couple of years earlier, he had come down with an infection that developed into rheumatic fever. The illness inflamed his joints and caused him much pain. Though he recovered, what Baker

Suffer the little children to come unto Me.
And He took them in His arms, put His hands upon them, and blessed them.—*Mark x., 14 & 16.*

Baptismal Certificate

This is to Certify that John Alec, child of
Mr & Mrs Wilfred J and Pansy K. Baker
was baptised in the name of the Father, and of the Son, and of the
Holy Ghost, at the London Road Congregational Church
Date October 10th 1926. Minister H Wallace Simon
Chelmsford

The baptismal certificate for J. A Baker, October 10, 1926.

and his parents didn't know was that this sickness foreshadowed the arthritic disease that would dog him through his adult years: ankylosing spondylitis. Baker's mother also suffered from arthritis, so it's possible that it was a condition to which he was genetically predisposed.

Despite the time lost at school from illness, Baker did well at Trinity Road. His father was strict and pushed him hard at his schoolwork, and Baker was a precocious child. When he left Trinity Road he was awarded the Junior Ann Johnson Exhibition, a cash prize that was awarded each year to a handful of children, and had done well enough to join the local grammar school, King Edward VI Grammar (KEGS, as it was known).

In notes made as an adult, Baker described the landscape around Chelmsford as he had known it as a child. Chelmsford had grown into a sprawling industrial town by the early decades of the twentieth century. The Bakers' house on Finchley Avenue was one of the rows of new semi-detached and terraced houses that were built around Chelmsford's factories. A few streets away the town ended and the pre-war English countryside began: pastures left fallow, quiet woodlands, and mile upon mile of hedgerows.

Back then the landscape around Baker's hometown was still largely unaffected by mechanisation. It was populated with villages clustered around church towers, small tenanted farmsteads with higgledy fields, and, to the east, the fleets and creeks plied by punts and sailing boats. Few farmers owned a tractor – the draught horse was still king of this world. The miles of meadows, woods and saltmarsh between Baker's home and the Blackwater Estuary, where so many of the events described in his books would be later witnessed and recorded, offered all manner of experiences to a curious boy on a bicycle. Baker was allowed to roam after school and on weekends, when he would cycle down the quiet lanes beyond Chelmsford, or sneak into pastures, or watch the local willow cutters with their hook knives at harvest. Baker called it a 'world of the senses – sight the least of them.'

When the Second World War began, drastic changes were wrought on this landscape. Few places familiar to Baker would escape the mark of militarisation. On the coastline east of Chelmsford, where Baker would later come for his days of 'hawk-hunting', the marshes were transformed into bombing ranges. Pairs of tramlines were laid across the tidal flats and strings of colourful pyramids placed to guide planes to their targets. Hexagonal structures made of concrete sprouted along the coast – pillboxes to defend against the possibility of Hitler's invading troops.

Inland, disused fields were sowed for crops to feed a population facing food rationing. Woodlands were earmarked for felling by the Forestry Commission, the timber to be used as pit props for coal mines in the north, a native source of power essential to driving the Allied war machine. The airfields close to Chelmsford – Boreham, Dunmow, Wethersfield – expanded at a phenomenal rate as new hangars and runways were constructed to cope with the influx of aircraft and Australian, Canadian, Polish and American crewmen who would come to the area over the war's duration.

American soldiers outside the Saracens Head, known locally as the 'American Club', Chelmsford, c.1942.

In addition to the warplanes, these same bases around Chelmsford saw the arrival of another new weapon in the Allied armies' arsenal. Dichlorodiphenyltrichloroethane (DDT) was a pesticide brought over by the tens of thousands of American soldiers stationed in the region during the later years of the war. Troops were routinely issued with small canisters of DDT dust to use against a different sort of enemy: mosquitoes (which thrived in the boggy fenlands around Essex and East Anglia during spring and summer), lice and bedbugs. The soldiers loved the stuff and would spray it all over their tents and barracks. Baker in all likelihood would have been unaware at the time of the local use of this revolutionary chemical; but the effects of DDT and other related organochlorine compounds would play a major role in his life, if inadvertently – for these pesticides would be credited later in the century for causing the crash in peregrine falcon numbers in England, the event that became the motivating force behind Baker's *The Peregrine*.

★

When war broke out in 1939, Baker had just turned thirteen. The region around his home soon became an unsettling place to live: over the next six years more than 300,000 bombs were dropped and a hundred enemy aircraft were brought down over Essex.

Those living in Chelmsford at the time later recalled how the air-raid sirens would wail with monotonous regularity, day and night; how, even though barrage balloons on long cables were used to deter low-flying planes, streets in the area would still be strafed by bullets from aircraft gunners; and how the spent clips and cartridge cases from guns both on the ground and borne aloft fell like rain so often that tin hats were placed on heads by habit, and children venturing outside were constantly reminded that 'what goes up, must come down'.

Why was Chelmsford such a target for bombing? Geography played a part in it: the town lay along the line taken by enemy bombers between the Low Countries and London. Many places in south-eastern England became incidental targets, as aircraft using the Thames as a guide off-loaded unused explosives on their return from bombing raids on the capital. Chelmsford lies about twenty-five miles from the Thames Estuary, north of Shell Haven, the location of an important oil refinery and fuel depot.

If, during a clear night in the early 1940s, you had looked southwards from the garden of Baker's house on Finchley Avenue, you would have been able to pinpoint Shell Haven on your left, and London to your right, from the flickering arc of ack-ack guns and the explosions overhead. Standing there in the flash and tick of these distant illuminations you would have heard the constant low rumble of aircraft and artillery as the wind changed direction or the searchlights found their mark. The thundering of the guns on the ground was more often for effect, however, than result. Only on occasion did they hit their targets, and many enemy planes would have continued on to London, or returned east over what was then still known as the German Ocean.

But Chelmsford was a significant target in its own right – so much so, in fact, that the Luftwaffe built a scale model of the town

Map plotting fall of long range V-2 across Essex, 1944–1945.

with which to train pilots to locate their points for attack. This provincial county town was a threat to the German war machine because of what it manufactured. A number of engineering firms essential to the war effort had made their home in Chelmsford; the three largest of these were the Marconi Company, Hoffmann Manufacturing and Crompton Parkinson Ltd.

Marconi's iconic Art Deco 'wireless' factory produced crucial communications equipment. More than that, its research laboratory worked on the top-secret project of developing radar, one of the most significant inventions of the Second World War.

Hoffmann, on the other hand, produced ammunition, along

West wall of the Hoffmann factory, Rectory Lane, Chelmsford, destroyed by a V-2 missile on December 19, 1944.

with some of the smallest and most crucial items for the Allied forces: ball bearings. These bearings kept every naval gun, every armoured vehicle wheel, and every airplane propeller shaft working. Upto 1,000 Chelmsford Hoffmann bearings went into each Spitfire's Rolls Royce Merlin engine – and 4,000 into the engine of each Lancaster bomber.

Crompton Parkinson was the smaller sibling to these two giants. The company manufactured munitions and electrical components; its factory stood on Writtle Road, the building recognisable by its yellow-and-red brickwork and the scalene triangles of its north-light roofs. It was a ten-minute walk from Baker's parents' house, and was where Wilfred Baker was employed as a draughtsman.

One of the most terrible bombing raids on the town during the Second World War targeted these three factories. The attack took place in the early hours of May 14, 1943. The moon had just passed its zenith when a large number of Dornier and Junker bombers were sighted over the Essex coast. Air-raid sirens sounded the alarm and three minutes later Chelmsford's residents heard the bass growl of the aircraft engines.

First, clusters of coloured target marker flares were dropped to guide the planes above; then, over the following hour, high explosives, incendiary bombs and parachute mines were dropped in a vast swathe across the town. The word 'aftermath' has its origins in the physical act of cutting down, of exposing the level of the ground – it describes how a strip of field looks after mowing (or 'mathing' in Old English). The aftermath of the Chelmsford raid exemplified that definition: explosives levelled a sharp arc running from the south-west to the north-east, as if a scythe had cut across the town. Fifty people were left dead and thousands of properties damaged. Finchley Avenue was just a few streets from the worst hit areas. Baker, then sixteen, would have had to cycle through the debris on his way to school the following morning; the sight and sound of the night's raid and its aftermath must have been frightening in the extreme.

At the same time that the town in which he lived was enduring the upheavals of war, Baker was going through private upheavals of his own. Later, he recalled that a kind of restless unhappiness had begun to grow inside him from this time.

A year or two into grammar school, Baker had begun to struggle. His difficulty was not in keeping up with the work; his friends recalled him being an able student when he had a mind to apply himself, but that was the problem. He was a daydreamer and easily bored – characteristics his teachers pigeonholed as 'lazy'. Though intelligent and articulate, even competitive when it came to subjects that he enjoyed, he couldn't get over his feelings of antipathy when confronted with teachers or lessons he disliked.

Another characteristic that developed itself in these years was Baker's tendency towards introversion. He wrote later in his life that, at this time, he had developed a feeling of 'captivity', which increased as he progressed through school. Baker would come to blame his mercurial temper as an adult on this childhood experience, throughout which, he said, he had felt a growing 'sense of being imprisoned, of being bound like a bird that has the power of flight.' He had always been a sensitive child, but as he reached his teenage years this began to contribute to his sense of being different from his classmates.

This didn't go unnoticed by the other boys. Jack Baird was in the same form as Baker at KEGS and recalled his impressions of Baker during their time at the school: 'Doughy' (a pun on Baker's surname and on his stocky physique), 'tended to be a bit of a loner and while we gone [sic] on OK with him and vice-versa he wasn't really a close friend of any of us.'

Baker wrote that it was around the age of fourteen that he first felt what he called an unaccountable 'sere of deprivation'. There was a sense of 'freedom lost', a feeling of absence that he connected strongly to a 'longing to be outdoors'. Such a longing was, in his mind, related to a freedom that belonged to nature and things beyond the human. His jotted notes ramble through a series of impressions from this time. What he wanted, he said, was:

> [to] get away, to be hidden, free because unknown, nameless, as an animal is nameless and unknown. ... [There was the]realisation (again) that there *was* another life, a life beyond, out there, where all that could ever really matter was happening unregarded.

This sense of there being a 'life beyond' everyday urban experience would come to be the driving force behind *The Peregrine*. In his introduction Baker wrote: 'I have always longed to be a part of the outward life ... to let the human taint wash away in emptiness and silence as the fox sloughs his smell into the cold unworldiness of water; to return to the town as a stranger.' According to his notes, Baker was already having these thoughts twenty-five years before he would come to write them down for publication.

Baker's feeling of estrangement had few positive outcomes in his early life. 'Aloneness became loneliness', Baker wrote, looking back on it in his twenties. Eventually his misery manifested itself in action. During a period of 'what almost seemed temporary mental aberration,' he found himself 'driven by inexplicable fear and still more inexplicable audacity to play truant for a fortnight.' No doubt he was punished for his truancy: caning was still a common penalty at the grammar school at the time.

For a while afterwards this impulse was somehow quelled, though clearly not forgotten. When Baker came to write his books as an adult, he connected freedom uncompromisingly with the outdoors and the feral, and sought to examine the lives of non-human creatures around him. His ability to both recognise and sympathise with the 'unregarded' status of British wildlife in the 1960s was what brought him his own recognition as a successful author. Baker himself, at least, was convinced that his progress to authorship had its roots in his difficult adolescent experiences.

Baker's early years were not without spells of happiness. His last year at school was one he recalled with fondness. At sixteen he had joined a number of boys who were entering the sixth form at KEGS to obtain their Higher Education Certificate (HEC), though Baker was not himself studying for that exam. The previous year, possibly due to illness, he had either failed or been unable to complete his studies needed to 'pass' grades in six subjects. In order to retake those exams, he had been given an extra year of study at the school.

Though he was not taking the HEC, Baker seems to have spent that year with the others in the Lower Sixth. Here he found four other boys who shared his interest in the arts: Donald Samuel ('Sam'), Edward Dennis ('Ted'), John Thurmer (often just 'Thurmer'), and Harold Cufflin ('Cuff'). Referred to fondly by Baker in his letters as the 'Happy Circle', the five of them would become fast friends into adulthood: Baker organised Cufflin's stag party in 1951; when Baker married Doreen in 1956, Dennis was his best man; and both Samuel and Thurmer kept many of the letters Baker wrote to them as a young man, some of which ran to sixty-odd pages.

Baker thoroughly enjoyed that year of school. He came out of his shell – so much so that he gained a reputation for being talkative to the point of garrulousness. He found that he had a gift for humour and became known for his parodies of friends and teachers. More than that, though, he felt himself intellectually stimulated in ways that he hadn't experienced before. He found himself among like-minded companions, and later he would recall how the boys would 'regale [their] burgeoning intellects' with spirited debates. In the years that followed he complained of comparative tedium in his work and colleagues, boredom being, as he defined it, 'my worst trouble ever since I left school.'

Meanwhile, during that extra year of study the seed of Baker's literary ambition was planted. He discovered a deep passion for literature, something he cultivated for the rest of his life. One schoolmaster in particular encouraged his reading: the Rev E. J. Burton, popular among the KEGS boys (who mysteriously nicknamed him 'Sally'), and who taught Literature, Language and Religious Education. Rev Burton became Baker's guide in his literary education, and it was under his tutelage that Baker first hit upon the idea of becoming a writer.

Baker's bumpy path through formal education ended in July 1943. He passed his School Certificate, but didn't do well enough (in Maths or French particularly, two of the subjects he loathed) to gain his 'matric exemption', the minimum required qualification to enter university. So Baker left KEGS with mixed emotions: while he had not enjoyed the school's rigid structure nor got on with many of his teachers, he had found the thing he truly loved. Now he had to find a way of making it into a career.

Baker's early years were thus in many ways not unusual, if not without incident. But there remains the question of the origins of Baker's unhappiness during his childhood, which would extend into his adult life. His sensitivity, reticence, feelings of loneliness and isolation, the moment of rebelliousness when he played truant and ran away from school for two weeks – where did they come from?

Baker's family life may be a cause. 'I would have been happier with brothers and sisters', Baker wrote to his friend Donald Samuel in 1946. 'To be an only child is a disadvantage to say the least.' It was a sentiment he voiced on more than one occasion.

A portrait of a young J. A. Baker by E. Nixon Payne, Chelmsford, c.1945.

In terms of his wider family, it seems that he had few close relationships there, either; though he had uncles, aunts and cousins who lived in Chelmsford or nearby, he made no mention of them in his notes and letters. His cousins were all at least ten years older than he was, and it's certain that he had few relations of a similar age to spend time with as a child.

At the age of nineteen or so, Baker became a regular in the household of his friend Donald Samuel. It was then that Baker began to make the connection between his family and the general sense of loneliness he had suffered from in earlier years. The Samuels' family dynamic was totally unlike anything he had been used to: they were a large household, loving, welcoming, boisterous and Catholic – a sharp departure from his own house, which consisted of just him and his parents, both of whom were reserved, private, and Protestant.

The Samuels lived on Writtle Road, a few streets from Baker's house. When, in 1945, Donald was posted abroad on military service, Baker would drop by after work on his way home. At first this was, as he said, 'just to learn how things [were] with them and with the absent heir to the estates.' But Baker's quick humour soon endeared him to the family and he became a friend to Donald's siblings, helping out the two older daughters, Gabriel and Jean, with their homework and playing with Donald's younger sister Chrissie. He even joined them on Christmas day and stayed for weeks when his own parents were away. With the Samuels, Baker found the sort of family life that he had missed all his childhood. 'I want you to know Sam,' he wrote in January 1946, 'how much I appreciate the invariable kindness and hospitality with which I am greeted. There's a domestic concord that prevails and an atmosphere of sympathy which means a great deal to me, for, as you know, my home-life has been a complete contrast.'

The Baker household was not harmonious. Once in 1946, after an episode of depressive anxiety, Baker confided some of his family's history to his friend Donald:

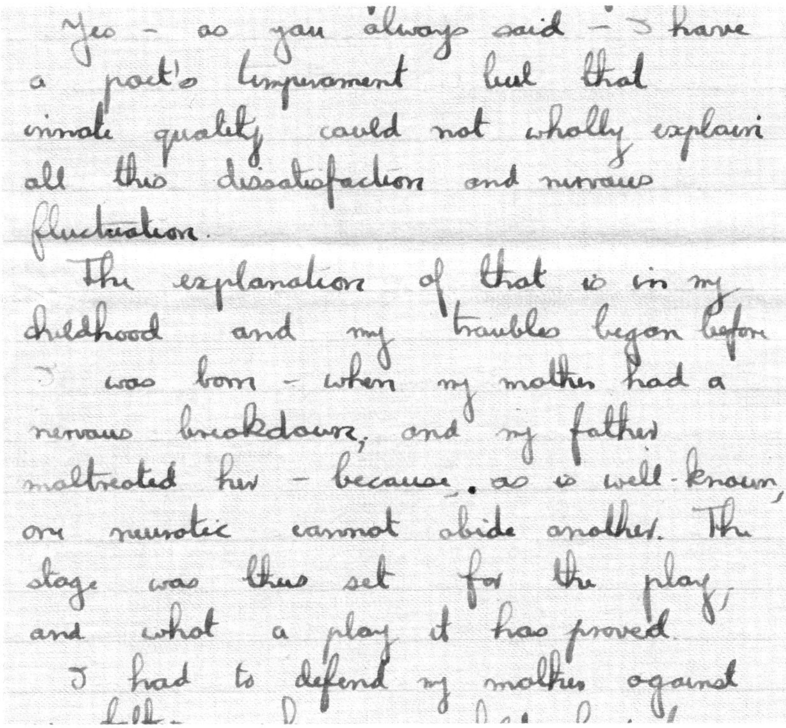
Yes – as you always said – I have
a poet's temperament but that
innate quality could not wholly explain
all this dissatisfaction and nervous
fluctuation.
The explanation of that is in my
childhood and my troubles began before
I was born – when my mother had a
nervous breakdown, and my father
maltreated her – because, as is well-known,
one neurotic cannot abide another. The
stage was thus set for the play,
and what a play it has proved.
I had to defend my mother against

Detail from a letter to 'Sam' (Donald Samuel), written from the Samuel family home on Writtle Road, September 15, 1946.

I have a poet's temperament but that innate quality could not wholly explain all [my] dissatisfaction and nervous fluctuation. The explanation of that is in my childhood and my troubles began before I was born – when my mother had a nervous breakdown, and my father maltreated her – because, as is well-known, one neurotic cannot abide another. ... I had to defend my mother against my father – who, as a child, had been bullied into submission by his father and lavished with every superfluous attention by a doting mother. The two extremes produced a person ill-adjusted in the extreme to married life and with the ruinous factor of being incapable of realising his own weaknesses. I grew up in that shadow – haunted ever by a scene when I stood between my mother, in tears, and my father, carving-knife in hand – his face suffused with an indescribable malice. It was against the kitchen sink – I couldn't have been more than seven years old. I accuse no-one. My father has been in hell and I do not

> believe that it was pathologically or humanly possible for him to have been other than he was. But Sam, I had no sense of security – I had my mother but though we could comfort one another – it had to be surreptitiously – my father was a jealous man. Everything – yes literally everything had to be hidden from him for fear that he would actively disapprove.

Such things, he concluded, had formed him; though, as Baker went on to tell Donald, he had discovered writing to be a kind of therapy through which some of the painful memories could be exorcised.

Baker's wife Doreen, in an interview after his death, confirmed the account of his father's unpredictable temper. Wilfred Baker was a violent man, she said, and her husband's parents had not enjoyed a happy marriage. Then she revealed something unexpected: Wilfred had apparently suffered from a neurological condition that caused him serious pain – so much so, Doreen said, that he had undergone a lobotomy.

This was a surprise. Wilfred was a man who designed electrical components; he was a Chelmsford town councillor for many years, and even became Mayor of Chelmsford in 1964. How, and when, could he have had surgery as drastic as a lobotomy? The fact that Wilfred worked and went on to have a responsible role in Chelmsford's community in his later years doesn't rule out the possibility that he underwent psychosurgery at a younger age; he died in 1973, and, as the practice of lobotomy (or leucotomy, as the procedure was also known) continued well up until that time in Britain, he could have undergone the procedure.

Nowadays most people will associate lobotomy with its most dramatic irreversible effects, with the terrors of the asylum, and with those whom it was most famously used to treat: the mad, sad and dangerous to know. But at the peak of its use in Britain in the mid-twentieth century, lobotomy was used to treat a large number of conditions: from physical symptoms like chronic pain and epilepsy, to what were considered purely psychological disorders, including anxiety, tension, melancholia, and 'affective states' as well

Wilfred Baker, Mayor of Chelmsford, photographed by E. Nixon Payne, in 1964.

as more serious depression and schizophrenia. For some of those who were treated, psychosurgery could offer an almost miraculous recovery, though its outcomes were variable and unpredictable.

Less drastic techniques had been introduced to psychosurgery during its development early in the twentieth century. According to a Ministry of Health report published in 1961, some 12,000 such brain operations were performed between 1935 and 1954 on patients in psychiatric hospitals in England and Wales. Almost 30 per cent of those patients recorded in the 1961 report made a total or almost total recovery, and they were able to return to their work and social environments with few or no symptoms.

The numbers of operations recorded in that Ministry of Health report fell short by several hundred a year at least. In part, this difference was accounted for by those patients who were given lobotomies for reasons other than mental illness: those treated for pain, or – more terribly – to control the behaviour of those considered 'mentally deficient'. But the survey also excluded patients who were operated on in general hospitals: those whom the author of the Ministry of Health report dismissed as 'probably neurotics'. For this last group especially, the results of surgery were thought to be better than average.

So it's more than possible that Wilfred Baker could have undergone some kind of lobotomy in a local hospital without suffering severe long-term effects. When this was isn't certain. His son made no mention of it in any letters or notes; the social stigma of lobotomy would have been more than enough to deter Baker and his family from discussing the details. But in the letter he wrote in 1946 to Donald Samuel, 'my father has been in hell', Baker described himself as a small child during some of the most violent episodes – could Wilfred have undergone treatment in the 1940s or earlier?

At the very least Doreen's comments confirmed the volatility of Baker's home life as he was growing up. Even as a young adult, the picture Baker drew of his relationship to his father was not an easy one. Both men were stubborn and had very different views on a number of topics, which meant they were often at loggerheads. Wilfred had never been a reader of poetry, and had what his son thought were ludicrous ideas about those who enjoyed verse (implying that they were latent homosexuals). Consequently he poured scorn on his son's loves of poems and his ambition to be a writer.

The differences between himself and his father, Baker felt, were fundamental and irreconcilable. His sensibility belonged to the world of imagination, while his father's was wholly practical and unimaginative. Antagonism between the two continued into Baker's twenties, fuelling what Baker described as 'hysterical' arguments. It also fuelled in Baker an increasing determination to prove his father wrong.

It was not long after Baker left school, however, that the emotional strains of both his home life and his work came to a head.

The gardens of Roffey Park Rehabilitation Centre, Horsham, Sussex.

Chapter Three
INSTABILITY

> [His mind] did not appear so much lost as suspended in its movements by the oppressive and permanent state of anxiety and fear.
>
> DR MATTHEW ALLEN, founder of High Beach Private Asylum, of his patient John Clare (c.1837)

> The malady by which the poet is lost to himself ...
>
> *The Athenaeum*, (c.1837) concerning an appeal for funds for the poet John Clare while in High Beach Asylum, Epping (Essex)

SIXTY MILES south-west of Chelmsford there's a long road that runs through a forest. In the month of May it's a tunnel of bright green oak, its verges overgrown with violets and forget-me-nots, the air soporific with the smell of wild chervil. A private lane leads off this road. It winds between rows of rhododendrons and past an old kitchen garden which is now a walled lawn, before emerging alongside the mock-Tudor gables of an imposing nineteenth-century country house, its sprawl of stables, lawns and landscaped gardens clasped by a gravel drive. This is Roffey Park House.

Now converted into flats, the house and its gardens were once part of an impressive 300-acre estate. A quarter of a mile down the road is a more modern building: 'The Roffey Park Institute', a centre for business leadership. It takes its name from the old country house nearby, the house that was known for managing the neuroses of its patients long before its name was connected to the neuroses of management. It was to Roffey Park House (then known as the Roffey Park Rehabilitation Centre) that Baker came in May of 1945, the day after victory over Nazi Germany had been declared in Europe. Signed in as one of Roffey Park's 120 patients, he stayed for the next seven weeks.

In the years that followed its opening in the summer of 1944, Dr T. M. Ling, Roffey Park's first medical director, called it 'one of the most interesting social experiments that has grown out of the war.' By the mid-1900s, clinicians had become increasingly interested in the study of psychological disorders. This had stemmed from the large numbers of soldiers returning from the First World War who were suffering from the effects of shell shock and other mental illnesses. Practitioners soon realised that more attention was needed to provide effective psychological care for what had become a silent epidemic among the British population – whether they had been on the front lines or not.

In the years after Armistice Day, health practitioners discovered many cases of 'neurosis' among the general population as well as those who had been in the armed forces. One pioneering study conducted in 1930 which examined 'nervous temperament' in Britain's workforce found that among 1,000 factory, technical, clerical and administrative workers, 16 per cent had 'serious or disabling' nervous and emotional difficulties; on top of this, a further 20 per cent had what were classed as 'minor' difficulties. The two psychologists who ran the study (May Smith and Millais Culpin) found these symptoms across all group and ages.

With the 1940s – and another war – came new strains on the working population. Many were malnourished from years of rationing, in constant fear of being bombed, and exhausted from the emotional and physical stress of working long shifts in factories that often ran day and night, seven days a week. Studies came to the alarming conclusion that up to one-third of all absences from work due to sickness were caused by neurotic illness. With employers already struggling under huge staff shortages as able men were called up to fight, the implications of these findings were grave.

Decisive action was needed; thus was born the National

Council for the Rehabilitation of Industrial Workers. The council's first move was to launch an appeal to create a treatment centre designed to handle what they dubbed 'industrial neuroses'. At least 175 employers contributed to this progressive project, companies that included giants like Courtaulds, Rowntree, Lever Brothers and Reckitt & Colman – as well as the Chelmsford-based companies of Marconi and Crompton Parkinson.

Money raised by the council went to buy a large estate in Sussex, nestled between the High Weald and the Surrey Hills, a few miles from the town of Horsham. At the centre of this estate was Roffey Park House. The building itself was converted to staff and patient accomodation, and opened in June 1944 as the first rehabilitation centre in Britain.

After leaving KEGS in 1943, Baker began a regular correspondence with two of his school friends: John Thurmer and Donald Samuel. Letter writing is, as Virginia Woolf said, the most 'humane art', and it's in his letters that Baker comes to life as an observer of people and places.

The earliest of these letters is dated September 1944. This month marked the start of a period of intense correspondence for Baker, as his friends travelled away from Essex on National Service – a period that was also one of intense loneliness. At this point Baker had started what would become a series of misery-inducing jobs in Chelmsford. Combined with other stresses, his work frustrations ended up resulting in what he later called 'a disaster of neurotic distemper'.

The build-up to this crisis had begun in the latter half of 1943. Around this time Baker had first fallen ill with ankylosing spondylitis. Much of this time he spent in hospital, in pain, waiting for the swelling in his joints to ease. It was a period of total incapacitation: 'long weeks of gazing at drab walls, inhaling the smell of ether that has an enervating hopelessness in its very essence,' as he described it.

After convalescing, Baker started work at the County Hall

in the centre of Chelmsford. During the later war years, Essex County Hall housed the Control Room for the local corps of the Civil Defence Service (CDS). The men and women of the CDS were responsible for protecting people and property during enemy air raids: they were in charge of evacuation, managing the shelters, and coordinating rescues and debris clearance, as well as processing damage reports. Baker's time at County Hall likely was spent working for, or alongside, the CDS.

This time was a period 'undiluted purgatory'. '[My] nerves became so affected,' he wrote, 'that I was afraid to use a public lavatory if there was anyone else there and spent half the night sifting out the foolish problems of the day.' There were a number of serious bombing raids on Chelmsford during this period, and the CDS was under a huge strain; it's no surprise that Baker's mental state took a battering. Though his body may have recovered from his long illness, his mind was still fragile. Twenty-first century medical studies have drawn links between the chronic pain suffered by patients with rheumatoid disease and psychological disorders such as depression or anxiety. Certainly from Baker's own accounts it seems that his bouts of illness coincided with periods of what he called 'habitual febrile imaginings and mental gymnastics', problems that would flare up over the rest of his life.

After a month of this, Baker managed to free himself from County Hall. Soon after, sometime in the middle of 1944, he started work at L. P. Foreman and Son, a willow specialist and packaging supplier in north-west Chelmsford. His school records show that at some point soon after leaving, Baker had taken up training as a draughtsman, like his father; most likely this training started at L. P. Foreman and Son, where he would have been put to use in the company's packaging offices. Today, the sole remnant of this large site is the old works building: a red brick warehouse with a large squared arch in the middle, through which traction engines and lorries delivered timber into the yard. The only indication of its former life is in its reliquary address, as the buildings are still called by the name it had locally: Foreman's.

In 1944 the end to the war in Europe still seemed far off. As the boys of Baker's 'Happy Circle' turned eighteen, they became eligible for conscription. His four friends received their call-up papers, and left Chelmsford to join the forces. Donald Samuel and Edward Dennis travelled first to Edinburgh for training, after which Samuel left for the South Pacific; Harold Cufflin was sent with the Queens Regiment 2nd of Foot to Chatham, in Kent, then later to Karachi, and eventually Indonesia; and John Thurmer went to train at the military barracks at Warley in Brentwood, later to be deployed in Palestine (where he survived the explosion in the King David Hotel, Jerusalem, when it was blown up in 1946). During the time they were away, the four of them and Baker exchanged hundreds of letters.

Though Baker also turned eighteen during this time, he managed to avoid being conscripted into the forces. His myopia has been suggested as a reason, but poor eyesight alone wouldn't have precluded being draughted. In 1944 the Government had ordered all men over the age of eighteen not suffering serious mental or physical illness to contribute to the war effort. If they proved unfit for the army, they could qualify for service as a clerk or storekeeper on the home front. There were also Reserved Occupations, jobs deemed vital to the war effort: brick-making, engineering, mining, and farming, among others. As Foreman's produced packing crates for transporting the various sorts of machinery and munitions that were manufactured in Chelmsford, Baker's work there as a draughtsman would have fallen into this last category of service.

The work at Foreman's began promisingly for Baker, in comparison with County Hall. He especially enjoyed being sent outside into the timber yard, which looked south over a stretch of water meadow broken only by the criss-cross of the streams that fed it and the willow trees that grew beside them. These rivulets were the tributaries that flowed eastwards into the River Chelmer, whose waters slacken through millpond, lock and irrigation ditches before emptying into the thick silt of the Blackwater Estuary.

Being outdoors helped Baker escape the feelings of confinement that had smothered him at County Hall. Writing to Samuel in October 1944 he described his pleasure:

> I have been measuring timber of late, at the bottom of our [Foreman's] yard which backs onto the flat water-meadows of the [River] Can ... On the hill, where the sky is drawn down to the mysterious trees and the clouds come drifting languidly past, stands Widford's Church and in a distant hollow nestles the square, rustic shape of Writtle surrounded by trees and crowding hedged fields ... To-day there was a wondrous lagoon above with feather-like shoals of cloud drifting in the opalescent waters ... "His head's in the clouds" is a term of contempt and derision applied to any who do not conform to the accepted standard of mundane vacuity; I would employ it as a great compliment for if a man has his head in the clouds [he] sees only the beauty of the world.

But cloud-gazing was not compatible with timber-measuring. As time wore on, Baker found that these moments of happiness became less and less frequent. He complained to Samuel that too often his enjoyment was interrupted:

> [Some] fool says, "Look – there's a Fortress," and another imbecile calls out to me that I am wanted up at the office ... and the [scenery's] delicate notes [are] drowned by the cacophonous cymbals of office routine.

Such mundane intrusions drove away Baker's peace of mind as the wind drove away the clouds above his head.

Though Baker didn't serve in the forces as his friends did, his experiences of the last years of the war were perhaps no less caught up in its violent effects. The 'Fortress' that he mentioned in his letter was the Boeing B-17 Flying Fortress, an American heavy bomber recognisable by the large white star on its flank and the bulbous glass nose that housed its forward gunner. Hundreds of Fortresses flew out of the airfields around Chelmsford during the war's later years. As the planes returned each day, those aboard

A V-1 rocket and a hunting peregrine falcon 'stoop' down on their victims in dreaded silence.

would throw out red flares to signal if there were dead or injured men aboard. So, though the sight of a Fortress was commonplace, local people would watch for them, as the augurs of ancient Rome observed the flights of birds to divine their fortunes.

Later, when he came to write *The Peregrine*, Baker described a sight that conjured other memories of wartime. Watching a falcon flying over a field, he reflected that though the bird was 'silent to me',

> to mice in the short grass, to partridges hidden and dumb in the long grass under the trees, his wings would rasp through the air with the burning whine of a circular saw. Silence they dread; when the roaring stops above them, they wait for the crash. Just as we, in the war, learnt to dread the sudden silence of the flying bomb, knowing that death was falling, but not where, or on what.

For Baker, the sight of a diving falcon conjured images of the 'flying bomb', the self-guided German V-1 missile that terrorised England during the summer of 1944. They were hard to detect and tricky to bring down, and devastated parts of London, Essex and Kent. With each rocket carrying almost 2,000 pounds of explosive, they created, when dropped, a shallow crater and a wide, destructive blast zone. These missiles earned another nickname, 'buzz bomb', from the sound their engines made; a sound that ceased abruptly when the bomb reached its controlled fuel limit and began to fall in silence, plummeting to land on whatever, or whomever, was beneath it.

Civilians in Britain hated the V-1 as much as they feared it. Common knowledge had it that you knew you were safe if you heard the crash of the impact. Those who never heard the crash were directly in its path.

The V-1 was succeeded by the far more dangerous V-2. One of these carried the same amount of explosive as the V-1, but travelled much faster – so fast that they appeared with no noise at all and were invisible to Allied early warning systems. A few days before Christmas in 1944, one V-2 fell close to Hoffman's factory. It was a devastating event: almost 180 people were killed or injured, mostly women who had returned to their night shift in the machine rooms after a break spent singing Christmas carols.

For someone of Baker's hypersensitivity, the effects of these attacks must have been devastating. But it was in his understanding of this fear that he was later able to sympathise with the lives of the wild creatures he observed. The peregrine became a paradoxical symbol of the war, embodying the violence that fell from the sky.

Back at Foreman's at the end of 1944, companionless and ground down by what he described as 'the dread' that the war induced, Baker retreated into himself and grew lonelier as the days passed. He could find no one at the company with whom he shared any interests; his artistic, intellectual nature singled him out as an outsider among his colleagues, and in his letters they came in for harsh criticism. 'Poetry', he wrote bitterly, 'is thrown overboard by these cultureless mariners as being too heavy a cargo whilst music and art were never shipped at all.'

Literature was a constant preoccupation. Since leaving school it had become Baker's focus, and the letters that he sent over the winter were strewn with references to his reading – titles, authors, potted biographies, even whole poems, carefully copied out over several pages. Without the guidance of teachers, Baker roved haphazardly through the British literary canon. He leapt from Shakespeare to Kipling and back to Shelley, from Milton to G. K. Chesterton, and Wordsworth to MacNeice.

Baker particularly admired Alun Lewis, ten years Baker's senior, who was celebrated for his writing about the war and his fluid, elegiac poetry which was often studded with acute observations of the natural world. Baker was drawn to the young poet, perhaps imagining a kindred spirit – Lewis, too, had been a grammar school boy from a middle-class family, though from South Wales rather than Essex. When Lewis died in Burma in March 1944, a likely suicide, Baker grieved his death as a loss to literature. His sadness lasted well into the end of that year, when he drafted several poems dedicated to the memory of the Welsh poet.

Yet even reading to keep himself occupied, Baker felt unhappy. Long hours at the timber yard restricted the time he could spend with his books, and to his work frustrations were added those of the heart. Early in the winter of 1944 he wrote to John Thurmer, quoting Shakespeare, that 'The lunatic, the lover, and the poet / Are of imagination all compact'. '[It] is my privilege to fill all these roles at this moment,' he said, 'though my performances in all but the first-named mark me as an indifferent actor. Yes – I am in love.' He had fallen for a woman who was several years older, and, to add to the hopelessness of the match, was already engaged (though unofficially) to another. Disconsolate, Baker could only tell Thurmer of the yearning and despair that he felt, and hope for its ending. 'Pah!' he wrote, in a wry sign-off, 'I will not burden you with disgusting details but merely charge you to retain the knowledge in your bosom – until I forget all about it which I shall do.'

But his infatuation was not easily forgotten. It continued well into the spring of 1945, and Baker's correspondence to his two friends recorded his increasing wretchedness. His writing took on a manic edge, filled with feverish parody and nonsense verse; several of his letters contained outbursts of anger, directed towards both himself and the object of his affections. Though all he offered (Baker said) was simple adoration, the one he loved couldn't, or wouldn't, understand him, and though he asked for little, all he got in return was scorn. The result was constant frenzy of emotion. His nerves were run ragged.

Though this sort of self-pity is common to many eighteen-year-olds who decide to be hopelessly in love, for Baker it became 'an obsession' without respite, as he later acknowledged. The cumulative stresses of war, work and unrequited love took their toll on Baker. Later, he recorded how his anxiety escalated, until, in April of 1945, he suffered a nervous breakdown.

At the time this happened, John Thurmer was visiting home on leave. Baker had arranged to meet him; the two friends spent an afternoon together joking and enjoying one another's company. The following day, Baker somehow heard that Thurmer was walking to Hatfield Peverel (a village seven or eight miles from the Bakers' house) and he was compelled by a sudden impulse to intercept him. Racing out on his bicycle, Baker covered the distance in twenty minutes, snapping a pedal and arriving at Hatfield Peverel in a state that must have seemed agitated. Thurmer was astonished to see him.

Afterwards Baker explained to Donald Samuel that this frantic rush to see Thurmer was a symptom of his mental fragility: 'God I was isolated in my imagination in those days – the knowledge that a temporary respite was to be found in an old friend's company – nearly drove me into a frenzy of eagerness.' The next day Baker had what he called a 'brainstorm', an incident during which he deliberately smashed a plate-glass window and covered himself in his own blood – something, he said, that 'was sheer relief, although it hurt.'

Three weeks of black despair followed during which he was unable to work or leave his bed, nor even able to concentrate on his books – a time when he was, as he said, 'on the edge of insanity'. He was diagnosed with a case of acute neurosis. The recommended treatment was a programme at the newly opened Roffey Park Rehabilitation Centre.

Only one letter from Roffey Park, written by Baker to John Thurmer, has survived. In it, Baker described how he came to the centre:

> Cher Ami,
>
> Forgive – if you can find it in your heart to do so – my failure to answer your voluminous tract with my usual alacrity. This omission was occasioned by the fact of my powers of concentration etc. being temporarily undermined by a 'nervous collapse'. On May 9th I came to the above address ... I had then been [away] from work for three weeks – wallowing in the depths of neurotic depression and instability. It was hell, and it is only

> during the last fortnight or so that I have begun to feel like my old self, or rather – my old self minus that 'nervous intensity' which rendered my happiness so precarious. This trouble had been threatening for a very long time – the immediate factor which hastened its approach being my idolatrous devotion to a certain lady. Years of misery occasioned by family quarrels and the like, however, have been the basic cause of my lack of confidence and introspection. But all that is past and I am confident that I shall leave here purged of all my doubts and dreads.

Being 'purged' of one's doubts and dreads was of course the sole purpose of the work at Roffey Park. Medical director Dr Ling stressed the need for each patient at the centre to understand 'the factors which have prevented [his] successful adaptation to life and thus brought him under medical care.'

'Successful adaptation' in the world of rehabilitative psychology in the 1940s meant returning to being a productive member of society. Roffey Park had what its staff called a 'morale structure': encouraged above all else were group activities, social living and practical endeavour. Boosting morale was 'perhaps the best form of treatment,' Dr Ling said, as 'neurosis is characterised by a failure to adjust to the environment, and the restoration of this adjustment is essential for recovery.' Learning how to 'keep calm and carry on' (as the wartime slogan went) was the essential message.

Restoring a patient to their environment involved a combination of occupational therapy, exercise and psychotherapy. In his letter to Thurmer, Baker described the average day of a patient at Roffey:

> 7.30 Rise (and shine, if possible).
>
> 8.15 Breakfast – porridge, bacon, bread & etc.
>
> 10.15 WORK. A little sweeping & polishing is done by patients. Insufficient labour renders this necessary.
>
> 11.10 A cup of coffee, or cocoa.
>
> 11.35 – 12.30 P.T. Strenuous physical contortions under a really first-class instructor. Very enjoyable for most.
>
> 12.45 Dinner. Quality – fairly good. Quantity – dubious.
>
> 1.30 – 2.15 Rest on beds.

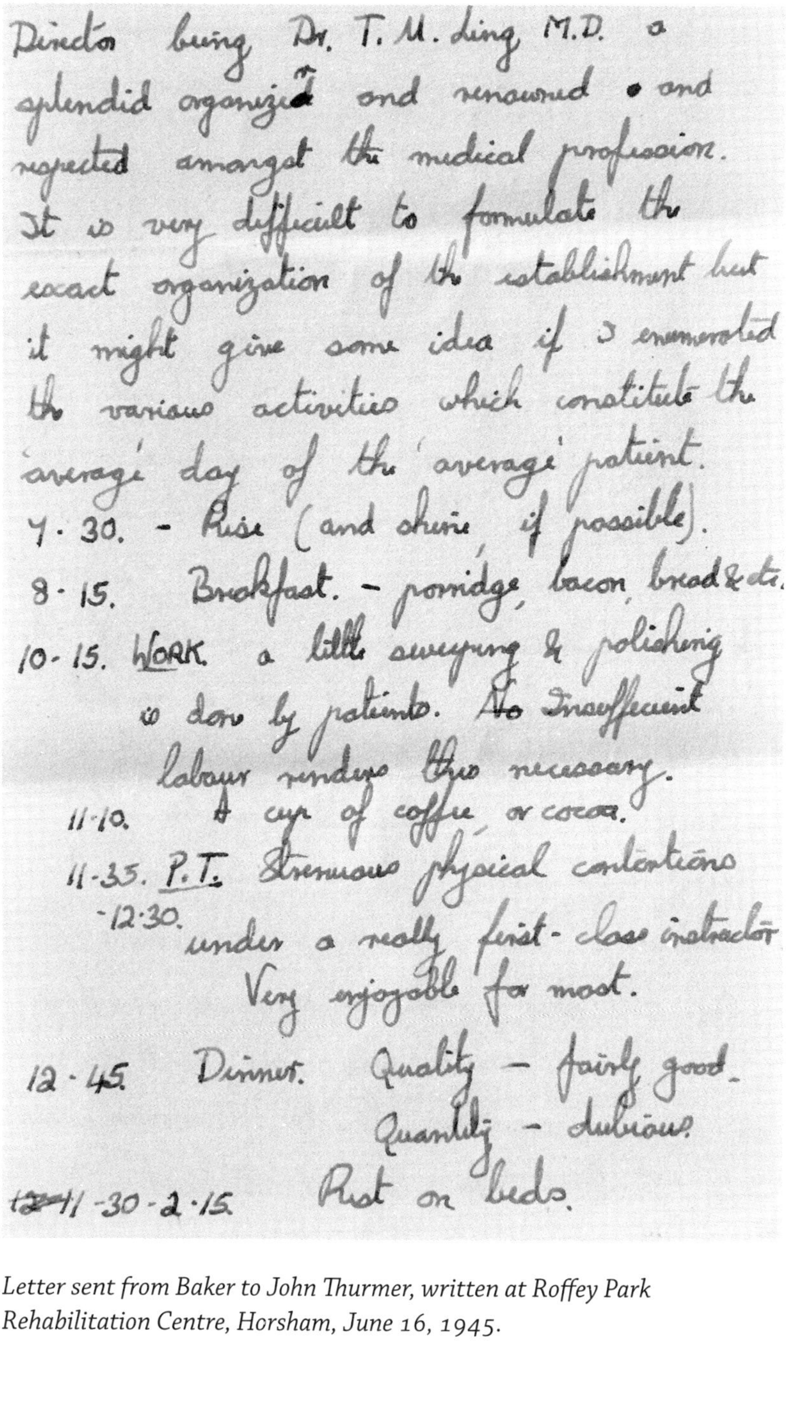

Director being Dr. T. M. Ling M.D. a splendid organizer and renowned and respected amongst the medical profession. It is very difficult to formulate the exact organization of the establishment but it might give some idea if I enumerated the various activities which constitute the 'average' day of the 'average' patient.

7·30. – Rise (and shine, if possible).

8·15. Breakfast. – porridge, bacon, bread & etc.

10-15. WORK a little sweeping & polishing is done by patients. ~~No~~ Insufficient labour renders this necessary.

11·10. A cup of coffee, or cocoa.

11-35. P.T. Strenuous physical contortions -12·30. under a really first-class instructor Very enjoyable for most.

12·45. Dinner. Quality – fairly good. Quantity – dubious.

~~12~~1-30-2·15. Rest on beds.

Letter sent from Baker to John Thurmer, written at Roffey Park Rehabilitation Centre, Horsham, June 16, 1945.

2.30 – 4.30 Occupations – either working in the extensive gardens or in the well-equipped engineering and carpenter's shops.

4.30 onwards is free. Tea at 5.00. Supper at 8.45. Bed at 9.30.

In the evenings various forms of entertainment were provided, often put on by the patients themselves. These included, Baker wrote, 'a Social and Dance in the fine ballroom on Saturdays, Debates, Brain-Trusts, Lectures, Games, etc.' Baker quickly became the chairman of the Debating Club – largely, he said, 'as a result of the fact that I can talk the majority of my colleagues under the table. Keeping up the old school tradition, you see.'

The axiom that 'what is good for the body is good for the mind' had been the approved prescription for mental illness far longer than Dr Ling had been practicing psychological medicine. Little, in fact, about this part of the treatment at Roffey had changed from methods of the preceding century. A hundred years before Baker's trip away from Chelmsford, and in an odd parallel to his experience, the poet John Clare (celebrated for his own bird writing) had been removed to Essex after suffering a mental breakdown. High Beach, the asylum where Clare was sent in 1837, was, like Roffey, a converted country house, in and around which routines of gardening and exercise were offered to all patients with the same belief in their curative properties. As the focus of remedy for mental aberration in the 1800s was religion rather than psychology, Clare was subject to prayer and Bible study – God being considered the best healer of the time.

Baker's more secular age had replaced faith with a different kind of spiritual recovery, though one that still required the ritual of confession and was no less immured in doctrine: the talking cure. What Baker omitted from his day's routine were the psychotherapy sessions undertaken by all patients at Roffey. These were (in the words of Dr Ling) 'directed along eclectic lines ... "Talking out" of problems, "counselling" techniques, and narco-analysis are extensively employed.'

If those techniques were a step forward from John Clare's day, there were still some methods used at Roffey that were no less

Roffey Park, near Horsham in Sussex, the rehabilitation centre run by Dr T. M. Ling, attended by J. A. Baker with others suffering from post-war and industrial fatigue.

brutal than those employed by the previous century, though they were disguised by the mask of modern science: electric convulsion therapy, modified insulin therapy and 'other physical methods of treatment' were utilised 'where necessary'. Baker doesn't say whether he underwent any of these treatments, but he would certainly have been exposed to their effects on others at Roffey.

The change of scene, combined with quiet but purposeful activities outdoors, did have a positive effect on Baker. As he recovered from his episode, his principal interests in nature and literature were the first things that returned to him. When John Clare reached Epping, where High Beach was located, he was in awe of its undulating countryside, so unlike the flattened fens of Northamptonshire that he was used to: 'I love the breakneck hills that headlong go, / And leave me nigh, and half the world below', he wrote. Baker was similarly enchanted by the new landscape he found himself in, with its uneven horizons and old forest of oaks and flowering horse chestnuts, so different from the familiar lowlands of Chelmsford. The parts of his letter to Thurmer in which he sounds the happiest are his descriptions of the Sussex countryside around Roffey:

> The view from the front door of the house is, I think, the most impressive and inspiring which I have ever beheld. In the foreground the lands [sic] falls away gently to a small stream in the valley. There is an expansive field studded with trees on which ewes and their lambs graze meditatively and, at sunset, fill the air with bleating which seems so in keeping as it is with the glorious fields and gills ... Across the valley there is a ridge of low hills largely covered with dark forest. From these hills – looking southward (the house faces NW) – you may see the glorious, sweeping downs of which you are so justly enamoured, crowned by the lone magnificence of Chanctonbury Ring – indeed 'Earth has not anything to show more fair'.

To Baker's delight, he found out that Wordsworth's fellow Romantic poet Percy Bysshe Shelley was born just a few miles from Roffey, at Field Place in Warnham. Baker was thrilled to think that Shelley, some 150 years earlier, had gazed upon the same woods and gills (the local name for streams) that he was then surrounded by. He told Thurmer, 'I wandered into the fields here in the early morning and heard, as he [Shelley] too heard, the glorious anthem of the skylark fading away into the heavens.' Baker's own situation at Roffey and the circumstances that brought him there must have made more poignant Shelley's fervent wish in his address to the skylark: 'Teach me half the gladness / That thy brain must know'.

Though Baker's stay at the rehabilitation centre lasted less than two months, the effects of his time there and the trauma of his breakdown were more long-lasting. Relationships with those close to him had changed and took time to recover – some of his friends found Baker's illness harder to deal with than others. Despite having written to John Thurmer very openly about Roffey, Baker thought Thurmer more distant. For a while afterwards, Baker felt acutely the change in Thurmer's close friendship, and it would take over a year for them to feel at ease together again.

As for his family, Baker wrote to Donald Samuel saying that after his treatment at Roffey he had learned to better tolerate his father's temperament (though not forgive it). This, for a while, improved things at home. Roffey's influence on his life ran further than this, though, and remained significant in his creative imagination long after. When, in his forties and fifties, he came to write out autobiographical notes and memories that he thought could be used for poetry, 'Roffey' was a name that cropped up in more than one instance – though if he ever did write anything about the Park, it has not survived.

One thing that was short-lived was Baker's hope that he would be forever purged of his 'doubts and dreads'. His struggles with them continued, probably for the rest of his life, though in less dramatic forms than those that had led to his referral to Roffey. Even in the few years immediately after his return home, his anxieties returned now and then. He wrote to Donald Samuel only eighteen months later:

> As to my changes of mood – I can't explain them. As you know – they are quite genuine, although so close together. God forbid that ever another Psychologist or Psychiatrist should come near me – I've had enough of that tribe, thank-you. I'm afraid they never made much of me, anyway ... I've always been like it – and I expect I shall always be the same, as I see no prospect of my ever growing out of my childhood. I think that's the real explanation of my nature, Sam.

J. A. Baker in his late twenties.

Chapter Four
TRIALS AND OBSTACLES

> There are doubtless many trials and obstacles ahead but I feel assured now – that I am going to overcome all these and, at last, justify the years of preparation and assimilation.
>
> J. A. BAKER, letter to Donald Samuel, 1946

SIX STOREYS UP, ON THE ROOF of the Oxford University Press headquarters on an evening in 1945, Baker sat and contemplated the view. The building, Amen House, was just off Ludgate Hill in the City of London, and he could hear birds calling in the plane trees and see St Paul's – so close it seemed a stone's throw away.

It was a striking panorama: the cathedral's pale dome rising from sooty, bombed-out cavities where buildings had once been; beyond, endless rooftops and the Thames; below, the bustling pavements of the City. Baker found it endlessly fascinating. Watching from his rooftop vantage point, he started to imagine what it would be like to see what St Paul's saw. 'Like', as he wrote in one letter to John Thurmer, 'a great bird, paused, majestic, aloft', while down below 'far, far below – Ludgate's teeming cliff – the avalanche of boulders – buses and cars thundering by – but the sound of pebbles on the shore.'

Such a view, he prophesied, would form 'the material with which, one not so distant day, I shall furnish my "house of sky" – my translucent world of poesy – my novel or whatever shape it may ultimately assume.'

Little did he know at that time how that 'house of sky', as he called it, would turn out to be *The Peregrine*, a work indeed preoccupied with the vertiginous perspective of a different bird, more literal but no less majestic. 'The typical watcher,' writes Charles Foster in his book *Being a Beast*, 'huddled with his binoculars in a hide, isn't concerned with Anaximander's vertiginous question, "What does a falcon see?"' But Baker was not a typical watcher, and this question became his obsession.

When Baker later came to write *The Peregrine*, he wanted to create a story that told not merely what it was like to just *see* a peregrine, but how a peregrine *sees*. He strove in his writing to inhabit the falcon's body – too see through its own eyes, feel through its body.

At the beginning of his book he asks: 'What does this bird understand? What does it make of the world that rushes towards its flight in bright, streaming points of magnification?' As in his descriptions of the view from St Paul's twenty years earlier, he found that to imagine the perspective of the peregrine was to be both empowered and humbled. Through its eyes he, too, could become aloof, free from the world below; he could also see the insignificance of humans and man-made things, insubstantial as flotsam on a distant beach. The lessons that could be learned from such a sympathetic view were, he found, increasingly needed, as the disregard with which people treated the natural world appeared to go unchallenged.

Until the end of his life, Baker was intent on trying to understanding what the world was like through the eyes of his birds. He hoarded books and magazine articles on the biology of animal vision and on aerial photographs, works with titles such as, *How Animals See: Other Visions of Our World*; *Britain: The Landscape Below*; *The Aerofilms Book of Aerial Photography*.

This last book was published in 1965 (two years before Baker's *The Peregrine*) by a company that had pioneered the use of aerial photography before and during the Second World War. In the 1950s and early 60s, batches of Aerofilms Ltd photographs were sent to public libraries, including Colchester Library, a short trip away from Chelmsford. Colchester Library still holds these miniature aerial photographs of southern Essex – Heybridge to

Woodford, and Basildon to Harlow – a great X across the region that has Chelmsford at its centre. These collections of Aerofilms photographs may well be the same ones that Baker's wife Doreen referred to when she mentioned that Baker, when he was writing *The Peregrine*, sought out aerial pictures of his local area in order to immerse himself in the peregrine's visual world.

Baker had reached the rooftop of the Oxford University Press after several frustrating months of unemployment. He had returned from Roffey determined that a change of occupation was needed. Foreman's had done him no good, and Baker was determined not to go back. If one wanted to destroy all creativity and original thought in a person, he told his friends, the answer would be to pack that person off to an office, where the mundanity of business would 'slowly deaden his faculties and quench his enthusiasm for everything except, possibly, cups of tea.' No, that line of work had not suited him – but what would?

His great desire was to be a writer; but he needed money, and the prospects of a jobbing author were poor. If he was not to give up his literary ambitions, he needed a career that could combine books with a reasonable income.

He was then nineteen. Several of his friends, soon to be demobbed, were looking to start university. Encouraged by them, Baker toyed with the idea of doing an undergraduate degree. He wrote to London University, but received little helpful advice. Then he went to the Essex education authority, hoping to find some financial support, but they informed him there was none.

To add insult to injury, the education board also told Baker that they had asked for a reference on his intellectual abilities from Norman Squier, his old grammar school headmaster. Squier was a man for whom Baker had little fondness, and the sentiment seemingly ran both ways – Squier wrote back to the board saying that he thought Baker was more suited to trade than university.

With this lack of support and no 'matric exemption' nor Higher Education Certificate, Baker concluded that the only way he would get to a university would be to resit some of his previous exams and then pay his own way, not a prospect greeted with rapture by his parents. Baker didn't relish the idea of taking up his schoolbooks again just to pass for an exemption, and so he gave up on the idea of university.

His next thought was to write to London publishers; perhaps the book trade would be a more appropriate occupation. Heinemann, Jonathan Cape, Allen & Unwin, Hodder & Stoughton all replied with polite but firm negatives, and from Cassells, Constable and Faber & Faber he received no response at all (Baker, tongue-in-cheek, suggested to Samuel that it was possible T. S. Eliot, editor of Faber at the time, caught the scent of a literary conservative and recoiled from his correspondence). After months of waiting, he finally received a single positive reply asking him to attend an interview. The meeting was a success, and so it was that on October 1, 1945, Baker started his new job as an assistant at the Oxford University Press.

The job in London liberated him from the confines of Chelmsford, but however much he was captivated by the city and the view from the roof of Amen House, Baker quickly tired of the role he was assigned. Within a matter of weeks he confessed himself 'heartily fed up of work that [is] entirely without interest.' He had started out with high hopes, thinking, with the arrogance of a bright nineteen-year-old, that his talents would be recognised and applauded. But being sent trotting from one office to another with letters, the occasional manuscript, and other sundries for a meagre wage was, Baker decided, not the job for him. And so, after only a month, Baker was once more back where he had begun, unemployed and at home in Chelmsford.

He was not disheartened. As far as he was concerned his real work was going very well: in the three months between returning from Roffey and starting work in London he had read almost sixty books; such 'aesthetic stimulus', as he called it, was far more important to his long-term goals. Now that he had time on his

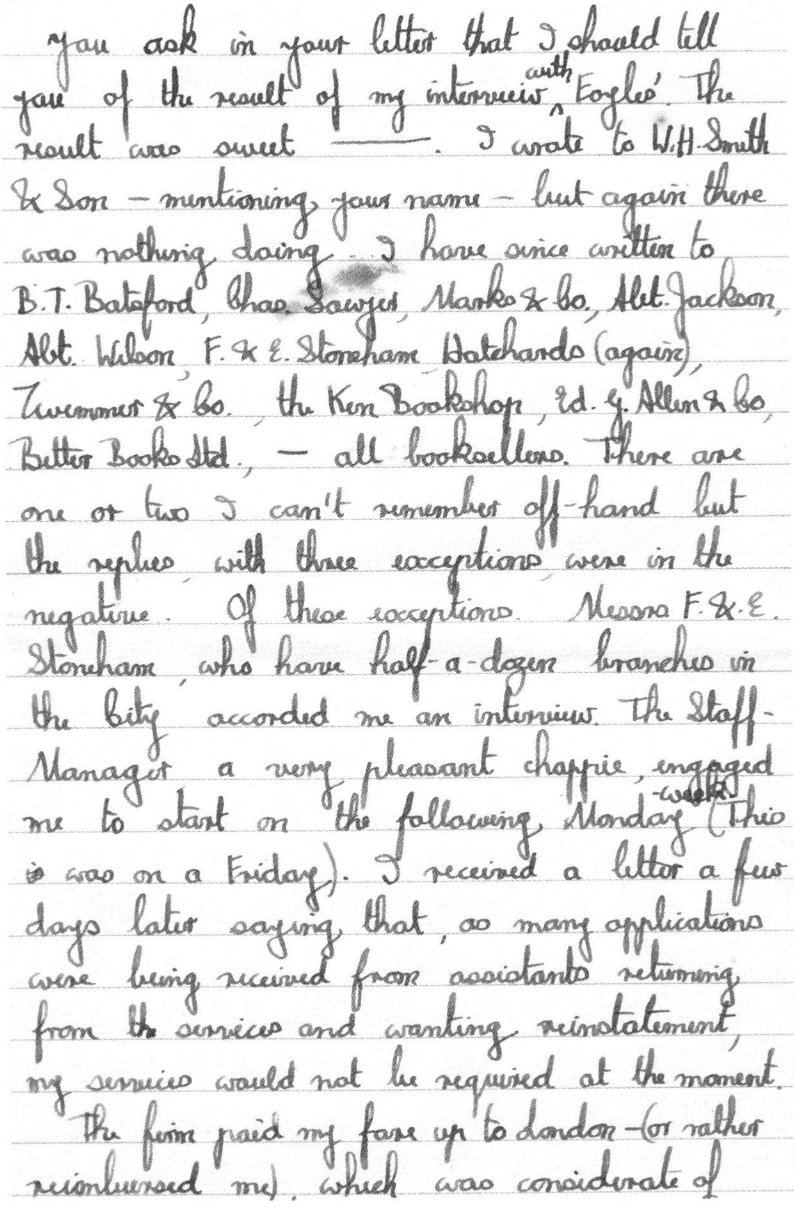
You ask in your letter that I should tell
you of the result of my interview with 'Eagles'. The
result was sweet ——. I wrote to W.H. Smith
& Son – mentioning your name – but again there
was nothing doing. I have since written to
B.T. Batsford, Chas. Sawyer, Marks & Co., Abt. Jackson,
Abt. Wilson, F. & E. Stoneham, Hatchards (again),
Zwemmer & Co., the Ken Bookshop, Ed. G. Allen & Co,
Better Books Ltd., – all booksellers. There are
one or two I can't remember off-hand but
the replies with three exceptions were in the
negative. Of these exceptions, Messrs F. & E.
Stoneham, who have half-a-dozen branches in
the City, accorded me an interview. The Staff-
Manager, a very pleasant chappie, engaged
me to start on the following Monday week (This
~~is~~ was on a Friday). I received a letter a few
days later saying that, as many applications
were being received from assistants returning
from the services and wanting reinstatement,
my services would not be required at the moment.
The firm paid my fare up to London – (or rather
reimbursed me), which was considerate of

Letter from J. A. Baker (known to his school friends as 'Doughy') to Donald Samuel, January 1946, recounting his fruitless search for employment.

hands, he was keen to devote it to his literary projects. Days and nights were spent feverishly reading and writing. He continued to send letters to London booksellers and publishers, but through the months of winter he had no luck. So he continued his intensive studying, desperate to absorb as much as he could.

By the end of January 1946, Baker's library had grown to remarkable levels. Dozens of books of poetry had been consumed as he made his way through the canonical writers of the nineteenth century, including Walt Whitman, Gerard Manley Hopkins and Robert Browning (as well as translations of the French and German poets Rimbaud and Rilke), and moved on to modern writers: John Masefield, T. S. Eliot (whom he had grown to like, despite not having been offered a job at Faber), Cecil Day Lewis and Stephen Spender. He discovered a love for the lilting style of the 'ultra-modern' Dylan Thomas, whom he thought perfectly mirrored his own memories of childhood and love of the countryside. Exercise books were filled with notes on form and metre, and hundreds of poems carefully copied out. Study was an outlet: it helped him to stave off the bouts of depression that continued to threaten. 'I have occasional spasms of that black despair that so harried me,' he wrote to Samuel, 'but, in the main, I am happier than I have been for a long time. Reason – I have started to write in earnest and can already say that I am progressing in great style ... Wish me luck Sam – I have found the key at last and if it doesn't unlock the door I shall batter it down with my fists.'

Many of Baker's own poetic efforts made during this time he sent to Samuel and Thurmer. Unable to share his writing at home and desperate to improve, he implored his friends to respond critically, and awaited their replies with impatience.

Baker's poems were very much those of a young man. He was still a teenager, and so perhaps can be forgiven for writing about unrequited loves, sunsets and being misunderstood. He was just embarking on what would become a lifetime of writing, and so, in terms of quality, many of the pieces he wrote at this time were poor. But a few showed glimmers of promise.

From the start, Baker understood that the best place for a writer to look for inspiration was in first-hand experience. His poems described what he found around him, everyday events, people, and encounters with nature. Already he was showing in his writing a skill for paying attention to the smaller events of life. Both of these gifts – noticing and recording the act of noticing – would come to maturity in his later works and would be the key to their success.

After months spent writing application letters, Baker finally found employment again. In February 1946 he joined the British Museum Library as an attendant librarian. He was cheerful at the prospect, thinking he had found the perfect place for his temperament and bookish ambitions; with naivety he thought he had 'come home to roost at last'.

Yet once more this opinion was not long to endure. While the duties of the young attendants were not strenuous, they were deathly boring. He was confined to the Museum's small Reading Room (the large one with its wonderful domed ceiling having been closed during the war and not yet reopened). There visitors would find the books they desired in the library catalogues, write the particulars onto little paper tickets (six tickets a day being the limit), and present them to Baker or one of the other attendants. They, in turn, would dispatch the tickets to the correct library section. Requested books were whisked to the Reading Room by a series of conveyor belts and paternosters to be delivered to the awaiting scholars. Baker struggled with the long hours of stifling mental inactivity, and the artificial light under which he had to work all day depressed him.

Most of all he found himself bitterly disappointed in his hopes of finding like-minded colleagues. The other library staff met his enthusiasms with disinterest or, worse, disdain. His ego slighted, Baker couldn't help himself from treating them with scorn. To his friend Donald Samuel, who was still undergoing training with the army, he wrote: 'My environment is every bit as moronic as yours these days, my fellow attendants being Civil Servants as well as stupid in the ordinary way ... I couldn't be in company where my gifts were less appreciated.'

Working at the library did, however, give Baker the opportunity for two pastimes he greatly enjoyed: reading and flouting authority. With access to two or three million books, he couldn't help himself from a bit of light-fingered borrowing: 'We are allowed to have any books we like from the library but *must* not take them away,' he wrote to Donald Samuel, adding 'I have two at home here now – I have to be very careful how I smuggle them out.'

These illicit activities didn't go down well with the senior Library staff. His attitude was deemed unsuitable, he was given his notice, and by August 1946 he was, once again, back to the drawing board.

In a fit of discontentment, and in the face of increasing antagonism between himself and his father, Baker resolved to leave Chelmsford and seek his fortune elsewhere. He wrote to Samuel to declare grandiosely that they lived in a bureaucratic age, one in which there was no settled job worth having; he was disgusted by the narrow-mindedness and regimentation he saw all around him, and longed for freedom; he had done with convention and would live instead for his writing. He planned to find work on a farm – though nothing was arranged. Gloucestershire, he decided, was to be his destination.

For his choice of Gloucestershire he had, of course, looked to poetry. Hilaire Belloc's 'Dedicatory Ode' pointed him to the 'western wolds' and the 'tender Evenlode' river. And so to Stow-on-the-Wold, a little town high in the Cotswolds, he went.

But this journey of self-discovery hit a snag almost before it had begun. He had set off ready to embody the romantic figure of the itinerant, carefree labourer. But when he got to Stow-on-the-Wold, the local farmers turned him away: he was too early for harvesting and they had no need of him.

For a week he dawdled at the Red Lion but the rooms were expensive and his funds were dwindling. From there he travelled

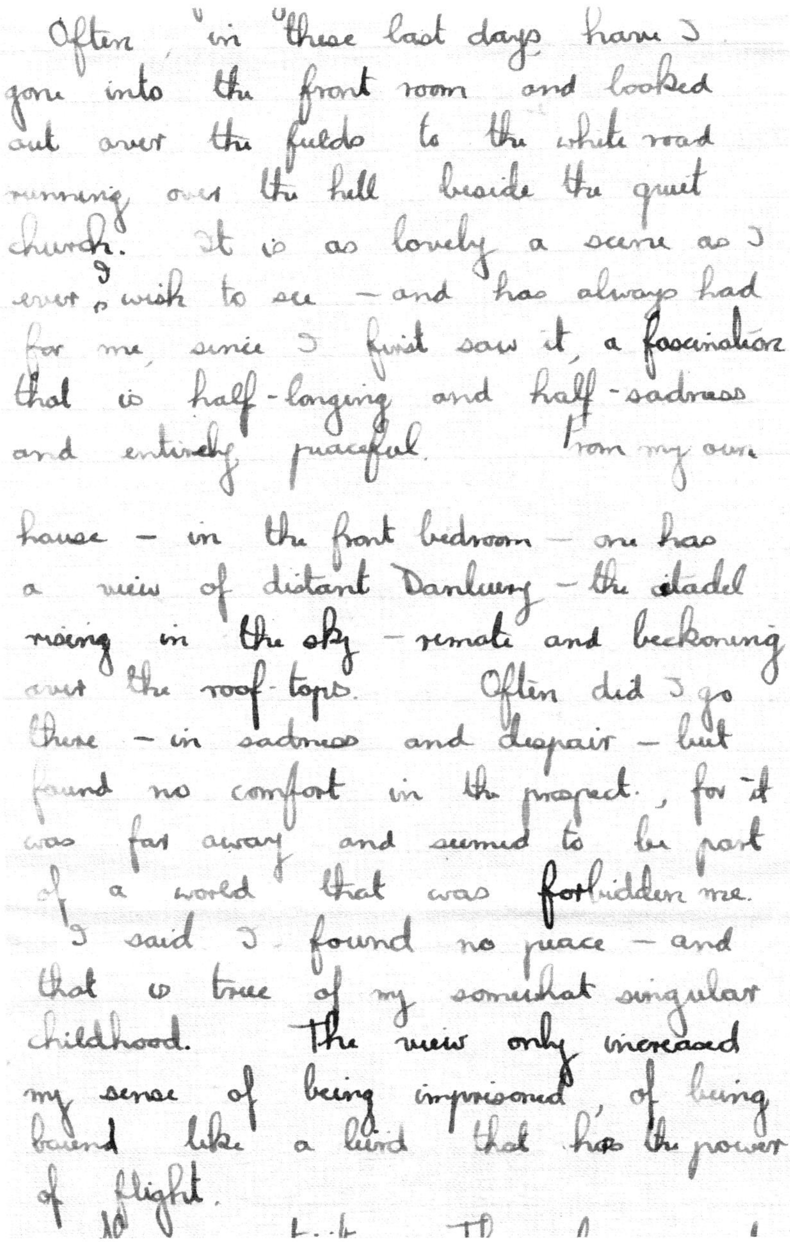

Often, in these last days have I gone into the front room and looked out over the fields to the white road running over the hill beside the quiet church. It is as lovely a scene as I ever wish to see – and has always had for me, since I first saw it, a fascination that is half-longing and half-sadness and entirely peaceful. From my own house – in the front bedroom – one has a view of distant Danbury – the citadel rising in the sky – remote and beckoning over the roof-tops. Often did I go there – in sadness and despair – but found no comfort in the prospect, for it was far away and seemed to be part of a world that was forbidden me.

I said I found no peace – and that is true of my somewhat singular childhood. The view only increased my sense of being imprisoned, of being bound like a bird that has the power of flight.

Letter from Baker to Donald Samuel, September 15, 1946, describing his feelings as a child of 'being imprisoned, of being bound like a bird that has the power of flight'.

to a guesthouse in the village of Bledington, Oxfordshire. There was little work to be had here either, though the novelty of the setting and his boldness in reaching it threw him into a turmoil of creative ideas. He wrote several long, furious letters to Samuel denouncing conservatism (political, literary, and otherwise), railing against government control and the old-fashioned restrictive values of their parents' generation, and vowing, in an outburst of pretentious rhetoric, that if by his writing he could bring some light into the dark world in which they lived, then he would have done all that a man could do.

Less than a month after he had left, on September 4, 1946, Baker wrote again to Samuel – but this letter was addressed from his parents' house on Finchley Avenue. With an air of gloom he told Samuel that he had left Chelmsford seeking experience, and by God he had found it – more than he had bargained for. While in Oxfordshire he had met a Land Girl named Pat, from the village of Kingham. After only the second meeting with her, he said, he knew he was in love. Never had he known anyone like her, nor the happiness he felt in her company.

But she loved another, an airman killed during the war. 'Consequently,' Baker wrote, 'she did not feel herself able to become seriously attached to anyone else. I was "anyone else." She was very fond of me – but there was just that abiding memory of the dead.' Pat told him that they couldn't continue, she couldn't see him again.

Like his last romantic failure, this crushing episode threw him into an emotional crisis. Shaken, convinced he could no longer remain in Oxfordshire without either making a nuisance or a fool of himself, Baker packed his bags that night, walked in the dark to the nearest station, and caught the first morning train home to Chelmsford. In all, from meeting to departing, he had known his Land Girl for eight days.

Baker pined for Pat over the winter of 1946. But there were other events to distract him; time passed and so did his despair.

Christmas came and went. By the spring of 1947 Baker still had no settled work. He gave up temporarily on his hope of earning money by his writing, and turned his efforts to getting employment in the only other area in which he had a keen interest: nature.

What he found was, as he put it, 'cold but congenial' work in the orchards and woods to the east of Danbury. This was for the English Timber Company, where most of his work consisted of managing and harvesting trees, so at least for some of the time he was outdoors rather than in an office. A year or so later he moved to another timber company, Sadds of Maldon, which managed other woodlands around Danbury.

With both companies Baker was working in woodlands, some of them hazel which had been coppiced for hundreds of years. During the coppicing process trees are cut back close to ground, leaving a 'stool' to grow new shoots, known as suckers. Once mature, these dense clusters of branches are harvested on rotation, forming a wonderful habitat for songbirds (particularly the nightingale) as they grow and regrow.

The coppices at Danbury might well have been where Baker first learned to listen out for the nightingale's distinctive call. Certainly when, many years later, he began the birdwatching diaries that would become the foundation of his published books, Danbury was one of his regular haunts – indeed, one of his earliest diary entries in 1954 describes hearing nightingales in the hornbeam and chestnut woods around Danbury Common. His time spent managing woodlands was a defining period in his development as a naturalist. In his notes the name of the English Timber Company is circled with an arrow pointing to the words 'love of nature' scrawled in large letters.

When his school friends Samuel, Thurmer, Dennis and Cufflin all returned to Essex, demobbed from the forces, Baker's regular letter writing came to an end. It's not until the summer of 1949 that Baker can be placed again, visiting John Thurmer in Oxford, where Thurmer was an undergraduate. By this point, Baker's career – 'that lugubrious chimera', as he called it – had taken another new direction. That summer he was waiting to take up his place at a teacher training college.

The idea of teaching may have been in Baker's mind for a while. He might have thought it a career through which he could advance his own ambitions as a writer. Three years earlier, back in Bledington where he met his Land Girl, Baker had shared the guesthouse with a number of young English teachers, and he had been impressed with their knowledge of literature.

Teacher training was a popular route taken by young men and women in the years following the Second World War. The country was experiencing a desperate shortage of teaching staff, so in 1945 the government created its Emergency Training Scheme, offered to those who had served in the Armed Forces or done other National Service. 'Emergency' teaching colleges were established around the country: students took courses that typically lasted a year, paid no fees, and received a generous maintenance allowance. Competition to get onto the courses was high. In the first few years of the scheme, applications were so numerous that the rate of acceptance was one in fourteen.

Which of these colleges Baker attended isn't clear, but he left a few scribbled notes that would suggest it was somewhere not far from Oxford, back in the Cotswolds once again. He also left a few choice phrases that summed up his memories of that time: 'College – beeches, P&E, frost, dormers pals.'

A little yellow cardboard wallet of black and white photographs, with 'COLLEGE' handwritten on it, confirms these impressions. Some of the pictures show only landscapes – a wide pasture with a group of Scots pines in the middle ground, a woodland climbing away into a low ridge. The next show Baker and another man in plimsolls and shorts, laughing and looking cold, followed by a group shot of a class of small, grinning boys in short trousers and long socks. There's a neat dorm room, presumably Baker's, with an old gut tennis racket on one wall and books on a shelf, a sheaf of papers cast across a desk. A youthful Baker appears in several others, his hands thrust into jacket pockets, standing with half-a-dozen other

ABOVE: *Baker (far right) stands at the edge of a group of young teachers-in-training, winter 1949–1950.* BELOW: *Baker's room during his brief time training as a teacher.*

Baker (bottom centre) surrounded by friends and colleagues at what is likely the Chelmsford Automobile Association's Christmas party, 1950s.

young men outside single-storey, creosoted prefabs, with fields and bare winter trees visible in the distance. Baker is smiling and happy, though never as relaxed or cocky as some of the other men, who pose rakishly for the camera. He is always on the edge of these groups, or at the back.

But soon teaching – just like draughting, publishing, library attending and woodland management – was added to the list of

Baker's failed occupations. He discovered an unplumbed loathing for the profession, and, though he trained for most of a year, seems not to have completed the course.

It was not until late 1950 or early 1951 that Baker finally settled. He began work at the Automobile Association's (AA) office in Chelmsford; this would be the one job, apart from writing, that he would manage to stick with for any length of time. As he told Thurmer in a letter, he had at last found something that was 'agreeable', or at the very least 'shows up no nasty neuroses before I go to sleep, as most of my previous jobs have done.'

This letter to John Thurmer is the last that survives from that period of Baker's life. It was written on August 6, 1951, Baker's twenty-fifth birthday. The tone is more mature than his letters from earlier years, as it was both addressed to and signed as 'John' (no more of the schoolboy nicknames 'Thurmer' and 'Doughy'), though Baker's language remained lighthearted, irreverent, and occasionally profane.

As well as describing his new job at the AA, Baker told his friend of his continued efforts to write. He had finally found some success in the area the previous October, when his first piece (as far as we know) was published in a magazine: an odd, surreal, single-page short story titled 'Always at Torquay'.

The rest of Baker's letter was taken up with news of their friend Dennis Cufflin's marriage. Towards the end, Baker wrote wistfully of his own dreams on that front: 'I was taken short later in the evening with an awful longing to get married myself ... You know, John, I really think I shall have to get married during the next twenty years. Can I be married out-doors? Preferably under an oak tree.' Baker wrote this little knowing that that same year he would meet Doreen Grace Coe, who worked as a wages clerk at the AA offices. Five years later they would marry – though not outdoors, or under an oak tree.

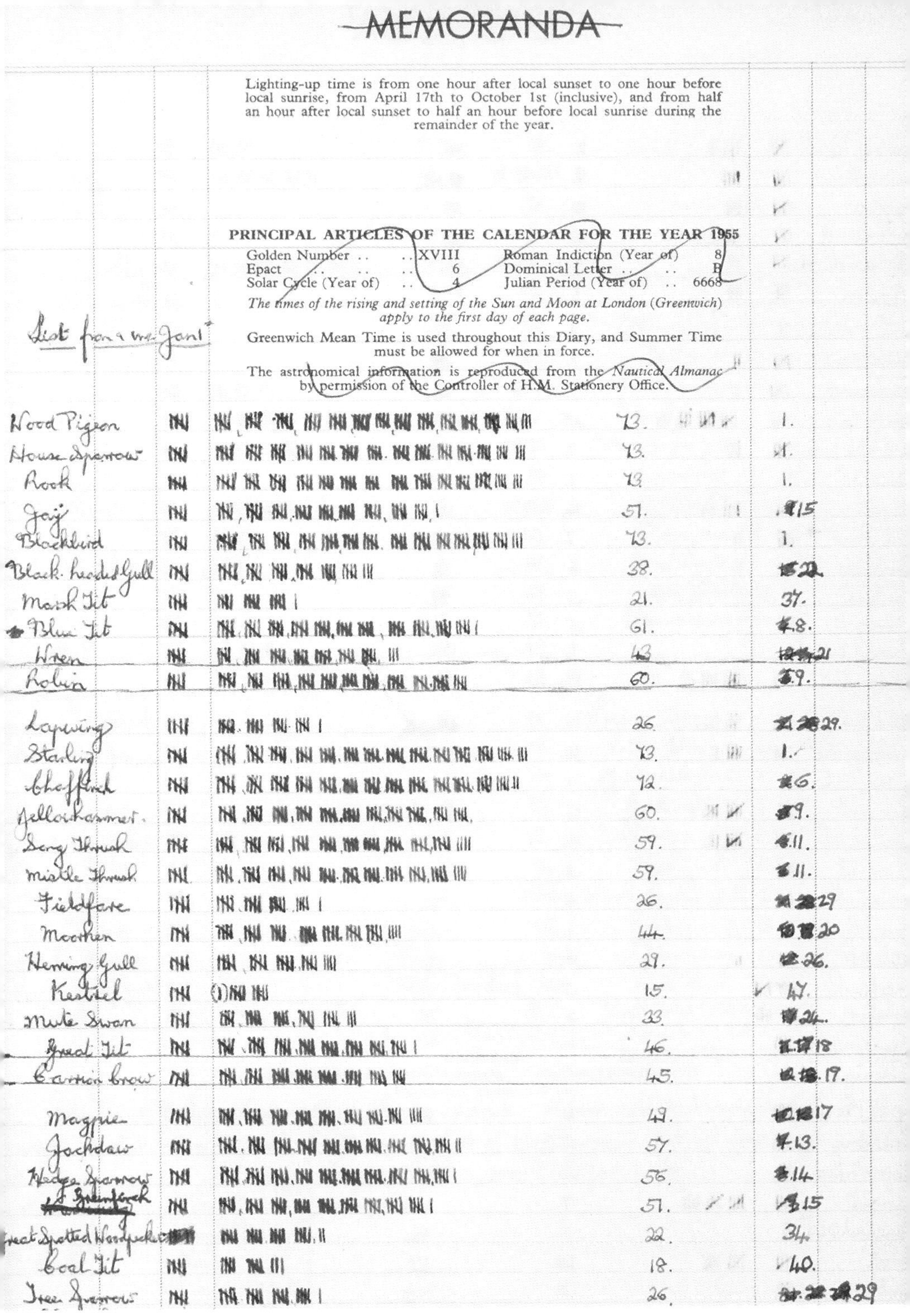

MEMORANDA

Lighting-up time is from one hour after local sunset to one hour before local sunrise, from April 17th to October 1st (inclusive), and from half an hour after local sunset to half an hour before local sunrise during the remainder of the year.

PRINCIPAL ARTICLES OF THE CALENDAR FOR THE YEAR 1955

Golden Number	XVIII	Roman Indiction (Year of)	8
Epact	6	Dominical Letter	B
Solar Cycle (Year of) ..	4	Julian Period (Year of) ..	6668

The times of the rising and setting of the Sun and Moon at London (Greenwich) apply to the first day of each page.

Greenwich Mean Time is used throughout this Diary, and Summer Time must be allowed for when in force.

The astronomical information is reproduced from the *Nautical Almanac* by permission of the Controller of H.M. Stationery Office.

List from the Jan 1st

Wood Pigeon	73.	1.
House Sparrow	73.	1.
Rook	73	1.
Jay	51.	15
Blackbird	73.	1.
Black-headed Gull	38.	22
Marsh Tit	21.	37.
Blue Tit	61.	8.
Wren	43	21
Robin	60.	9.
Lapwing	26	29.
Starling	73.	1.
Chaffinch	72.	6.
Yellowhammer	60.	9.
Song Thrush	59.	11.
Mistle Thrush	59.	11.
Fieldfare	26.	29
Moorhen	44.	20
Herring Gull	29.	26.
Kestrel	15.	47.
Mute Swan	33.	24.
Great Tit	46.	18
Carrion Crow	45.	17.
Magpie	49.	17
Jackdaw	57.	13.
Hedge Sparrow	56.	14.
Greenfinch	51.	15
Great Spotted Woodpecker	22.	34
Coal Tit	18.	40.
Tree Sparrow	26.	29

A running tally of species in the front of Baker's birdwatching diary, 1955.

Chapter Five
SYSTEMATIC WATCHING

> The world reveals itself to those who travel on foot.
>
> WERNER HERZOG, *The New Yorker*, January 12, 2016

> There is no limit to the extent to which we can think ourselves into the being of another. There are no bounds to the sympathetic imagination.
>
> J. M. COETZEE, *Elizabeth Costello*, 2003

> All a poet can do today is warn. That is why the true Poets must be truthful.
>
> WILFRED OWEN, draft preface for a collection of poems, 1918

SOMETHING STRANGE WAS HAPPENING in the spring of 1961. On farms and in woodlands, across fields and gardens, all around the English countryside, hundreds of bodies were being discovered. A search in Lincolnshire turned up 5,934 corpses in just 6 square kilometres, while 4,000 more victims were found in Cambridge, and in a third case 500 bodies turned up near a single spot, seemingly struck down where they had come to rest for the night.

But the true number of victims was almost impossible to estimate: the corpses were small and hard to find, and were often scavenged by animals before they could be counted. This was because the casualties were all birds – most of them woodpigeons, stock doves, pheasants and corvids.

The incidents were met with shock. What mysterious epidemic was killing these birds? It soon became apparent that crows and game birds were not the only creatures affected: barn owls, sparrowhawks, kestrels, buzzards and peregrines were also found, some in alarming numbers, and otters, foxes, and even pet cats and dogs succumbed. Before they died, some of the wild animals seemed to lose their fear of man, and were reportedly found staggering and confused, as if drunk. One disoriented fox was even discovered wandering in the yard of a Master of the Hunt.

In fact, that spring had not been the first in which such cases had occurred – though it was the worst. Since 1956, significant deaths of wildlife had been noted every spring, especially among birds like woodpigeons and pheasants, and particularly in the east of England. The cause had, at first, puzzled naturalists. A joint committee of the British Trust for Ornithology and the Royal Society for the Protection of Birds was set up to investigate. By the early 1960s the committee had published a series of reports with alarming conclusions: a great number of animals were affected, and it was clear that something was harming entire ecosystems, not just individual species.

The committee's conclusions confirmed long-held suspicions: agricultural pesticides were to blame – specifically, several insecticides belonging to the cyclodiene group of chlorinated hydrocarbons, including aldrin, dieldrin and heptachlor. These had been available since the late 1940s, but only became widely used around the mid-1950s. Aldrin and dieldrin in particular were popular among farmers, used to protect crops of carrots and wheat from the ravages of insect populations, and the seeds of cereals in particular were dressed with the chemicals before sowing.

But insects were not the only seedeaters, and the pesticides were far more fatal to other animals than had been predicted by scientists. The spring of 1961 was very wet; the rain saturated the soil, and when that year's dieldrin-dressed seed was sown it was not buried deep enough or was stuck to the surface of the ground, where it was easy for birds to retrieve. A woodpigeon that fed on only a handful or two of dressed grain would be poisoned within days. Though the seed-eating birds were hit hardest, the hunters and carrion-eaters that fed upon them in turn also suffered.

Strangely, it was around this time that Baker was recording his most regular sightings of peregrines. From 1959 onwards he had greater success in tracking these birds than he had in any of the previous years. In 1961 he noted down periods in January, February and March when he was travelling out many times a week and finding peregrines in the same places over consecutive days, sometimes four or five times in the same day; and in March 1962 he managed to track the same peregrine almost every day over a fortnight.

But it was many years before those deadly springs of the early 1960s that Baker's falcon obsession had begun.

In the years that followed the last letter written to John Thurmer in 1951, Baker had continued to find life at the AA agreeable, and not just in his work. For the AA was also where he had found love – and this time it had been reciprocated.

Doreen Coe was only sixteen when she and Baker first met – according to Doreen's brother, Bernard Coe, she had missed the last bus home and Baker gave her a lift on the handlebars of his bicycle. Doreen's father wouldn't allow her to marry until she was twenty-one, so she and Baker courted for five years, and married almost exactly a month after her twenty-first birthday, on Saturday October 6, 1956, at London Road Congregational Church, before moving into a rented house half a mile away from Baker's parents.

A number of black and white photographs taken of the ceremony show the couple outside the church. In one, the photographer caught the moment that a gust of wind fluffed up Baker's blond hair, and as Doreen pressed her bouquet against the front of her dress to stop her petticoats doing the same. In appearance the two of them were strikingly dissimilar. Baker, often the shyer of the two in front of the camera, was tall, thickset, and light-haired, with blue eyes and a soft, full-lipped face that made him appear younger than he was; Doreen was petite and slender, with shoulder-length dark curls and dark eyes that look out confidently from pictures.

Baker's birdwatching began during the early years of his and Doreen's courtship. It was through the AA that he met Sidney Harman (Sid), an enthusiastic and knowledgeable birder. Baker joined Sid on his excursions into the Essex countryside, and learned from him the names, songs and behaviours of many local species.

At first, they sought after one bird in particular: the nightjar. Known as 'nighthawks' or 'corpse fowls', and associated with superstitions of ill-fortune because of their crepuscular habits, nightjars could be found in the woodlands south of Chelmsford. Baker was searching for nightjars from at least 1953, the year he recorded discovering an oak tree where the birds would perch in spring to start their eerie churring song as the sun went down.

As Baker's birding experience grew, he began to venture out more and more without Sid Harman. On a few occasions Doreen joined him, but mostly he went alone. He would take his old Raleigh bicycle and pack its saddlebag with a handful of Ordnance Survey (OS) maps, a notebook, a thermos flask and sandwiches, slinging the leather straps of his binoculars and telescope across his chest and pedalling along the lanes that led into the countryside.

It was around this time that Baker started to write the first of his field diaries. Its opening entry, on March 21, 1954, was marked with the decisive words: 'Start of systematic watching'.

There was something about 'birding', as it was known, that appealed strongly to Baker – or perhaps more accurately, to his obsessive, systematising tendencies. Along with his diaries, he started to collect information on birds in the same way that, as a younger man, he had gathered information on books and writers. He filled notebooks with meticulous columns listing all the names of species found in Essex. He wrote pages of notes on plumage, moulting, migrations, songs (even going so far as to transcribe them into musical notation), feeding habits: everything he could discover.

He was not alone in his obsession. Sir Dudley Stamp commented

Doreen Coe photographed by J. A. Baker during a trip to what looks like the Blackwater Estuary, mid-1950s.

in 1969 that, since the end of the Second World War, 'Bird-watching, otherwise prying into the private lives of birds, has become a national sport and the ever-present danger is that birdwatchers may become more numerous than the birds to be watched.' It was, however, Stamp thought, understandable that avifauna took pride of place in the public's interest: '[They] are largely diurnal and sleep by night,' he wrote, 'as do the best people; though many delight in display, the majority, again like the best people, hide sufficient of their charms or charming customs to be intriguing.'

In truth, the pastime had grown in popularity because it had been made easier, cheaper and more widely accessible. More people in the UK owned cars, and could afford to travel outside of cities for a day's nature watching. More places had also been made available to promote birdlife and birdwatching. The Royal Society for Protection of Birds (RSPB) bought its first nature reserve in Romney in 1930, and the charity increased its land holdings during the 1950s and 1960s to cater to an ever more engaged public. When, for example, the RSPB opened their osprey hide at Loch Garten in the Cairngorms, 14,000 visitors arrived in the first six or seven weeks. By 1960, membership of the RSPB was well over 10,000.

The tools for birdwatching had also improved. Two world wars had increased demand for optical instruments such as field glasses, binoculars, gun sights and periscopes. The optics industry had been transformed from an expensive, small-scale craft to one that produced cutting-edge technology in volume. Brands such as the Ross Prismatic (British), Bausch & Lomb (American), Zeiss and Hensoldt Wetzlar (both German), became well known. The quality of German lenses was so high that field glasses were one of the first things that would be taken from dead or captured soldiers during the Second World War.

After the war, birders who had been in the Armed Forces quickly adapted what they had to the needs of their hobby. Companies were quick to fill the gap, and soon the market was flooded with instruments that far outstripped the optics that Baker owned,

J. A. Baker photographed by Doreen Coe, mid-1950s.

most of which were made in Germany during the interwar years. His Harwix Mirakel binoculars were weighty, black-coated alloy in a worn leather case, with the red velvet lining rubbed bald like the fur of a well-loved toy; true to their engineering, they still work with remarkable sharpness.

But the real revolution in birdwatching was brought about by publishing affordable and accessible books. For the first few decades of the twentieth century, ornithological literature had been dry stuff, books that were stultifying in their academic language and even more stultifying in their length: they they often ran to several volumes and were useless in the field.

In the 1930s a new kind of bird book appeared. It represented a bridge between the scientific world of ornithology and the novel sport of birdwatching. Written in language that could be understood by the beginner, amateur, or professional, these books were clear, concise and were small enough to carry into the field. They took the emerging popular science market by storm: the *Observer's Book of British Birds*, for example, when first published in 1937 sold a staggering three million copies.

Many of these books offered more than just a digestible format – they taught amateur birders how to identify species in the field with ease and speed. In the years prior to the Second World War new methods of field identification were developed, one of the most significant of which came from the USA. In 1934, American naturalist and artist Roger Tory Peterson produced a new kind of identification system for birds, which he published in his *A Field Guide to the Birds of Eastern and Central North America*. Previous guides had relied on biological observations and measurements that could only be understood by trained ornithologists and were best performed on a dead specimen. But Peterson's *Guide* focused on prominent, distinctive characteristics to produce a visual system not bound by scientific classification – so any beginner, with no prior zoological training, could use it.

Peterson's system used schematic illustrations with arrows to direct the observer to each bird's most distinctive 'field marks' –

physical characteristics easily seen from a distance or in motion, such as spots or marks in plumage, the shape of the tail or wing or beak, or a flight pattern. This new method was both simple and effective – so much so that the Peterson Identification System was taken up by a whole host of nature guides thereafter. Peterson was even asked to adapt his system to produce a plane-spotting guide for the US Army Air Corps in an effort to reduce 'friendly fire' incidents.

What had been accessible only to professional ornithologists became literally an open book, and identifying wild birds took off as one of the twentieth century's most popular pastimes. These amateurs, whose interest in birds had shifted from shooting, skinning or egg-collecting to behavioural study, conservation and protection, called themselves 'bird watchers' or 'birders'.

One of the earliest popular British birding books was written by E. M. Nicholson, a pioneering ornithologist whose 1931 manual, *The Art of Bird Watching*, developed ideas of field observation and identification. Nicholson's guidebook urged a scientific approach: he emphasised the need to make records of bird behaviour, locations, dates and times, as well as numbers of individuals and different species. Writing these down, he insisted, was crucial to the work of the birdwatcher: 'the only article for bird watching that can rank with field glasses, if not before them,' he wrote, 'is the note book.' Baker, likely under the direction of a writer such as Nicholson, always carried a notebook in which to collect his field notes.

Along with field notes (which, according to Nicholson, had to be made *in* the field within the first few minutes of the sighting), Nicholson also advised his readers to make another, more detailed and permanent record. This, he said, should be something like a card system, and most certainly 'not a record in diary form which', he remarked, 'soon becomes unmanageable'.

Yet a record in diary form was exactly what Baker chose to write when he started his 'systematic watching'. At the end of each outing he would come home and write up the day's field notes into the exercise books he kept in the spare bedroom which he had converted into his study. Here he kept other kinds of birding notes that also went beyond Nicholson's remit of a useful permanent record. Sometimes these included flowers or feathers that he had brought home, often for Doreen but also for himself as tokens of the day's expedition and inspiration for his writing.

He kept cardboard folders, too, for his other natural history research, on the covers of which he wrote lists of suggested contents. One read: 'Speculations / Introductions / Valley / Topography / Geology / History / Species Occurring / Peregrine in Essex / Essex Generally / Arrival & Choice of Territory ... ' 'Unmanageable' might have been Nicholson's description – and perhaps this was just part of Baker's unmanageable nature – but in any case Baker seemed to manage it quite well.

What Baker did have difficulty with, however, was the art of identification. Robert Macfarlane has remarked that Baker seemed to lack the ability to read what birdwatchers call 'jizz'. When birders boast of being able to identify a bird at the merest fleeting glimpse, they are talking about knowing it by its so-called jizz: a combination of appearance, location and movement, rather than specific field marks that one would need a clear view to see. ('Jizz' is thought by some ornithologists to be the phoneticised acronym for 'General Impression of Size and Shape'; but its etymology is just as likely that described by T. A. Coward in his *Bird Haunts and Nature Memories* as being from 'gis' or 'jis', an obsolete variant of 'guise'.)

Like many newcomers to serious birdwatching, recognising jizz was something that Baker struggled with, though his myopia wouldn't have helped. The birds he saw first-hand, as he noted on several occasions in his diaries, were often unlike their pictures in illustrated bird guides – either slimmer or fatter or brighter or duller. 'Birds are like people', he wrote on March 3, 1955, 'faces in a crowded street – by a principle feature you think you recognise a friend, but it turns out to be a stranger – so with species'.

Learning to know birds by their jizz was not his only difficulty. Baker's notebooks give a good account of the other frustrations encountered in perfecting his birding skills. In the excitement, say, of trying to train his telescope on an interesting-looking bird while in the teeth of a strong easterly wind, he would end up in a tangle of gaberdine, bicycle, and map, sweating profusely and swiping helplessly at the condensation that kept obscuring both his glasses and his optics – while the bird, alarmed at the sight of this flailing monster, had since taken wing, or stayed long enough to afford him only the briefest of glimpses. Such an occurrence, he said, was typical of his early birdwatching style.

The part of Essex where Baker did most of his birding has some of the most evocative place names of anywhere in Britain. They record the rich history of the land. The village of Skinners Wick has a name that betrays the presence of Romans in the area, 'Wick' coming from the Latin *vicus*, meaning 'street' or 'neighbourhood'. Layer de la Haye takes its name from the Norse *Leire* or *Leger*, meaning 'mud', a reference to the marshland around the village, which after the Norman conquest was owned by the de la Haye family. The name of another village, Goldhanger, comes from the Old English for 'grassland where marigolds grow', and the island of Foulness from the Old English *fulga-naess*, which translates as 'wild birds nest'.

One thing Baker became very good at was finding the best locations for his birding trips, and many of these place names found their way into his diaries. His outings usually took him through the farmland east of Chelmsford to the creeks and saltings around the Blackwater Estuary, though he also spent time at the Hanningfield and Abberton reservoirs. Some parts of the marshes here were privately owned; typically, Baker was not one for following the rules, and would clamber over the barbed wire fences. Sometimes he was caught trespassing by a gamekeeper and turned back, though this never put him off trying his luck another time.

On his collection of OS maps Baker left a fascinating record of his excursions through these areas. He would mark his most frequented trails in ink, labelled with little arrows and distances, or would shade areas in red or green pencil. Each map was scribbled over, every one showing his idiosyncratic method of notation where sightings of birds were marked with their initials: 'P' for peregrine, 'SH' for sparrowhawk, 'LO' for little owl, and so on.

The dates in Baker's diaries were filled out patchily. Some entries were a mere line of data, others were lengthy descriptions. Even when he was unable to go out birding because of illness or work, he would still write in his notebooks of the birds he saw or heard in his garden or from his office window at the AA: a redwing calling outside the AA building on London Road; or three spotted flycatchers on the Bakers' coalshed roof in 1955; or, the same year, a green woodpecker, 'dowdy and sheepish', flying across a neighbour's garden.

Some weeks of the year – noticeably those during the summer months – Baker left almost completely blank. This had a lot to do with his locality. East Anglia is part of what is known as the East Atlantic Flyway, a migration route that takes birds from northern breeding areas to wintering grounds in the more temperate south. So, for the months of winter, tens of millions of birds following the Flyway make Essex their home; this explains why, for those months, this part of the coastline is of most interest to birders. From above, the Blackwater Estuary's wetlands look like an enormous coronal section of a kidney – a thousand watery veins draining from the claggy soil into the sea. The landscape functions in ways that are similar to a kidney, too, sieving particles from the streams of ebbing and flowing liquid. Channels slow the river- and seawater, and allow suspended nutrients to be deposited onto the tidal mudflats, home to the plants, invertebrates and fish that feed migrating shore birds. Waders such as knot, dunlin and curlew flock to the estuary, where geese and ducks, from teal and wigeon to diving merganser and goldeneye, join them. Along with these migrants, of course, come the hunters that prey on them – including peregrines.

Any birder's success depends on paying attention to the rhythms of life at play in a landscape such as this. From the beginning Baker wrote up his field notes to include details such as wind direction, weather, and tides. A good example can be found in his first autumn of writing in 1954. After an outing one Friday, six months after he had started his 'systematic watching', he made this entry:

> October 1st: Goldhanger. A steady S[outh] W[est] Wind, with mainly high cloud, breaking towards sunset. S[lack] W[ater]—2.50[pm]. H[igh] T[ide]—3.40[pm]. Gore – Greenshank picked out by dazzling white underparts. A beautiful sunset, on the mud reddening the breasts of thousands of gulls. A Curlew from Lauriston Marsh, well inland, with a very grating and rusty call. In the same place as I heard a similar call a week before. E[ast] side of Joyce's Bay, at dusk, a bird went up from the mud and saltings, with shrill call, like a boy's whistle, with fingers in mouth [...] [a] Spotted Redshank. Grey Plover feeding on mud at Gore, reminiscent of Thrushes in the way they listen, & thrust into mud, leaning forward like Pointers on a leash.

Baker's description of grey plover pointing like tracking dogs is as accurate as it is charming: these piebald birds softly stalk worms burrowing in ooze, as a pointer hunts partridge hiding in foliage.

This entry shows that Baker had learned to pay attention to the environment as well as the animals in it. The birds Baker was watching could only feed where intertidal mud was exposed, something that only happens at certain times of the day. That is why he also made a note of the tide times. Knowing these tidal states would have been essential to getting the best view of coastal wading birds as they gathered to feed over shallow submerged mudflats either side of low tide. Calculating slack water (the point at which there's the least tidal current) can be quite tricky as it's very specific to location. So whatever might be said about Baker as an ornithologist, it's clear that he worked hard to understand the effects of this changeable environment on the birdlife. Before, such detail had been all but invisible to him – as he would write in *The Peregrine*, 'the hardest thing of all to see is what is really there'.

On the same Friday outing in October 1954 when Baker saw the grey plover, he also thought he saw something else more exciting.

At the bottom of that day's diary entry he wrote:

> It may have been on this day, or possibly on a September day, that I saw a bird [that] I spoke to myself about as a Peregrine. I was at the angle of Lauriston Marsh, between Joyce's Bay and Lauriston Beach, when a Pigeon-like bird flew over, high and fast, going W[est] S[outh] W[est], into wind. I thought at the time that I couldn't see a Peregrine in such a locality, being ignorant of their movements. Something unfamiliar about the fast, flapping flight, made me try to get a better view. I failed to do so.

This was one of his first encounters with a peregrine.

A couple of pages later, on December 8, Baker recorded another meeting with the raptor in an entry squashed into a page's margin. This time, he had a better view and was far more certain that the bird he had seen was indeed a falcon. The day had been wet, with a strong wind, and Baker had cycled about an hour's ride from Chelmsford. He was pedalling along a road near the village of Heybridge when he was sure another peregrine flew across the road just in front of him.

From this early point of contact on that December day in 1954, Baker's birdwatching became focussed around his pursuit of the peregrine. He had what Derek Ratcliffe called 'the fever' – an all-consuming drive to seek out these marvellous creatures. Sceptics of Baker's ornithological skills question whether he could indeed have managed to track these rare birds as he said he did. It's notoriously difficult to find a wild peregrine; but others had achieved it much as Baker did, and in less forgiving country. Ratcliffe himself described how, some ten years before Baker had his first sighting of a peregrine falcon, he had successfully started out hunting for peregrines as a teenager in Galloway, returning over many years equipped with little more than a bicycle, a handful of one-inch maps, some books of the local countryside, and a couple of ropes. At least in the Essex marshes Baker didn't have to scale any granite crags, and so could dispense with the ropes.

The bulk of Baker's notes that survive were written between 1954 and 1962. Most of the locations he recorded are in Essex, around

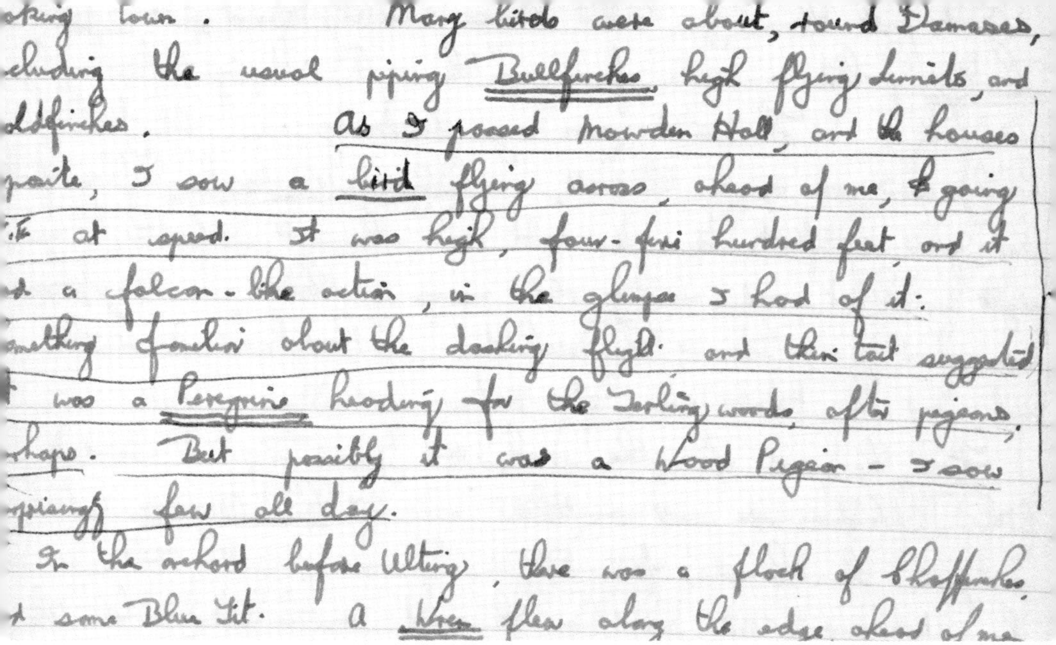
oking town. Many birds were about, round Danbury,
cluding the usual piping Bullfinches, high flying linnets, and
oldfinches. As I passed Mowden Hall, and the houses
posite, I saw a bird flying across, ahead of me, & going
it at speed. It was high, four-five hundred feet, and it
d a falcon-like action, in the glimpse I had of it:
mething familiar about the dashing flight and thin tail suggested
it was a Peregrine heading for the Terling woods, after pigeons,
rhaps. But possibly it was a Wood Pigeon - I saw
springs few all day.
In the orchard before Ulting, there was a flock of Chaffinches
& some Blue Tit. A Wren flew along the edge ahead of me

An entry from Baker's birdwatching journal records what might have been one of his earliest encounters with peregrines.

the Chelmer and Blackwater rivers, but there are a few others. He wrote about having seen peregrines while on honeymoon in Folkestone in 1956; and again, the following year, on the Sussex coastline at Seven Sisters and over Belle Tout, a few years before the peregrines that nested there were reported to have vanished.

The same year that Baker noted down his first sighting of a peregrine was also the first year in which the species had become protected under British law. The falcons appeared on a list published as part of the Wild Birds Protection Act 1954. This act was intended to safeguard a number of owls, birds of prey and other wild species and their eggs from being destroyed by individuals, though some (including pigeon enthusiasts and gamekeepers, who blamed the falcons for taking their young birds) deliberately defied the act. Peregrines, controversially to some, appeared on the protected list because it had become evident that their population numbers were in serious decline, though at the time the Act was instated experts were not sure exactly why.

During the post-war years pesticide use had grown to massive proportions around the world. In the UK alone the Ministry of

Agriculture included just fifteen chemicals on its list of Approved Products for Farmers and Growers in 1950; this increased to forty-seven in 1960, then to 163 in 1970, and to almost 200 by 1980. By the mid- to late-1950s, when Baker first started to learn about the peregrine, attention was being directed to the effects of organochlorine insecticides, in particular to dieldrin, aldrin, heptachlor and DDT.

These chemicals were unlikely to poison a predator outright; rather, it was the persistent nature that posed a threat. They could remain in the environment for decades. Predators like the peregrine were susceptible not because they ate the poisoned insects or laced seed, but because they ate the creatures that had consumed the chemicals directly. When you think that a barn swallow is estimated to be able to eat an average of sixty insects an hour, it's not hard to imagine how quickly these toxins could accumulate as they travelled up the food chain.

Another contributing factor to the effect of these chemicals was the way they were processed by the body. The toxins were stored in the fat of the animal – where initially the poisons were inert, and did no harm. But as a warm-blooded predator, a peregrine must expend a great deal of energy hunting for its food; their lives are a lived on a constant knife-edge between survival and starvation. So, as a bird of prey stored up and then burned off its fat reserves as the seasons changed, migrations occurred or pickings were good or slim, these toxins would be metabolised. First they entered the blood and then the brain, damaging the bird's reproductive and nervous systems.

Derek Ratcliffe was the wildlife biologist who recognised the connection between thinner, more fragile eggshell production in peregrines and pesticides such as DDT. The embryos might fail to develop or the parents would crush the eggs by accident. As DDT can remain in the soil for well over a decade, its impact on birds that only have a lifespan of seven to fifteen years in the wild was dire; with far fewer viable offspring to replace them, numbers crashed.

In addition to the cumulative effects of DDT, there were the swifter impacts of other insecticides such as dieldrin. Poisoning epidemics like that of the spring of 1961 were most likely caused by the use of dieldrin, and, as the variety of affected animals found in 1961 showed, it wasn't just the occasional species that were vulnerable to its indirect effects. In the UK, owls, kestrels, peregrines and sparrowhawks were especially at risk, but many others were also affected, including geese, herons, bats and other insectivorous or carrion-eating mammals. England, especially the south and east, which had the largest areas of agricultural land, experienced the worst of the effects. Here both native sparrowhawks (which were not protected by the Wild Bird Protection Act 1954) and peregrines became almost extinct. By 1964, it was estimated that 80 per cent of the British peregrine population had been wiped out.

By the early 1960s scientists finally had the technology to identify for certain the high levels of organochlorine pesticides in the bodies of wild birds and mammals. By 1962 – the same year that Rachel Carson's book *Silent Spring* exposed the hazards of chemicals like DDT to a horrified public, and became the seminal work for the burgeoning environmental movement – a phased withdrawal of some organochlorine pesticides, including dieldrin and aldrin, was introduced in the UK. Yet this was only a voluntary withdrawal; it would take many years for the compounds to be banned outright, and more still for the effects on wildlife to diminish. Even in 1973, it was thought that 28 per cent of incidents of wildlife death were attributable to dieldrin alone. That same year, extremely high concentrations were found in the brains and livers of two peregrine falcons found dead in Stirlingshire.

To make all this worse, a perfect storm scenario was brewing that threaten English wildlife at the same time that Baker was searching for peregrines in Essex in the early years of the 1960s. In addition to the perils of pesticides, wild animals were faced with surviving the coldest period for more than 200 years. The winter of 1962 to 1963 was known as the Big Freeze: temperatures plummeted to -20°C, blizzards left snowdrifts and foot-long icicles across the country, and in some places it was so cold that the sea froze. Much of England was covered in snow from January until early March.

Hundreds of thousands of wild creatures were starved or killed by exposure to the terrible weather. Others survived by scavenging. Peregrine falcons are very rarely seen eating carrion, and only when they have more trouble in finding their usual prey – as they likely did during that extreme cold spell.

The winter Baker described later in *The Peregrine* was strongly influenced by the Big Freeze, though he pooled incidents and details from the ten-year period that his diaries had covered. The account that he gave of that winter in his book follows the progress of one juvenile tiercel peregrine in particular. Baker also explained that during this time woodpigeons made up more than half the peregrine kills that he found. It's possible, even probable, that some of the 'kills' he was finding, marked with signs of having been eaten by hawks, had been scavenged rather than killed over that terrible winter.

This might give a clue also as to why Baker was so easily able to track the peregrines, as well as supporting the truth of his sightings. In his book *Silent Spring Revisited*, conservationist Conor Mark Jameson goes so far as to suggest that Baker could have been basing his peregrine sightings on falconer's birds that had escaped or been released, which was why the birds were so tame. But Jameson touches, too, on the effects of chemical poisoning on animals during the period and the unusual number of bird corpses that were the result. He comments in passing that 'perhaps poisoning might even explain the unusual or lethargic behaviour of closely studied raptors at the time.' Could this have been the case with the birds that Baker was 'studying' in particular? Putting together what we know of the ongoing problems with dieldrin-dressed seed in East Anglia into the early 1960s, and how the seed was eaten in large quantities, especially by woodpigeons, it might well be that Baker managed to record so much interaction with the peregrines precisely *because* they were suffering the effects of pesticide poisoning after scavenging the carcasses of pigeons that had themselves succumbed to dieldrin. A juvenile falcon still honing its hunting technique, like that which Baker described himself following, might be more drawn to scavenging if it couldn't find fresh prey. If the symptoms recorded in other animals are anything in comparison, then peregrines made sick from pesticides might also have behaved strangely and lost some of their normal secretiveness and fear of people.

Did Baker have any suspicions of this at the time? It can't be said for certain – though books like *Silent Spring* (which he read after its publication in 1962) may have given him an idea. He certainly knew something of it later, when he described in his introduction to *The Peregrine* how many peregrines in England at that time 'died on their backs, clutching insanely at the sky in their last convulsions, withered and burnt away by the filthy, insidious pollen of farm chemicals.'

Such an explanation would support Baker's claim that everything he wrote about really did happen. It would make sense, too, in the light of his diary records. And it would acknowledge the fact that Baker was not, probably, an extraordinary birdwatcher. He was just in the right place at the right time. That is, the wrong place and the wrong time for the peregrine.

Baker's motivation for writing his first literary work came from seeing this crisis first hand. He saw, too, the subsequent need for justice and reform: in an early draft of *The Peregrine*, Baker wrote with biting anger of 'armed men, those who carry guns, who set up traps, who scatter poison on the fields.'

'The survival of hawks,' he argued in an early draft of *The Peregrine*, 'will not depend on consideration of their place in nature, or on their usefulness in maintaining balance, though these are valid arguments. Their survival will depend on the magnanimity of each individual person who has in his power the means of death.'

If those who killed hawks – deliberately or otherwise – bore a responsibility, then Baker felt it was *his* responsibility as a writer to hold them accountable. Many years earlier, not long after the end of Second World War and when he had first committed himself to writing, Baker told Donald Samuel what he considered the purpose of the author to be. 'It seems to me,' he wrote, 'that, in view of the world's condition today, we who have creative ambitions and, perhaps, a genuine creative ability, are bound by our conscience to give all that we have to the cause of working for a better way of living.'

Of course, he was writing then in reference to the atrocities that 'armed men' had dealt each other – six years of bloody warfare culminating in the atom bomb. But as had grown older, Baker's conscience had directed him to the world beyond humankind and how it, too, deserved a 'better way of living'. Now confronted with the cruel indifference of people in Britain to that most remarkable of birds, the peregrine, Baker was, as he said, bound by his conscience to give all that he had. The peregrine was becoming a *cause célèbre* for nature conservationists; a symbol, as Derek Ratcliffe wrote in his book *The Peregrine Falcon*, for 'one of the foremost trends of our time – the relentless domination by Man, the supreme competitor, of the rest of the living world.' Since the time that he had first started writing with serious intention as a young man, Baker had been searching for the thing upon which he could try, as he put it, his 'prentice hand' – and in the peregrine he had found it.

Throughout Baker's books, he insists on calling his peregrines 'hawks'. This name is technically inaccurate: peregrine falcons are of the family *Falconidae* and not true hawks, which are of the *Accipitridae* family. Because Baker ignored this difference, his critics have accused him of having been ignorant. If he couldn't even tell a falcon from a hawk, what sort of birder was he?

There is, however, one explanation for his use of hawk instead of falcon. 'Hawk' was, and still is, an historical term used by falconers to refer to any of the birds they use, regardless of modern zoological categories. The question is, where did Baker pick up the term?

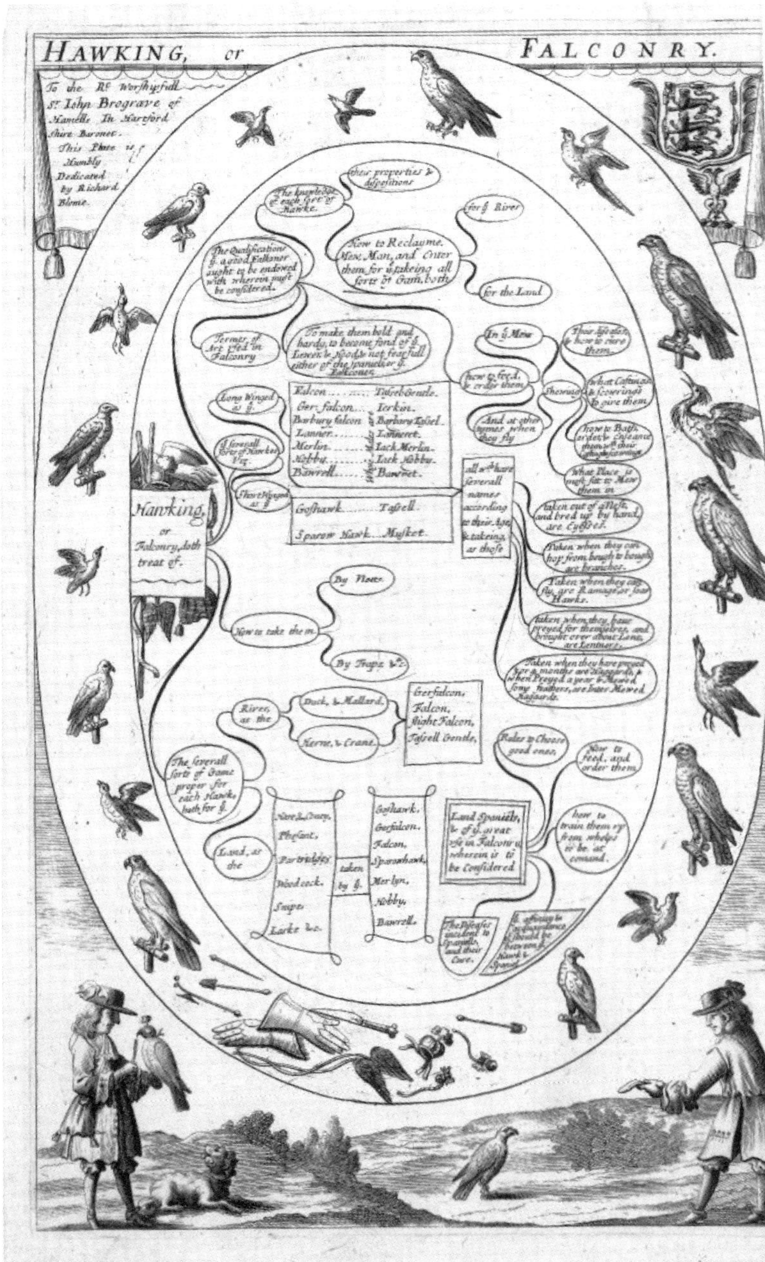

Illustration from Richard Blome's 1686 guide Hawking, or Faulconry. *The page shows various species of 'hawk' – the peregrine is perhaps the one beneath the heron (centre right), as peregrines (alone, or in pairs) were often flown at herons and could even kill them.*

Firstly, there was a small and informal falconry group whose members flew peregrines out in the fields around the Blackwater Estuary during the 1950s and 1960s, as well as later. In his books and his diaries, Baker made passing reference to having seen falconers practising in the area; he may well have spoken to them and asked them about their birds and the sport.

Secondly, he did in fact own books on the subject of falconry. Michael Woodford in *The Manual of Falconry* (1960), a copy of which was in Baker's library, used 'hawk' throughout to mean loosely both hawks and falcons, trusting, as he said, that 'the reader will bear with these generalisations.' Presumably Baker trusted his readers to do the same.

Baker took an interest in the language of falconry and its history. At one point in *The Peregrine* he wondered whether the phrase 'taken by surprise' came from hawking. He might well have been correct: many of these terms from falconry have since crossed into everyday use and lost their hawking roots. 'Disclosed', for example, comes from an Old French word that described a hawk that had just hatched. 'Reclaim', also from Old French, meant 'to make a hawk tame, gentle, and familiar', or to call it back to the glove. To 'make a point' in an argument, say, comes, too, from hunting: used of dogs but also of hawks, it describes the action when a hawk throws herself up into the air above the spot where her quarry has been driven into a covert.

Richard Blome in his seventeenth-century *Hawking, or Faulconry* described how a falconer could attract a kite by releasing an owl with a fox's tail tied to one leg – a sight that lures the kite to investigate out of curiosity: 'when the *Kyte* is descended pretty near her, then let fly your *Hawk*, and the *Kyte* perceiving the surprize, doth endeavour to preserve herself by mounting up.' So it's possible that Baker was right, and 'take by surprise' does have falconry roots – as 'surprise' derives from the Old French *surprendre*, 'to overtake', itself from the Latin *prehendere*, 'to seize, grasp', and thus sounds quite hawkish; or at least like the sort of language that could have developed out of a hunting term. (Most of our English words that relate to falconry come from French: after the Norman invasion of the eleventh century, the French-speaking ruling class replaced the English used in hunting sports with those of their native tongue.)

There's more to connect Baker's writing to falconry that just his language. In his introduction to *The Peregrine* Baker writes that he had learned to 'hide in my own stillness', to stay downwind, and to keep his movements deliberate in order not to alarm the bird that he was trying to see. These were all methods recommended by Woodford in his *Manual*, in which he insists that the best falconer must learn stillness and slowness, and never make panicked or jerky movements; such skills, he says, are what are needed to soothe wild hawks from their fear of man. Woodford also directs the amateur falconer to take care with his clothes: to wear the same type and colour of clothing when dealing with birds. 'Hawks can see colours and recognise their trainer mainly by sight,' he said, going on to caution that, 'they will not know him if he trains them in shirt-sleeves and comes one day to them in a raincoat. Inattention to details of this sort can easily result in the loss of a hawk.' Baker took such advice seriously as his years of peregrine hunting progressed. Doreen said he always wore the same kit while out birding: flannel trousers, shirt under an old woollen jumper, and a tweed jacket; an outfit finished off with a cloth cap and his brown gaberdine raincoat to keep off the worst of the weather.

Surely in Baker there was something of the falconer as well as the birder. He sought a more active, intimate relationship with the peregrine than that of the merely passive birdwatcher. He wanted to be 'recognised and accepted by the peregrine' (as he wrote in his book's introduction), to create a 'bond' between himself and the bird. This sort of bond is more in the remit of the falconer than the birder – and it requires more of both the hawk and the woman or man. *The Peregrine* has been called 'a love story of sorts', and in many ways its narrative chronicles the sort of love that James Campbell described as belonging to the ideal falconer in his *Treatise of Modern Falconry* of 1773. This, Campbell wrote, 'must be very intense, to animate him to undergo, undaunted the numberless inconveniences of attendance, weather, and soil, wherewith it is generally accompanied ... To do these things effectively, he must understand [the hawk's] temper and constitution, and ought to possess much patience and mildness in the application of his knowledge.' This doesn't sound like a bad description of a man who wrote, 'For ten years I followed the peregrine. I was possessed by it. It was a grail to me.'

In 1962, Baker and Doreen moved into a council flat in Chelmsford. Over the next few years Baker continued his peregrine expeditions, though, it seems from his diaries, with less success each year. As the reasons for this decline became widely known, Baker committed himself to creating something that would mark the peregrine's loss as a tragedy, and one not just experienced by birders. When asked why her husband had chosen the peregrine as a topic for a book, Doreen said that it was because the peregrine was a dramatic symbol. A hunting falcon embodied drama; it captivated Baker and could captivate a reading audience too. According to Doreen, one of Baker's favourite books was Melville's *Moby-Dick*. He saw in the peregrine a parallel with the white whale – a wild creature of awesome power and beauty, persecuted by mankind to the limits of its territory.

Baker did this his own way. The book was, as Doreen put it, part observation, part fiction. What Baker saw, she said, he embellished to make more poetic – though this embellishment was in the way of description rather than invention. Baker insisted that all the events he wrote about really did happen, as his diaries corroborate.

'Peregrine', as has been mentioned before, has its roots in the Latin for 'pilgrim', and Baker's book certainly describes a pilgrimage of sorts, its rituals and acts of devotion performed under a cold sky beside a muddy field track or the long horizon of a sea wall. The journal structure he chose emphasises this sense of pilgrimage, as 'journal' literally means 'a day's travel'. When in the mid-1960s, Baker began to write up the first manuscripts of *The*

Doreen and John pose together, late 1950s.

Peregrine, he pored over his old diaries. By then he had material that covered more than a decade of outings, with which he turned lapidary: each day's record was cleaved, bruted and polished before being set, gemlike, in the rosary of the book's narrative.

In order to concentrate on this task, Baker gave up his job at the AA. From his diaries alone it's not clear when he resigned, but it seems that by 1965 he had committed himself to writing full time. This was a serious undertaking, as he and Doreen had to live for a few years solely on their savings and National Assistance.

Baker later told his publishers that he rewrote the text of *The Peregrine* five times. Two of these manuscripts survive, both of them handwritten. The earlier draft he wrote out in sections, each held together with paperclips and the whole lot bound together

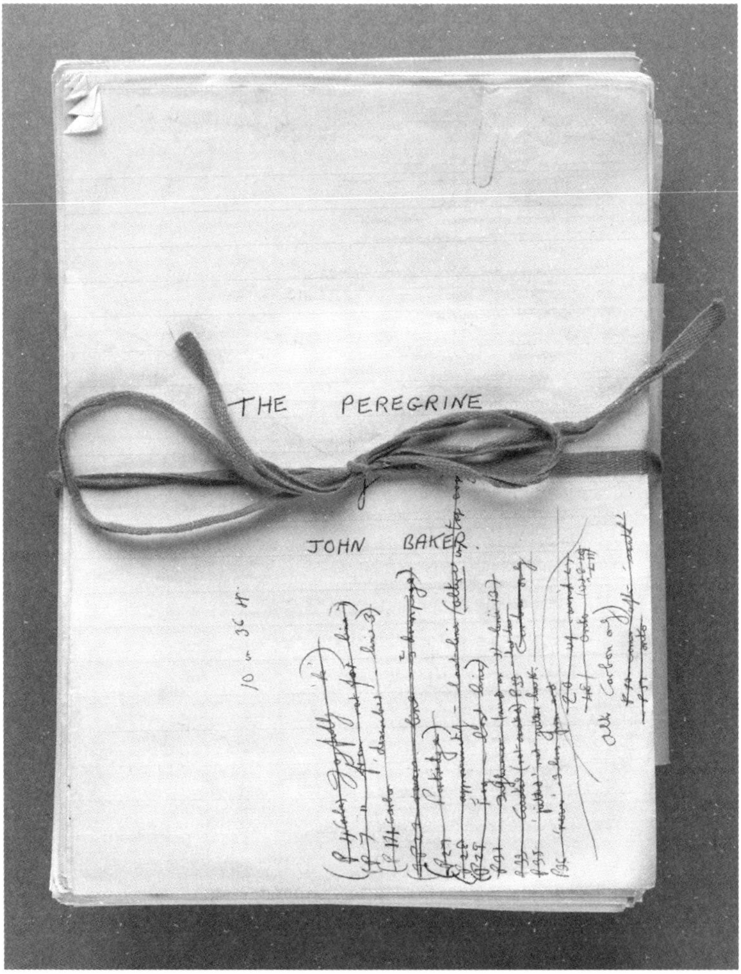

An early handwritten draft of The Peregrine.

with a large rubber band. The other, possibly penultimate, draft showed the book in almost its published state. Both manuscripts would have been laborious to put together, as they ran to nearly 400 handwritten pages each.

To add to that effort, Baker's health had deteriorated. His ankylosing spondylitis caused painful arthritis; it often made him short-tempered and prickly. To write was an uncomfortable labour, as the joints of his hands had begun to fuse, causing his fingers to seize and clench into painful claws, something that can be seen in the author photograph that was taken by Collins for *The Peregrine*'s dust jacket.

By May 1966, Baker had completed his manuscript. He sent it off to Collins publishers, where it came to the attention of Michael Walter, one of the editors. Walter was impressed by the work, and within a matter of weeks Baker had a contract promising him an advance of £250.

Not long after, Walter passed on *The Peregrine*'s manuscript to John Moore, an author famous for his *Brensham* trilogy about rural Britain and for his pioneering conservation work. Moore wrote back to Walter that Baker's work was 'something quite exceptional in the way of nature writing … Gilbert White himself would have admired it.' And not just Gilbert White, in Moore's opinion: 'T. H. White would have loved this book. So would Hemingway, and so would Gerard Manley Hopkins, because it's like a huge and glorious extension of his poem – that was about a kestrel, I know, not a peregrine, but no matter!' To be mentioned in such company as Manley Hopkins and his 'Windhover' was no doubt a wonderful affirmation for Baker, who had desired so long to have his writing acknowledged.

Moore also voiced to Walter the same interest in Baker's life that was to be repeated by countless readers:

> Occasionally I speculate what sort of chap he can be who takes ten winters out of whatever work he does simply for the purpose of watching peregrines. One must inevitably feel curious about anyone possessed and driven by such a monomania. I experienced a kind of awe, an astonishment, and a real excitement … No bird has ever had such a Boswell.

J. A. Baker out on the Blackwater Estuary, 1950s.

Chapter Six
THE POET-NATURALIST

> Never in a lifetime of reading academic books about birds have I learned a tithe of what I find here about the true ecology of bird life; never in the last ten years have I read descriptive writing of this quality.
>
> MAURICE WIGGIN, draft article for *The Bookman*, March 1967

IN FRONT OF A SMALL but crowded London room early in 1968, Baker was waiting to speak. He was to give a speech accepting the Duff Cooper Memorial Prize, an award given annually to an exceptional work of non-fiction writing.

The guests began to gather, glasses in hand, to listen. Among these was Michael Walter, Baker's editor at Collins. Walter watched him take the floor with trepidation: only minutes before, Baker had rolled up to him, bright-eyed, and remarked what fine stuff the reception's champagne was. Walter knew that his author drank little as a rule, and, though Baker had a rather dry sense of humour, Walter had not thought he was joking about the champagne. He had watched Baker disappear back into the crowd with a growing sense of dread that his author was looking and speaking like a man who was tight as an owl.

Quiet was finally called for and the chatter in the room died down. John Julius Cooper, 2nd Viscount Norwich and son of Duff Cooper, stood to welcome Baker and other guests – a mixed collection of journalists, broadcasters, publishers and literary types. Viscount Norwich gave Baker a warm introduction. *The Peregrine*, he said, was a worthy winner of the prize. When the judges had first been handed the book, their enthusiasm had been lukewarm – none of the five men were birdwatchers, nor keen or knowledgeable naturalists. But they had been overwhelmed by Mr Baker's sensitive style and the poetry and evocative beauty of his writing. The judging panel's decision to select *The Peregrine* had, Viscount Norwich said, been unanimous.

Now it was Baker's turn to speak, and Walter, who had kept one eye on the rosy-cheeked writer all the while, couldn't help murmuring a quiet prayer under his breath. But to Walter's surprise – and possibly because of the alcohol – as Baker began to speak both his awkwardness and habitual prickliness fell away. Everyone agreed afterwards that he had performed brilliantly: he was relaxed, his speech was deft, funny and graceful; there was not a word too many, and he didn't go on past the limits of his listeners' enjoyment. Baker's editor was amazed – none of these attributes were, to Walter's knowledge of him, the normal Baker at all. After the speeches were done the party continued, and Baker was the hero of the hour.

A couple of months earlier, in early December 1967, Baker had received the telegram that awarded him the Duff Cooper Memorial Prize. The prize consisted of a copy of Duff Cooper's autobiography and £200. Sir Duff Cooper's son, John Julius, had sent his warmest congratulations to Baker: 'The award is made annually,' he wrote, 'for an outstanding work in the field of history, biography, politics or poetry; yours falls squarely and incontestably into the last category.'

The year 1967 had been full of plaudits for Baker and *The Peregrine*. As well as the Duff Cooper, Baker was given the *Yorkshire Post*'s Book of the Year for best first work, an award he accepted at a ceremony at the Queens Hotel in Leeds. Baker kept a copy of the photograph that was taken of him accepting the award from the newspaper's editor.

Around the same time in December that he received the telegram from Viscount Norwich, Baker had also just been given an Arts Council grant of £1,200. Having never written a book before or had any ornithological training, he was (according to the report in *The Daily Telegraph*) 'the most unusual of the 14 [grantees]' to be given money. Even so, the Arts Council had commended *The Peregrine* as 'a work of extraordinary talent and total maturity.'

The book had picked up praise abroad, too. The same month it was published in Britain, Harper & Row had put their edition of *The Peregrine* on sale in the US, where excellent reviews had flooded in from New England to Texas. By the following year Baker was signing contracts for *The Peregrine* to be translated in French and Japanese editions.

At home *The Peregrine* had met with similar enthusiasm from the British press: 'Is fine natural history writing coming in again?' wondered Richard Fitter in *The Times*. The author and journalist Maurice Wiggin went so far as to call *The Peregrine* 'the greatest wildlife document of our time', and Clancy Sigal said it was 'a beautiful and astonishing book, perhaps one of genius.' It was John Moore who called Baker 'the man who thinks like a hawk', in his fervent review in *The Birmingham Evening Post*, an article that was accompanied with a large cartoon illustration of a peregrine falcon, wings and talons spread, bearing down on a terrified partridge. Baker liked this so much that he kept an extra copy.

Baker kept cuttings of many of *The Peregrine*'s reviews, trimmed from a remarkable array of newspapers and journals. He pored over them and made little tables listing details of publication, date, author – even the number of words in each and whether it was good, bad, or fair. In some, he underlined passages that he liked; usually it was a line or two praising his poetic style that was singled out, especially when it was compared favourably with other writers. In *Wild Life and the Countryside*, for example, the reviewer wrote: 'Mr. Baker can *write*, with a power and an imagery and an economy that recalls Dickens or Dylan Thomas' (no doubt Baker would have been especially tickled to be included in the same company as Dickens and Thomas, two of his favourite authors).

Elsewhere Baker was applauded for writing that was 'thematically reminiscent of Hemingway's *Old Man and the Sea*, though more gentle.' One reviewer in *The Sunday Times* described his work as having an 'instant' quality only seen in the best poetry, and ranked him alongside Gilbert White, Dorothy Wordsworth, Francis Kilvert and Hopkins as a writer of nature's 'immediacy'. Elsewhere Kenneth Allsop, the well-known author and broadcaster, went one step further, extolling *The Peregrine* in *The Evening News*:

> It instantly takes its place among the great triumphal affirmations of man's search for his lost place in the universe, his inner need for oneness with Nature. It has within the same passion as the novels of Faulkner, the poetry of Blake, the music of Debussy. This is a religious epic of a bird, a symphony to a vanishing killer.

Baker made sure to hold onto several copies of Allsop's review.

The Peregrine also made its way onto the airwaves. The BBC radio series 'Woman's Hour' featured a review of the book in its programme on June 8, and a reading from an abridged version of Baker's book aired over a week in February 1968 on the same series.

Baker himself had taken a turn in the radio studio. Kenneth Allsop interviewed him on the BBC radio programme 'The World of Books', which aired on the evening of March 28, the week after *The Peregrine* had been released. Later the same year he spoke again, this time to Ted Ellis, the Norfolk naturalist, at the BBC's Norwich Studio. Ellis had read a preview copy of Baker's book, and when it was suggested to him that he might like to meet the author, he jumped at the chance. During the interview Ellis questioned Baker about the ten years that he spent intensely observing the peregrines in Essex. No recordings of either programme seem to have survived.

The Peregrine and its author were offered a spot on television, too. On BBC2 at 9.05pm on May 30, 1967, Baker appeared in the series *Life in the Animal World*. This episode was titled 'Feathered Fury', and was introduced by Desmond Morris, who discussed great predatory birds of the world and their 'unique place in man's culture.' Baker was among one of the several guests being interviewed: others included Leslie Brown, author

24, BLOMFIELD ROAD,
LONDON, W. 9.
CUNNINGHAM 5050.
01-286-

December 17, 1967.

Dear Mr. Baker,

I am writing to confirm my telegram of last Friday, telling you that your book has been awarded the Duff Cooper Memorial Prize for 1967; and to repeat my warmest congratulations. There are five judges for this prize - the Warden of New College, Oxford (Sir William Hayter), Cyril Connolly, John Bayley and V.S. Naipaul and myself - and our decision was unanimous. The award is made annually, for an outstanding work in the field of history, biography, politics or poetry; yours falls squarely and incontestably into the last category. None of us are particularly keen or knowledgable naturalists, but this in no way lessened our enthusiasm for the evocative power and sheer beauty of your writing.

The prize consists of a specially bound copy of my father's autobiography, "Old Men Forget", together with the annual interest on a sum of money contributed by all his friends after his death - amounting normally to between £150 and £200. It is awarded in the course of a reception held in London, usually by some distinguished person whom we invite to perform the ceremony. I wonder if there is anyone you would particularly like us to ask? We thought vaguely of the Duke of Edinburgh - because of his interest in the preservation of wild life - or perhaps Sir Solly Zuckerman, but if you have any ideas we should be only too pleased to consider them. Thursday morning of this week. It would be so nice to meet you and to have a chance of telling you in person just what a masterpiece I consider "The Peregrine" to be.

Please don't hesitate to let me know if there are any queries or problems. I look forward so much to hearing from you.

Yours sincerely,

Norwich.

Letter to J. A. Baker from Viscount Norwich, awarding him the Duff Cooper Memorial Prize, December 17, 1967.

J. A. Baker receiving the Yorkshire Post's *'Book of the Year 1967.' He is shaking the hand of the paper's editor Mr Guy Schofield at the Queens Hotel in Leeds.*

of several zoological guides to birds of prey; Dr Bijleveld, an ornithologist from the Netherlands; and Roger Upton and J. G. (or 'Jack') Mavrogordato, both of whom were experts on falconry and hawking. How Baker, the aspiring middle-class writer from Chelmsford with no qualifications to speak of, felt among this group of specialists is anyone's guess. The last two in particular would have been intimidating, if only because they came from levels of society that Baker likely had never come across before: Roger Upton trained and flew hawks for the royal family, and had travelled extensively in Arabia to learn the falconry techniques of the Middle East; and Jack Mavrogordato – born into the Greek nobility, educated at Oxford, trained in law – was known for his work as an advisor to the Governor General in Sudan and as the president of the British Falconers Club. How these experts felt about Baker's writing is also anyone's guess.

There were those that didn't approve of Baker's subjective style.

One reviewer in *The New Statesman* commented that Baker's 'observations seemed accurate' but his lyricism meant that 'it could hardly be respectable ornithology'. Another remarked how Baker must have been a rather poor sort of birder – his insistence on describing peregrines as 'hovering' meant he was clearly confusing them with kestrels. Most reviewers, regardless of their knowledge of birds, threw up their hands at the prospect of evaluating Baker's observations. Readers would either love it or hate it, warned *The Times Educational Supplement*: 'There can be no compromise with a book of this type.'

That Baker took part in promoting his work on television and radio does suggest that he was not as much of a misanthrope as some of his writing (and some of his reviewers) made out. It's a shame that none of these recordings seem to have survived – so many tapes were wiped, recorded over or destroyed by the BBC and others in those days. According to Doreen Baker, her husband had a deep voice and loved to read aloud; it would be a wonderful thing to hear him speak about or read from his own books. Perhaps copies of the recordings do still exist, tucked away on a dusty shelf somewhere and forgotten about, as so much of Baker's life has been until now.

In 1967 Baker and Doreen moved to a new house on Marlborough Road, only a couple of streets away from where Baker had grown up. They had help from Doreen's family to paint walls and move furniture, work that Baker was unable to do because of his arthritis. His health, however, had not stopped him from starting work on a new writing project.

Even after finishing *The Peregrine*, Baker had continued to keep diaries of his birdwatching trips, but these were now fewer and further apart. His diary entries show a graphological portrait of what was happening to the rest of his body: the words hunched over the lines in a scrawl, his writing grown smaller and spikier in sympathy with his seizing finger joints.

In this painful way, he began to collect both old and new material for his next book. The success of *The Peregrine* had spurred him on, and, encouraged by Walter at Collins and helped along by the money he had received, Baker came up with an outline for *The Hill of Summer*.

Where *The Peregrine* was set over the months of winter, *The Hill of Summer* traced the other half of the calendar; each of the six chapters a study of the months from April to September. Baker drew on many years' worth of memories, mining his extensive collection of diaries for the shimmering encounters that make up *The Hill of Summer*. If his first book was for the dying peregrines, then his second was for England's other endangered birds of prey, owls and kestrels and marsh harriers. 'The golden eyes are shallow,' he wrote of a sparrowhawk, 'a raging surface, like a storm-driven haze of Magellanic water.' Where Blake saw the world in a grain of sand, Baker saw galaxies in a sparrowhawk's eye.

In line with its season, the book is more languid and drifting than his previous work. When conceiving the idea of it, Baker wanted to fulfill the name of 'poet-naturalist' that he had been given in the wake of *The Peregrine*. And so his vision for the new book was for a work that captured the essence of English landscapes – downland, heath, hill, estuary, among others – in the same poetic style that he had honed while writing *The Peregrine*. As it turned out, it was this poetic ambition that was his undoing.

Collins published *The Hill of Summer* on June 16, 1969. It was met at first with some excitement. Like *The Peregrine*, Baker's second book featured in an abridged version on BBC Radio, with an excerpt read each summer month to correspond to the months described in its pages. It also earned a spot on television that year. *Survival* was a leading nature documentary series produced by Anglia Television, and in August of 1969 both *The Hill of Summer* and *The Peregrine* were featured in one of its programmes.

Ultimately Baker's second book suffered in comparison to *The Peregrine*. He had written it with more speed but without the same sense of purposeful anger that had driven him before. One reviewer complained that the book's cast was too large, there was too little

Baker's folder with his collection of reviews of The Peregrine.

action, and it lacked the crucial concentration of Baker's first work.

As other reviews of *The Hill of Summer* began to trickle in, the general consensus was that it fell short of his previous book. While *The Times* admired his lyricism and said his skill for observation had 'more in common with poets like Hopkins or Ted Hughes' (a comparison that would have delighted Baker, an avid reader of both poets), many others considered it as 'too literary, too poetical'. The BBC's science correspondent John Newell was of the opinion that:

> it would be fair to say that Mr. Baker has written a very long and perhaps rather self-indulgent but nonetheless often very good, perhaps great, poem.

The New Statesman's Frederick Laws seemed to sum up the prevailing attitude of ambivalent praise: 'He gives no common view of nature, and he only seems embarrassing because he is so whole-hearted.'

Baker's second book was, as his editor Walter later described it, a commercial flop. And though *The Hill of Summer* appeared the following year in a French translation, and a decade or so later in Italian, during the remainder of Baker's lifetime Collins would never print another edition.

Baker was crestfallen by *The Hill of Summer*'s reception. At some point in the years that followed, he went back over the book's proof copies with pen in hand, vigorously chastising his own writing: 'Poor', he scrawled in the margins, 'Very Poor', 'Rubbish'. It was a disappointment that was hard to recover from.

There was further disappointment for Baker in the ongoing fortunes of *The Peregrine*. Though his first book had fared far better than his second, *The Peregrine* had struggled to find a mainstream audience in the first few years after its publication. When the initial wave of enthusiasm for the book had passed, Maurice Wiggin mourned the fact that the public had not taken it into their hearts as they had done with *Ring of Bright Water* or *Tarka the Otter*. '[*The Peregrine*] is to my mind the most miraculous piece of writing about the natural creation since the war,' Wiggin wrote. '[But by] denying himself a self-indulgent "homocentric" narrative, this author possibly denied himself the reward of best-sellerdom.'

Neither Baker nor Wiggin could have imagined that, fifty years on, readers would be finding *The Peregrine* as relevant to the twenty-first century as it had been to the twentieth – as vivid, startling and disturbing as it was on the day it was printed.

Perhaps it is *The Peregrine*'s lack of 'self-indulgent "homocentric" narrative' that has made it so resistant to being dramatised in film, unlike the works of Gavin Maxwell and Henry Williamson. Though this has not been for lack of trying.

During the 1970s a number of requests were made to Baker, through Collins, about film rights for *The Peregrine*. Each time Baker turned them down; any film that would be made would have to be true not just to the action but also the experiences of the book, Baker said, and he doubted such a thing would be possible.

But early in 1984, one proposal piqued Baker's curiosity. A man from the BBC's Natural History Unit got in touch with him through Collins. He told Baker he had long been an admirer of *The Peregrine*, and cherished the thought of making a film worthy of the book – would Baker agree to a meeting to discuss it?

This man was John Sparks. He was a zoologist and naturalist with a particular passion for birds, and had worked at the London Zoo under Desmond Morris (whose other research students included a young Jane Goodall). Sparks had then joined the BBC during the mid-1960s, and had worked on a number of groundbreaking programmes, notably David Attenborough's series *Life on Earth*, which aired in 1979.

At the time he wrote to Baker, John Sparks had just written a book on animal behaviour and not long been appointed Head of the Natural History Unit (where he would go on to commission the long-running programmes *Nature* and *Birdwatch*). Sparks was born and raised in Colchester, not far from Chelmsford, and the Essex and Suffolk coast had been his stamping ground, too. *The*

Peregrine's descriptions resonated deeply with Sparks' memories of the places of his childhood.

Baker mulled over the Sparks' idea. Ten days after receiving the letter, Baker sent a reply: he wanted to meet, he said, to talk about the project, but his health was not good and they would have to wait until his arthritis had stabilised. Sparks wrote back quickly with both thanks and sympathies, hoping Baker would contact him as soon as he felt strong enough for a conversation.

It wasn't until the autumn of 1984 that Baker found the strength to write again to arrange a meeting. Sparks was overjoyed, and suggested coming to meet Baker at his home in Essex, rather than risk Baker's health with the long journey to Bristol.

They met towards the end of November. Sparks travelled to Chelmsford accompanied by his producer Peter Jones. Ten years earlier Jones had produced what was, at the time, a controversial *Horizon* programme called 'Science is Dead, Long Live Science' that had featured such contentious environmental science issues as energy-generating windmills, biological water filters and natural fertilisers.

The pair explained their idea to Baker over tea and cake brought by Doreen. They wanted to make a fifty-minute documentary film based on Baker's work. Afterwards, Sparks wrote to Baker thanking him for the meeting:

> It was fascinating to hear you talk about the experiences which led to you writing *The Peregrine* and [we] were reassured by your analysis of the relationship between your experiences over 12 years and the book, and by your thoughts about how the film should relate to your book. As I said to you, it is our intention to see that the film that we should eventually make will be as faithful to your writing as is possible given the constraints of programme making.

Baker was clearly impressed by the pair's abilities and their sincerity, and gave Collins permission to negotiate with the BBC for television rights for *The Peregrine*.

There was some delay, however, and it was not until well into 1985 that Collins informed Baker that the BBC had offered a fee of £1,700 and were ready to go ahead with the production. More delays held up the project, and Baker didn't receive the first half-advance for the rights until five months later – the other half, he was told, he would receive when the programme aired.

Baker never did receive the second half of his rights fee. After its slow start the project failed to get off the ground. It's not certain whether the BBC binned the idea or decided to postpone it indefinitely when faced with the realities of just how expensive and difficult the film would be to make. Every so often since then, though, the idea of producing a film of *The Peregrine* has surfaced (David Cobham got so far as drafting a full screenplay), before quietly being shelved once more. As the strength of Baker's text is so bound up in the power of his language perhaps it's for the best that nothing thus far has come of it.

Detail from Baker's Ordnance Survey map of Southend-on-Sea (1945), showing the areas around the Blackwater Estuary marked with peregrine sightings.

Chapter Seven
PRESERVATION

And if there is some scenery,
Some unpretentious greenery,
Surviving anywhere,
It does not need protecting
For soon we'll be erecting
A Power Station there.

JOHN BETJEMAN, 'Inexpensive Progress', 1966

FOULNESS WAS APTLY NAMED. At least that was the opinion expressed by Sir David Renton, MP for Huntingdonshire, to those attending a late afternoon sitting of the House of Commons in early March 1971.

Foulness was, Sir David said, a flat, desolate and unattractive piece of estuarial coastline. Yes, he had been told that numbers of migrating brent geese fed there; but were Foulness to be repurposed, they would no doubt find other feeding grounds. Sir David was himself a member of the RSPB – but there were much more attractive birds, at least to his mind, than the brent goose, and dozens of species of *them* would be destroyed if a site for the new development were chosen further inland.

The development in question was London's third airport. That day's debate focussed on the report of the Government-directed Roskill Commission, which had been tasked with investigating a number of possible locations. Around fifty members from the front and the back benches were straining to have their say, and, despite being asked by the Speaker to be brief, few of them were managing to stay within the ten-minute limit.

Sir David was not alone in favouring Foulness Island, part of the broad, sandy expanse of Essex's south-east coast, used solely as an artillery range. Later that month the Cabinet would follow his lead and nominate the area for the project, despite the fact that the Commission had rejected the estuarial airport on the grounds of its expense, remoteness, and environmental impact.

Planning began immediately. The Foulness project was shrewdly renamed 'Maplin Sands Airport', after the mudflats that extended from the island's shore into the North Sea. The planned development included more than just the airport: there would be a large deepwater port to cater to the new breed of vast container ships; motorways and a high-speed rail line to link it all to London; and a new town covering an estimated 82 square miles that would house the thousands of people employed in the venture. As the Government phrased it, Foulness would become an international transport hub to carry Britain into a 'better tomorrow'.

One person who didn't agree with this vision was J. A. Baker. Maplin Sands Airport looked to be an environmental disaster for his beloved Essex coast. Later that summer, after the announcement was made official, Baker walked, as he had done hundreds of times in search of peregrines, along the sea wall that stretches along the Dengie, a haunch of land that thrusts into the sea between the estuaries of the River Blackwater and the River Crouch. The Dengie, its mud and marsh crowded with migrating birds, was directly in the path of the airport.

Baker described his walk in the RSPB's magazine *Birds*. This seemingly dreary expanse of sea-washed silt, he wrote, was home not just to the brent geese slighted by Sir David, but something more: a 'very old silence'. 'It is rare now,' he wrote. 'Man is killing the wilderness, hunting it down. On the east coast of England, this is perhaps its last home.' Foulness and the land around it had been a refuge for birdlife for millennia; for this ancient beauty to be brushed aside by 'indifferent politicians' was inexcusable.

In ten years without intervention, he wrote despairingly,

ON THE ESSEX COAST
J A Baker
The Essex coastline is threatened by development. J A Baker, author of *The Peregrine* and *The Hill of Summer,* shows that it has aesthetic as well as scientific value.
Andrew Dodds
281

Title page for J. A. Baker's article 'On the Essex Coast' in RSPB Birds *(Sep–Oct 1971). The illustration is a view of the Saxon chapel of St Peter-on-the-Wall at Bradwell-on-Sea, on the eastern edge of the Dengie peninsula.*

the coastline would be destroyed by a web of roaring jet-engine noise, motorway traffic and emissions from electricity-generating 'temples' that would dominate the land and air. Baker probably had one such temple in mind: the Bradwell nuclear power station had been sited on the Dengie since 1957, its pair of imposing concrete and steel reactors looking like something on the cover of a J. G. Ballard novel.

Baker lamented that the effects on wildlife of such rampant energy production and consumption were often left unreported and unchallenged. During his walk across the saltings that day, Baker found a black-throated diver on the sand, dead, coated in a slick of sticky black oil. To readers of the magazine this would have been a reminder of the *Torrey Canyon* oil disaster, which had happened only a few years earlier.

On March 18, 1967, The SS *Torrey Canyon*, carrying 120,000 tons of crude oil, struck a reef off the coast of Cornwall. At the time, it was the worst environmental disaster ever recorded. Television news ran footage of Cornish beaches awash with oil and dying marine life, grim-faced men with flame-throwers and cans of kerosene doing the only thing possible to clear the oil: set it alight. The military firebombed the oil slicks, with ineffectual results. These images would have struck Baker: he had holidayed there in the 1940s, and had spoken fondly of hiking along its shores as a young man.

Now, Baker was faced with the possibility of his own countryside being desecrated. The other airport site recommended by the Roskill Commission was in Buckinghamshire, but that idea had been killed off by mounting public concern about the environmental effects. When Foulness came out top of the list, the RSPB began a vocal campaign against it, hoping that their environmental arguments would have a similar effect. Baker, a prize-winning writer local to the area and known to bird lovers, was an obvious ally to help the resistance. He wrote in blind fury against those proposing the new airport: they showed how man was insatiably, thoughtlessly plundering resources, lured by the 'stench of money'.

Both money and oil, however, would also become the rescuers of the Dengie and Foulness. Not long after the plan was confirmed, the cost of relocating the army's munitions testing ranges to Shoeburyness was found to be too high. To make matters worse for supporters of the project, by October 1973 inflation in Britain was at 10 per cent and there were fears that investing in Maplin

Airport would overheat the economy. That same month, the first 'oil shock' occurred: Arab petroleum states placed an embargo on oil and the price per barrel quadrupled. Maplin became a public expenditure the country couldn't afford, and a General Election in October 1974 sealed its fate: the newly elected Labour government branded Maplin a Tory prestige project. The idea was abandoned.

'GLORIOUS DAY', Baker wrote in spiky capitals on a page torn from a small, lined notebook, on Tuesday. October 7, 1975. It had been four years since the publication of his RSPB article, and that day he enjoyed an outing, unblighted by airport development, to the Old Hall Marshes, which lie along the north shore of the Blackwater.

The record he made of this trip is the last diary entry to be found among his papers, hidden away in a collection of cardboard folders, newspaper clippings and letters from the *Dictionary of National Biography*. It was one of a dwindling number of expeditions that Baker was able to undertake during the last decade or so of his life.

His disease had left him unable to take on office work, and so he and Doreen lived on benefits from the Department of Health and Social Security. His arthritis now affected his hands, knees, hips and back, and it would in a matter of years permanently cripple him. Though Baker still enjoyed some freedom of movement during the early 1970s, cycling became too much; he and Doreen bought a car, driven always by Doreen, as Baker never got a licence.

And so it was that they would head out in the car to his favourite walking spots. Doreen would leave him with a flask and packed lunch, and return several hours later to collect him and drive home. On his good days, when his condition wasn't troubling him too much, Baker could spend most of the daylight hours outside like this, slowly traversing his old haunts: the familiar woods and coastal paths, lanes and sea walls, his binoculars always to hand.

The diary entry that Baker wrote that day, in the autumn of 1975, was squashed into dense lines of blue biro, very small and crabbed, though recognisably his, written, no doubt, with increasingly unyielding fingers. Still, he managed to record the details.

Most of that day he spent on the coastline near Tollesbury, watching the birds that flocked around the Blackwater Estuary until the sun began to fade. He had set out along the sea wall where the ground was rough; the path had been churned up into thick mud after the previous day's rain, and Baker found the walk easier on the eye than the feet. As he started out a brittle sunshine was sweeping the marshes – perfect conditions for birdwatching.

Slowly, Baker picked his way around the shore of Tollesbury Fleet. Streams of cloud began to draw over from the north-west. The wind was strong and, Baker wrote, 'amazingly cold' and wintry; though, as he noted, there was too much ploughing and fishing activity going on for it to have any of winter's feeling of 'wildness'. It was also too early for the vast numbers of overwintering migrant waders that he had seen come and go over the last two-and-a-half decades. The wind was especially biting, he wrote, 'out on the marsh, past [the] lost hedges.'

A great many of the hedgerows in England had been grubbed up on farms to cultivate larger fields. This had had a more dramatic effect on the Essex shoreline: without the hedges acting as windbreaks, the strong prevailing south-westerlies scoured the foreshore, stripping vegetation and drying out the ground.

The Blackwater may have escaped being turned into an airport flight path, but a number of threats still imperiled its wildlife. Without the hedgerows to hold back or soak up the run-off from fields, rain washed pesticides and fertilisers into the marsh, killing many of the tiny creatures on the lower trophic levels: the phytoplankton, worms and snails upon which the rest of the marsh's ecosystem still depends. Combined with the impacts at this time of other waterborne contaminants along the East Anglian coast, particularly tributyltin (TBT – an extremely toxic biocide used in anti-fouling boat paint), the marsh was under attack from all sides.

Baker had known the Old Hall saltmarsh for nearly twenty years: it was an area that he criss-crossed with annotations on

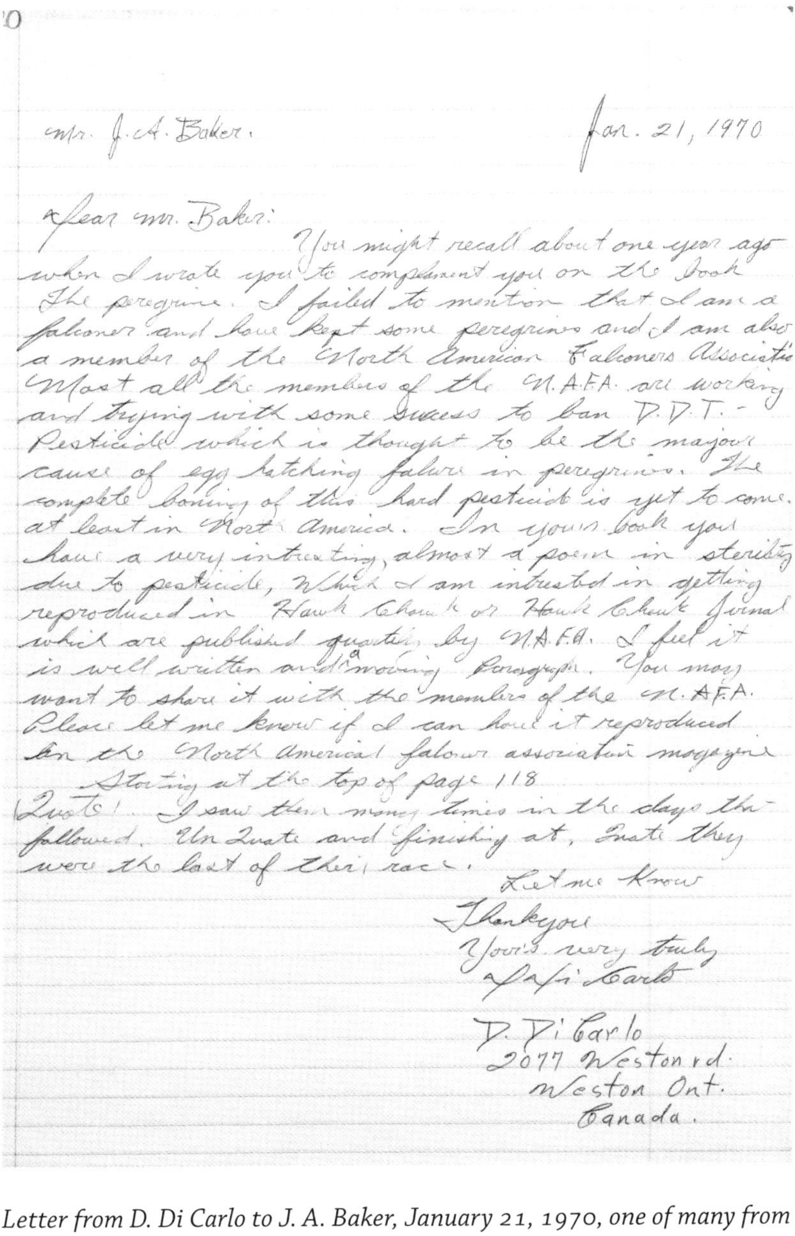

Mr. J. A. Baker.   Jan. 21, 1970

Dear Mr. Baker:
You might recall about one year ago when I wrote you to complement you on the book The peregrine. I failed to mention that I am a falconer and have kept some peregrines and I am also a member of the North American Falconers Association. Most all the members of the N.A.F.A. are working and trying with some sucess to ban D.D.T. - Pesticide which is thought to be the majour cause of egg hatching falure in peregrines. The complete baning of this hard pesticide is yet to come at least in North America. In your's book you have a very intresting, almost a poem in sterility due to pesticide, which I am intrested in getting reproduced in Hawk Chalk or Hawk Chalk Jurnal which are published quarterly by N.A.F.A. I feel it is well written and a moving Paragraph. You may want to share it with the members of the N.A.F.A. Please let me know if I can have it reproduced in the North American falconer association magazine
Starting at the top of page 118
Quote! I saw them many times in the days that followed. Un Quote and finishing at, Quote they were the last of their race.
Let me know
Thankyou
Your's very truly
D. Di Carlo

D. Di Carlo
2077 Weston rd.
Weston Ont.
Canada.

Letter from D. Di Carlo to J. A. Baker, January 21, 1970, one of many from fans of The Peregrine *and* The Hill of Summer *that Baker received from around the world. This, from Ontario in Canada, was written by a member of the North American Falcon Association working towards a ban of DDT.*

his birding maps from the 1950s. Now in his diary he noted with sadness that the saltmarsh looked 'drier than ever, v[ery] yellow, v[ery] hard to pick up [*sic*] brown or yellow birds.'

The birds he was most interested in seeing were, of course, raptors. Those that he saw that day are listed at the top of the page: first a kestrel, and then what he thought might have been a hen harrier. From the sea wall, looking out across the creeks of the Fleet, he also caught a glimpse of what he thought was 'Poss M / Poss P' – possibly a merlin or a peregrine.

Even then, many years after writing his books and more than two decades after his first sighting, Baker remained captivated by the peregrines. Every chance he got he would scan the Essex skies, trees and telegraph poles for them. October was prime time for spotting an early migrant beginning its winter hunting. He couldn't be sure, though. Here the mudflats spread themselves wide at low tide – not an easy landscape to judge size from a distance or distinguish between the grey-brown plumage of a peregrine and the brown-grey feathers of a merlin. A sight of either falcon, though, would have been something special, as both were still rare all across East Anglia.

When, in his RSPB article four years earlier, Baker had called for this part of the Essex coast to be made into a nature reserve, he couldn't have known that his wish would become a reality. It would have pleased him to know that Old Hall Marshes, the same yellowing reed beds upon which he had stood that day in 1975, and more besides, would be protected by the early 1990s as a Site of Special Scientific Interest. It's now the Blackwater Estuary National Nature Reserve, one of the first places in the world to successfully model both the 'managed retreat' of coastal flood protection and the best ways to re-establish saltmarsh. Many a glorious day's birdwatching there today will yield sightings of kestrel, merlin, peregrine and harriers from Tollesbury sea wall – unthinkable from where Baker stood in 1975.

We shouldn't be too complacent, however. Not all of the Essex coastline has been immune to the conflict between business and nature that threatened it in 1971. Directly across the Blackwater from Tollesbury Fleet, is Bradwell nuclear power station. In 2015, the site was in the process of being decommissioned and debates were being had about the possibility of constructing a new station on the same site. The multimillion-pound decommissioning project was brought to a halt, however, when a pair of peregrines, one of a small local population, were found to have built a nest on the reactor roof. The site's director told local newspapers that protection for the birds had been put into place, and would remain until the eggs could be relocated.

Within a matter of days the nest site was found mysteriously destroyed, the eggs smashed. The parent birds have since vanished, and the work continues.

Portrait of J. A. Baker, likely taken as an 'author' photo in 1967.

Chapter Eight
MEETING THE WEATHER

> ... strain towards the master-
> Fulcrum of violence where the hawk hangs still,
> That maybe in his own time meets the weather
>
> Coming the wrong way ...
>
> TED HUGHES, 'The Hawk in the Rain', 1957

THOUGH THERE ARE NO MORE diary entries after 1975, there are other fragments that give clues to the last twelve years of Baker's life.

One scrap of notepaper, for example, contains a list he wrote of outings made by car between 1976 and 1984, presumably taken from diaries that no longer exist. Dates, times, temperatures and weather conditions were all noted down with precision. All of the trips seem to have taken place during winter and early spring – the best times of year for seeing peregrines and other migrants to the Essex countryside. The list isn't a long one: it covers less than a single side of A5 paper, and with each year the number of outings got fewer.

During the last decade of his life Baker bought a number of maps. Each one is covered with his usual bird-spotting annotations: SH, P, M, or O, often accompanied with little notes like 'Prob', 'Poss', 'Winter', 'Small', 'Big'. One 1976 map of the Essex coast is scribbled all over with Baker's handwriting; on another from the 1970s, of the Midlands, Baker marked in pencil: 'SNIPE', 'WOODCOCK', and 'HERON'. These were areas fairly local to Chelmsford – within a couple of hours' drive at most – so there's a good degree of certainty that they record Baker's own sightings. Certainly he was managing the odd outing until the early 1980s, sometimes as far as Suffolk and Norfolk.

Some of Baker's maps appear to record sightings that couldn't have been made by him. There's one of County Mayo in Ireland, not published until 1982; given the state of Baker's health at that time, he wouldn't have been able to make such a trip himself. Often on these later maps the only mark is 'P' – peregrine. At this time, Baker was also making a collection of magazine articles and birdwatching society records on peregrine sightings, not just from the UK but from around the world. In all probability he was sourcing the sightings from these and transferring them onto his maps.

His retreat into this kind of documentation was a symptom of a life lived largely indoors. For his entire adult life Baker had been obsessed with recording and making lists. Now, heading into his fifties, increasingly housebound, he turned again to his first passion: books. He continued to build up his library, both fiction and non-fiction, and read and reread vast swathes of literature. In a return to his teenage habit, he catalogued his reading. A small sheaf of notepaper, attached in the top left-hand corner with a rusting paperclip, contains dense columns of titles that Baker copied down around this time. Each list appears under one of a number of headings: 'Great Novels', 'Very Good Novels', 'Acceptable Novels', and so on. In total there are about 260 titles listed on these pages.

Nor did he restrict his work to reading. Ever since the publication of *The Hill of Summer* he had been mulling over what his next writing project would be. Baker kept proof copies of both his books, and these provide clues as to the direction of his thinking. During the last ten to fifteen years of his life (taking the acicular deterioration of his handwriting an indicator of time), he went through these proofs with meticulous attention. Every page (and the red paper covers, too) was scribbled over with arcane notations. In two proofs he underlined every metaphor and simile, verb, adjective and personal pronoun, and made running

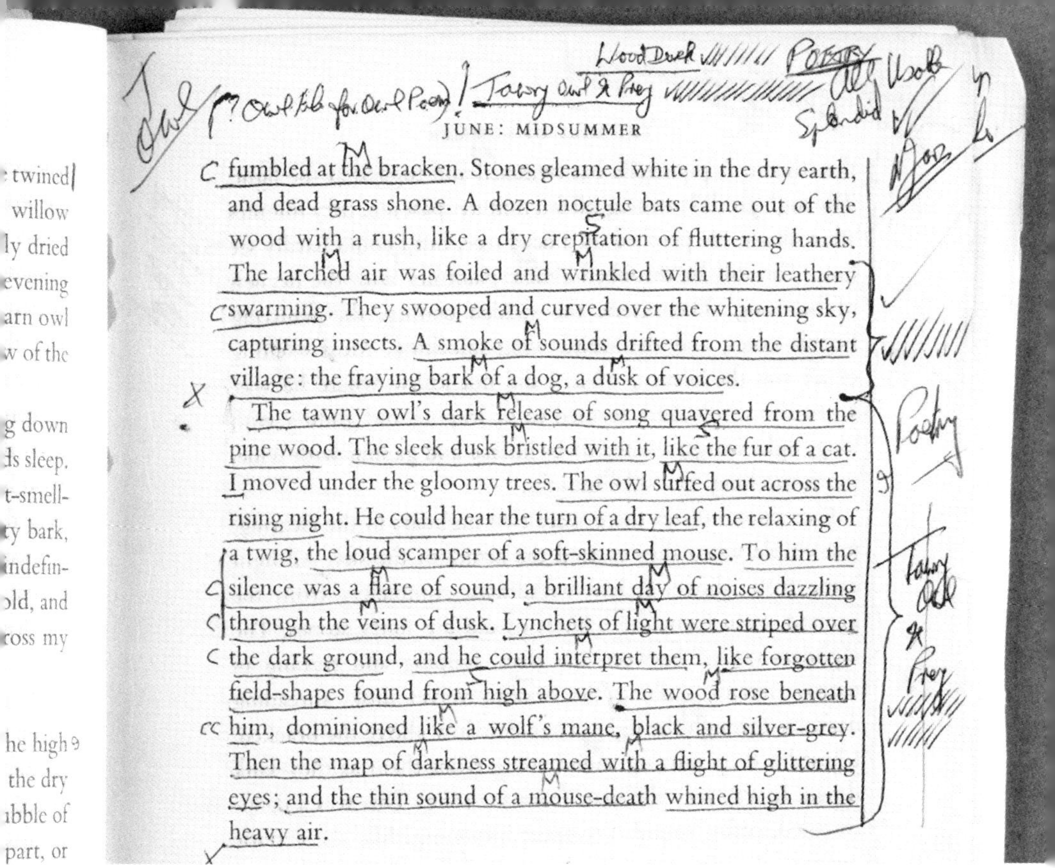
JUNE: MIDSUMMER

fumbled at the bracken. Stones gleamed white in the dry earth, and dead grass shone. A dozen noctule bats came out of the wood with a rush, like a dry crepitation of fluttering hands. The larched air was foiled and wrinkled with their leathery swarming. They swooped and curved over the whitening sky, capturing insects. A smoke of sounds drifted from the distant village: the fraying bark of a dog, a dusk of voices.

The tawny owl's dark release of song quavered from the pine wood. The sleek dusk bristled with it, like the fur of a cat. I moved under the gloomy trees. The owl surfed out across the rising night. He could hear the turn of a dry leaf, the relaxing of a twig, the loud scamper of a soft-skinned mouse. To him the silence was a flare of sound, a brilliant day of noises dazzling through the veins of dusk. Lynchets of light were striped over the dark ground, and he could interpret them, like forgotten field-shapes found from high above. The wood rose beneath him, dominioned like a wolf's mane, black and silver-grey. Then the map of darkness streamed with a flight of glittering eyes; and the thin sound of a mouse-death whined high in the heavy air.

Pages from a proof copy of The Hill of Summer *(1969), heavily annotated by Baker.*

totals of each at the bottom of every page. In the third he marked every stressed syllable, as poets like Gerard Manley Hopkins had often done. Another proof was filled with ticks and crosses, and little notes saying 'Good', 'Excellent', 'Very poor', and 'Poetry'. The cover of one of the proofs he labelled as 'Possible Poetry'. Was that what he was planning, a return to his first love – to writing verse?

'Possible poetry' was of course not Baker's only project. He was still aggrieved by his second book's lacklustre reception, and wanted to achieve again the acclaim that had greeted *The Peregrine*. Admirers of his books sent letters to him asking if there would be more, and Baker wrote back with assurances that he was indeed planning something new: a novel. In one reply, a researcher at the Royal Ontario Museum in Canada wrote to him in October 1971 expressing delight upon hearing that Baker was 'working on [a book about] people and their place', and wishing him 'the best success and joy in working on your novel.' Kenneth Allsop had said that *The Peregrine* was a book about 'man's search for his lost place in the universe'; did Baker's plan for a new work, on 'people and their place', have similar themes?

Three years later there was still no book. The desire to write had not left him, but he was frustrated by illness: in the autumn of 1974 the journalist Maurice Wiggin wrote to him, saying: 'Don't be put off writing your new stuff by your present immobility ... I do understand your writing problems – that the style, the imagery, is always available for writing about the natural creation, but not for novels ... Do try to bring the new peregrine book to a conclusion, if you can.' Somehow the peregrines remained elusive, even after all Baker had written about them.

Without the inspiration afforded to him by his excursions into the countryside, Baker was struggling to find his authorial voice. He was forced to retreat into a world of second-hand nature. He began a sort of scrapbook, stuffed into a brown cardboard folder. The contents of this folder, written out on its cover and variously crossed out and replaced, suggest that his interests here never strayed far from their usual posts: 'Poetry', 'Saker', 'Gyr[falcon]', 'Peregrine + Some Landscape Etc', 'Landscapes Actual/Metaphorical', 'Aerials', 'Sea'; and a list of geographical locations, 'West Ireland', 'North Cornwall', 'Seven Sisters', 'Dorset', 'Beachy Head' (at the time, these were UK and Ireland's remaining peregrine nesting sites).

Kept inside this folder were sheaves of glossy colour magazine photographs, illustrations, articles, and cuttings taken from newspapers and books – even Christmas cards. The contents range further than the titles on the folder might suggest: kingfishers, owls, robins, trees and tigers join the ragbag collection, all carefully cut or torn out by Baker then squirrelled away for safekeeping.

As he grew less mobile from the mid-1970s onwards, Baker started to supplement his researches with information gathered

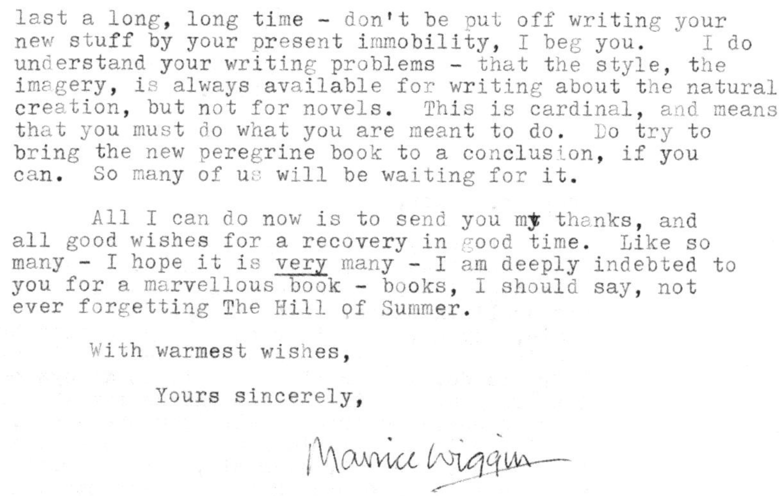

last a long, long time - don't be put off writing your new stuff by your present immobility, I beg you. I do understand your writing problems - that the style, the imagery, is always available for writing about the natural creation, but not for novels. This is cardinal, and means that you must do what you are meant to do. Do try to bring the new peregrine book to a conclusion, if you can. So many of us will be waiting for it.

All I can do now is to send you my thanks, and all good wishes for a recovery in good time. Like so many - I hope it is <u>very</u> many - I am deeply indebted to you for a marvellous book - books, I should say, not ever forgetting The Hill of Summer.

With warmest wishes,

Yours sincerely,

Maurice Wiggin

A letter of encouragement from the author and journalist Maurice Wiggin to J. A. Baker, September 8, 1974.

from others who had tracked peregrine falcons. He received letters from a number of correspondents in reply to his questions: 'I am very happy to give you any help I can in the matter [of peregrine falcons],' wrote one. 'I am grieved to read of your sad state of health; but cheered by your brave determination to win through.'

This sort of outsourcing was fruitful: that same correspondent sent him several letters filled with details about a number of eyries on the south Kent coast, particularly between Dover and Folkestone (an area Baker was familiar with, having honeymooned there with Doreen). From another peregrine watcher he received letters about nesting pairs in Dorset, on Old Harry Rocks near Poole Harbour. The writer told Baker to please 'include these in your work. One will look forward so much to a volume about this fine bird.'

But whatever it was that Baker had in mind to write, whether it was a novel, guide, or volume of poetry, he could never settle to complete it. He was still making promises about a 'new' publication towards the end of 1980, when he sent a letter to an admirer of

The Peregrine in which he made mention of there being 'a third book' in progress.

What this third book might have looked like is pure speculation. Whatever it was that Baker was writing, no sign remains of any drafts. Perhaps somewhere in an attic in Essex there's a manuscript waiting to be found. But for the time being, the trail of Baker's third and final book has run cold.

J. A. Baker died on December 27, 1987, at the age of 61. He was cremated at the Chelmsford Cemetry and Crematorium nine days later. There was no record made in the crematorium's formal book of remembrance; his ashes were scattered over the public lawn, but he asked not to have a specific memorial.

During the last few years of his life, Baker's health had gone into a steep decline. Like the hawk in Ted Hughes' poem that is blown from the sky and hurled to earth, the weather, too, had changed for Baker. The year before his death, he was diagnosed with cancer. Over his life a number of treatments had been prescribed to ease his arthritis: injections of gold and blood transfusions had alleviated some symptoms. For many years he had also taken the drug Imuran, an immunosuppressant, which, like most drugs of its class, carries with it an increased risk of cancer. Six months of chemotherapy couldn't stop the spread of the disease. Doreen cared for him until the end.

Hughes' poem 'The Hawk in the Rain' was one of Baker's favourites. He left a number of subtle references to it in *The Peregrine*, and scribbled quotations from the poem among his notes. In particular, Hughes' lines on the hawk as the 'diamond point of will that polestars / The sea drowner's endurance' were ones that seem to have resonated with Baker. Struggling against the pain of his illness as he crossed the saltmarshes in search of peregrines, Baker must have felt both a deep connection and envy of the raptor flying without effort in the skies above. He was one and the same with the narrator of Hughes' poem, the hawk-hunter who drags 'heel after heel' through the ploughland's clutching

Feb.II	One off Cuckmere Haven. Was a female and was carrying a kill.
Mar.3	One female over Glynde Levels.
Mar.I7	One female at Glynde Levels. Perched on cable tower.
Mar.I8	Pair at Friars Bay, Peacehaven. The falcon called as she left the cliff.
Mar.30	Pair at Friars Bay, Peacehaven. Birds were silent.
Apr.2	One male at Friars Bay. Was silent
May I3	One flying up the Ouse Valley.
May 20	Between Seaford & Hope Gap at least one adult and one juvenile were seen from the beach below the cliffs. The juvenile identified as such by grey -brown back & wings and by general 'unfinished' appearance. Was seen to fly into the cliff and perch there. It was joined by an adult which perched just above the young bird.

Australia, as you know, is a glorious bird country and the Peregrine seems to be holding his own; at least here in Victoria I know of several nests; some in trees (dead, 60ft gums) which have been used for as long as people can remember. Even if you don't see the bird, his kills are not uncommonly found - parrots' feathers on the side of a country road and a carcase with a chipped breast bone.

Indeed, I own one, an assertion to counter my family's claim that he owns me. He has a permanently dislocated shoulder but enjoys leaping from his block for about 2 yards. He now enjoys the mice I breed for him and has accepted pets' meat; which means I no longer have to shoot sparrows for him too often.

There is some irony in the fact that he has forced me to become a traffic hazard. When I abruptly stop to pick up a recently-killed bird for him. As if he is determined to pay back the species that crippled him, with the same steel.

Recently I camped in a valley where a Tiercel each evening dashed up and down pacing spine-tailed swifts. Without difficulty, excellently he put to rest the controversy.

He is the fastest. Watching him, whole paragraphs of your book came back.
Once again I thank you.

ABOVE: *Note from 'Charles' to J. A. Baker attached to a record sheet from the Sussex Ornithological Society. The sheet gives details of peregrine sightings around Horsham, Sussex between January 23, 1956 and March 29, 1959.*
BELOW: *Letter of appreciation for* The Peregrine *from Vic Dolby to J. A. Baker, sent from Melbourne, Australia, February 11, 1975.*

clay, suspended forever in pursuit of the bird.

The hawks had become Baker's own polestar: they were at the centre of everything that he wrote. Perhaps he saw them as a lifeline, anchors for his creativity and ambition, but also for knowing his place in the world – in the landscape of his beloved Essex, and in himself as a writer. Baker wrote that as a child he had been struck by the abiding feeling that he belonged 'out there, on the edge of things', a feeling that pursued him into adulthood. 'Out there' had been a hazy approximation of the distant horizon beyond Chelmsford's suburbs, past hedgerows of elm and through farmers' fields to the no-man's-lands of woods and desolate saltings. But being 'out there, at the edge of things', seems to have been the story of the rest of Baker's life, too.

As well as 'pilgrim', *peregrine* in its original Latin could also mean 'foreigner' or 'outsider'. Baker was, according to his friends, his wife and his editor, a natural loner – and looking at his life experiences it's not so hard to see how this aspect of his character came to define him. He had felt himself an outsider for most of his life: as the only child of an unhappy, sometimes violent, marriage; as an overly sensitive and highly strung teenager; in the separation from his friends as they left Essex for active service during the war; in his mental breakdown and rehabilitation; in his repeated failures at work; in his sometimes debilitating physical and mental illness – and so on. Even as a birdwatcher he made his own way, and had, in Doreen's words, 'no truck with birders'. In the pursuit to which he dedicated so much of his life, Baker chose to be on the outside of the accepted, always skirting the edges.

It's possible that being an outsider helped Baker to develop his gift as an acute observer. And, perhaps, too, it was his own sense of himself as an outsider that made him uniquely able to identify with the peregrines, and uniquely qualified to tell their story.

When Derek Ratcliffe mentioned Baker's work in his own guide to the peregrine falcon, he called it a 'remarkable' book, if written in a 'somewhat extravagant style'. 'Extravagant' is perhaps the best description of *The Peregrine* – it was a term favoured by Henry

David Thoreau who knew its Latin roots from *extra* (outside of, beyond) and *vagari* (to wander). To be 'extravagant', as Thoreau had it, was to 'wander beyond the boundaries'.

Wandering beyond the boundaries is what Baker's writing was about. His acts of trespass were physical and psychological: climbing over fences, walking along sea walls, always moving between the fringes of the town and the changing tides of the coast, probing the unsettling hinterland between the human and non-human animal. To confuse a book of non-fiction with fictionalised autobiography would be a mistake. But in Baker's case, it's not too much of a leap to see how his elusiveness as a writer stemmed from the experiences of his life, experiences that pushed him to inhabit and translate the 'other life' that he had known:

> *another life, a life beyond, out there, where all that could ever really matter was happening unregarded.*

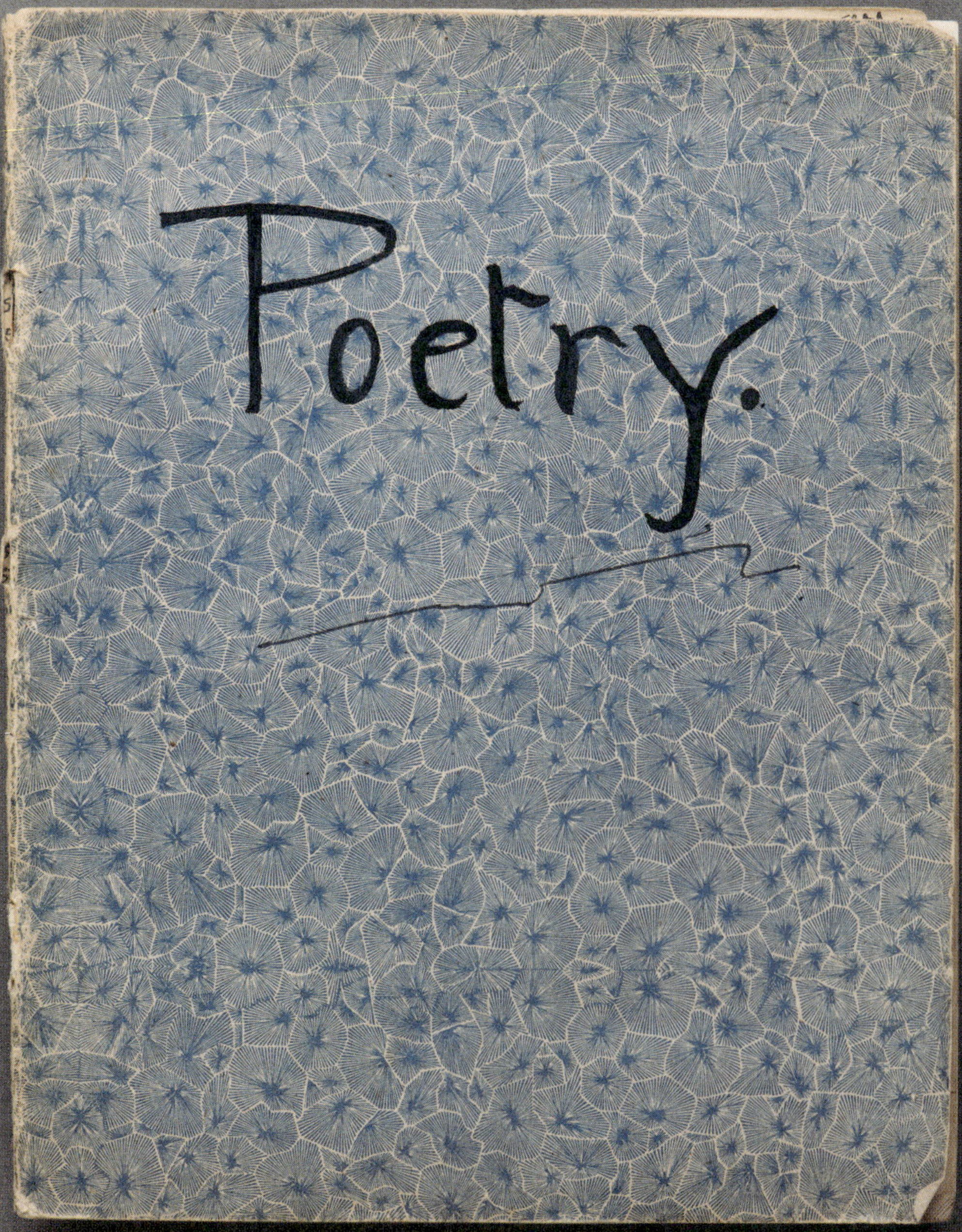
Poetry.

Owl Light

This is the country of desperate love
Where gipsy fires crouch among long-legged
                    shadows.

The sun has enriched the west with light
And left sadder clouds to rise above his dwelling.

The trees of the ride beseech the stirring owl,
'Speak poet, and soothe the troubled sky
That no evil spell may sour the falling dew.
Make gentle the coming of the night
For the last breeze has passed into the wood
To sleep with the frail lizard under the same grey
                    stone'.

And the poet speaks,
And his breath, like a loosened shaft,
Becomes a star.

To Alun Lewis, Poet (Killed at Arakan, 1944)

Friend that I never saw
You had a poem of the rain
As you pondered the weary hours
Of waiting for the high moment
That was planned for you.

And now, in a little Cornish village
I, too, ponder the deep future
And wonder,
Nor is my hope greater than yours
Though my burden – so much less.

The rain soaks into the leaves,
Into the patient soil
And I know
That at Arakan also
The rains are pouring their endless grief
Above your grave.

Friend that I never knew
Who speaks to me of Christ –
I give you my integrity,
My faith in trust.
I shall not rest
Till I have raised
Love from the ruined cross,
And seen the coming
That your words foretold.

June 25, 1946

"To Alun Lewis, Poet" (Killed at Arakan, 1944)

Frind that I never saw
You had a poem of the rain
As you pondered the weary hours
Of waiting for the high moment
That was planned for you.

And now, in a little Cornish village
I too, ponder the deep future
And wonder,
Nor is my hope greater than yours
Though my burden — so much less.

The rain soaks into the leaves
Into the patient soil
And I know
That at Arakan also
The rains are pouring their endless grief
Above your grave.

Frind that I never knew
Who speak to me of Christ —
I give you my integrity,
My faith in trust.
I shall not rest
Till I have raised
Love from the ruined cross,
And seen the coming
That your words foretold.

June 25th

"To an airman killed over Germany, 1944"

I glimpsed your name in the paper
And so I recalled your face
And, strangely – began to remember.

At cricket in parks at evening
I made you my make-shift hero,
A timid child in my dreaming
– Yet I tired of that soon
For so seldom you smiled
And made no meaningless gesture.

Later – I lost you,
A face among many faces
And heroes were easy to come by
When I was a thoughtless schoolboy.

So – the war came,
Though long before that I had forgotten
And never thought of you
As an airman.

War has no laughing heroes,
Only the tired and human faces
Masked for the daily execution,
For which the long summer evenings
Of playing in the park
Were such useless preparation.

Now it seems that I can see again
Your solemn face
Shadowed with some foreboding,
Framed in those careless years.

Airman – you were nothing to me
Till your death was signed on a paper.
Sad I assemble
The fragments that are left,
For me – your life that has ended
Begins with your death.

July 19th

To An Airman Killed over Germany, 1944

I glimpsed your name in the paper
And so I recalled your face
And, strangely – began to remember.

At cricket in parks at evening
I made you my make-shift hero,
A timid child in my dreaming
-- Yet. I tired of that soon
For so seldom you smiled
And made no meaningless gesture.

Later – I lost you,
A face among many faces
And heroes were easy to come by
When I was a thoughtless schoolboy.

So – the war came,
Though long before that I had forgotten
And never thought of you
As an airman.

War has no laughing heroes,
Only the tired and human faces
Masked for the daily execution,
For which the long summer evenings
Of playing in the park
Were such useless preparation.

Now it seems that I can see again
Your solemn face
Shadowed with some foreboding,
Framed in those careless years.

Airman – you were nothing to me
Till your death was signed on a paper.
Sad, I assemble
The fragments that are left,
For me – your life that has ended
Begins with your death.

July 19, 1946

The Lost Kingdom

In my careless childhood I was a wanderer,
Far from the harsh red roofs
And the forbidding silence of the suburbs;

Happy to run free – over the lovely fields,
Along the summer hedgerows
Where only the shy rabbits had their home.
Beneath the twisted hawthorns
To be alone.

With the brown twigs
Fallen from the thick hedge
I made my nest,
Dry and warm in a sandy hollow.
The red rose-hips were my winter's store,
And only the shy rabbits saw
My kingdom come.

Through the dusty leaves
I watched the world that was the distant houses,
And tall, intrusive pylons
Lurching across my sight
Like slender giants in armour.

Never then was I afraid
For I had found my warmth and security –
The only needs of every child.

Now – all this is changed.
Across the green fields lie long rows
Of the sharp red roofs.
They have built over my childhood dreams,
There is no way back
To the bright fields of my youth.

September 26, 1946

"Waiting in the Train"

Pebbles of rain soft-falling,
Flecking dark pools on the platform;
Lamps huddled in mist,
And the rain slow-falling.
Dark pools reflect the station arches,
Sombre against the fading day.
Occasional passers
Splash to pieces
The mirrored frescoes of the arches.
From the compartment,
Through the window hazed with breath,
I watch the passers
Treading out beauty,
Unaware.

Feb., 1946

Waiting in the Train

Pebbles of rain soft-falling,
Flecking dark pools on the platform;
Lamps huddled in mist,
And the rain slow-falling.
Dark pools reflect the station arches,
Sombre against the fading day.
Occasional passers
Splash to pieces
The mirrored frescoes of the arches.
From the compartment,
Through the window hazed with breath,
I watch the passers
Treading out beauty,
Unaware.

February, 1946

Rain

The sad clouds steal furtively across the sky
And only the grey and huddled houses
Oppose the drifting rain
That taps soft fingers on the window-pane.

The street is sleek and shining, like a seal's back,
And there are shadows and reflections
Of the huddled houses,
And their yellow-lighted rooms.

The hills are hidden,
And now only the drifting rain
Breathes moist upon the window-pane.

November 14, 1946

"Rain"

The sad clouds steal furtively across the sky
And only the grey and huddled houses
Appose the drifting rain
That taps soft fingers on the window-pane.

The street is sleek and shining, like a seal's back,
And there are shadows and reflections
Of the huddled houses,
And their yellow-lighted rooms.

The hills are hidden,
And now, only the drifting rain
Breathes moist upon the window-pane.

Nov. 1145

Death of the Birch-Tree

Lean is the dull steel flashed white in the sun
Like a sudden lifting of the white-leaved abele,
Flushed from the raw thongs of the birch-tree,
The white wood flies through the mists of morning.

The ringing singing of the axe-blade widens,
The keen cold frost edge fishing with dew,
The smell of the bruised sap darkens the air,
Haw and lithe is the air that shivers.

Sheer from the cruel north of my cleaving arms,
Fierce falls the arctic fang of the axe-blade,
And the light is shed from the heart of the birch-tree.

The Rooks

Orange and red,
The wild-rose-hips waver on their brown, beak-thorned stems,
And behind the hedge
The orange and red sun descends
Into the autumn mist.

Across the field, where the earth has tumbled rough
In the brown wake of the plough,
The last glow stains on the windows,
Making the grey farmhouse fierce and fiery-eyed,
While, over the farmhouse and the dark, shaggy wood,
The rooks curve and fall raggedly
Like scraps of burnt paper
Upon the wind – tossed carelessly.

In little groups divided – so restlessly wheeling,
With their frantic lament
Filling the wide forum of surrounding air,
Noisily there they assemble,
And, sounding ever their prehistoric cry,
They fly out – high and together
Into the sun-drenched west.

November 7, 1946

"The Rooks"

Orange and red,
The wild-rose-hips waver on their
brown, beak-thorned stems,
And behind the hedge
The orange and red sun descends
Into the autumn mist.

Across the field, where the earth has
tumbled rough
In the brown wake of the plough,
The last glow stains on the windows,
Making the grey farmhouse fierce and fiery-
eyed,
While, over the farmhouse and the dark, shaggy
wood,
The rooks curve and fall raggedly
Like scraps of burnt paper
Upon the wind - tossed carelessly.

(Over.)

In little groups divided – so restlessly wheeling,
With their frantic lament
Filling the wide forum of surrounding air,
Noisily there they assemble,
And, sounding, ever their prehistoric cry,
They fly out – high and together
Into the sun-drenched west

Nov. 4th

Pilgrimage

I will venture into the supreme evening
When cool webs of sunlight are straying to the sea
And calm sails are soothing the forelands and the speechless hill.

This staff I carry is winter madness,
I have stripped it of seasons
Down to the livid bone
The immemorial winter;
With it I will cut the shapes of birds upon the air
Stir the passionate waters to infinite dreams
Or follow the fading of some glorious cloud.

Upon the Journey – A Place to Sleep In

The way has led to this forsaken field,
While winds are resting in quiet shapes of thorn.

The woods that enclose this place
Are light overgrown by trees;
When darkness comes
I shall watch the trees grow tall.

A great oak has struck down through the heart of the field
That its vampire summer beauties never wander;
To-night, for comfort and safe-keeping,
I shall sleep with the oak's dark sorrow.

Boxes containing the J. A. Baker Archive at the Albert Sloman Library, University of Essex.

John Fanshawe

INTO THE ARCHIVE

ON A BALMY CORNISH AFTERNOON this May, my son Jack and a trio of friends spotted a young peregrine jousting with two kestrels over a coastal meadow. Sloping away to the sea, and pockmarked with thickets of blackthorn, bramble and gorse, the field often yields trails of feathers where falcon kills have taken place. The kestrels weathered the larger bird's attentions, calling in mock anger at its lazy passes. After a few minutes the bird returned to the cliff scrape from which it had recently fledged, and keened peevishly.

Among the slate bluffs that withstand north Cornwall's battles with the Atlantic, a quiet resurgence has occurred since the 1960s. Half a century ago, peregrines were scarce here, but now these impressive cliffs host a growing population. One of Baker's many correspondents, the artist and falconer Dick Treleaven, spent decades patiently recording the recovery of peregrines north of Boscastle. As a young birder, it was often on those cliffs that I would meet him to seek out the thunderbolt falcons. When Dick died in 2009, friends erected a seat at his favourite vantage point overlooking the steep precipice at Buckator. More than seventy pairs now nest in Cornwall, three within walking distance of where I write. As Hetty Saunders has noted, Cambridge has joined the cities where urban peregrines thrive, treating the great buildings as cliffs from which to hunt the wood pigeons and their feral cousins that flourish in college gardens and on the streets. It was after a meeting to discuss Baker's biography that she and Robert Macfarlane found a pigeon corpse flayed on a pavement, as if, Hetty recalls, Baker's 'ghost had left us his bloody blessing.' Peregrines breathe wildness into cities like no other bird, and provide moments of mesmeric ferocity for a lucky few. My early encounters were giddy with the promise of birding adventures ahead, though I had no idea then that I'd spend my life working in international bird conservation.

In 2010, when I collaborated with Mark Cocker on the complete works, details of J. A. Baker's life were scant. At times, he appeared to have arrived fully formed as a voice for nature. A geography had started to emerge from the 500 plus locations Baker mentioned in his diaries. As Mark and I walked many of his paths near Chelmsford, over Danbury Hill, along the River Chelmer, and beside the Blackwater Estuary, we acquired a feel for Baker country.

That world was defined by long views and great skies, where Baker found his peregrines in 'a pouring-away world of no attachment, a world of wakes and tilting, of sinking planes of land and water,' or the intimacy of close looking that yields a wren 'like a small brown priest in a parish of dead leaves and wintry hedges.' It was possible to sense Baker mining the woods, river and estuary for moments of encounter.

The contemporary Chelmsford landscape is now greatly changed, with the unforgiving thrum of the A12 that snakes east of the town dominating a stretch of the river Baker loved, and the hedges shorn of mature elms by the Dutch beetle, and the fruit orchards grubbed up. As our knowledge of Baker's world emerged from the diaries, and after the complete works were published in 2010, it was hard to resist the pull that there must be more to learn. The film-maker and author David Cobham had met Baker's wife Doreen to talk about a possible film of *The Peregrine*. Both the diaries and a series of photographs of Baker's library emerged during that visit. Soon afterwards, the books were sold, so the pictures have made a massive contribution to our understanding of Baker's influences. From them we learned not only of his love of literature, especially poetry, but his interest in aerial photography, history, walking, cricket, cookery, opera, and more.

When the collected works were published, new stories came to light from friends like Jack Baird and readers like Michael Weston, who also explored Baker's routes, including Grace's Walk and Hurrells Lane. It was during these early conversations and correspondences that I became something of an accidental archivist. As a second edition of the complete works of J. A. Baker beckoned, Mark and I started a new conversation with Doreen's brother, Bernard Coe. It seemed possible that other material existed, and Bernard kindly agreed to search for it. I remember well the excitement sifting through the material stored in two cardboard boxes, which with the diaries, photos, and letters later secured, forms the core of what we now know.

Ahead of writing this biography, Hetty recorded all these items in *A Descriptive Catalogue of the J. A. Baker Archive*, published by the University of Essex. In an index, she lists and describes in meticulous detail the personal, financial, ornithological and other correspondence, the manuscripts and notebooks, maps, photographs, contracts, press cuttings and reviews. Opening the boxes that first time in Bernard's kitchen, with a trail of finches and tits visiting the feeders in the garden like a rag-tag cast of Baker familiars, it was definitely the manuscripts of *The Peregrine* that transfixed me. Rusting paperclips held each section together, but Baker's script was still so sharp and clear. Yet it was the contents of Hetty's section D, 'Optics Belonging to J. A. Baker', that yielded a presence of the man. Three monoculars, and two pairs of binoculars just like the first I had owned, a now battered pair of Janik 8 x 30s, which felt like relics of a foregone age. Unable to resist, I picked up the smaller pair – the Mirakel 8 x 40s – and watched a male chaffinch hanging sheepishly on a feeder in the garden, aware of the encircling tits. Many months later, after a day in the archive, Robert Macfarlane tried all the optics, and picked up the same Mirakels to watch wood pigeons 'clap-clap-gliding' across the Essex campus, and a wagtail 'figure-eighting for flies' on the roof of a lecture hall.

Writing about Baker in *Landmarks*, Macfarlane considers

binoculars, and how they allow the viewer to see an object 'in crisp isolation, encircled in blackness – as though at the end of a tunnel.' He believes they are the 'perfect emblem of Baker's own intense, and intensely limited, vision,' and 'thought of him out in the field towards the end of his decade of hedge-haunting and hawk-hunting; how difficult it must have been to hold the binoculars, as his finger joints thickened and fused, and his tendons tightened.' It is a tough vision of Baker's later years. Perhaps, despite his infirmity, Baker used the Mirakels to watch the domestic comings and goings of birds in the gardens and trees and across a stretch of sky from his upstairs study window in the quiet cul-de-sac of Marlborough Road.

Among the local newspaper clippings in the cardboard boxes was a description of John and Doreen's wedding on October 6, 1956, which mentions his best man, Edward Dennis. By tracking down Ted, who had moved from Tansley, near Matlock, to an address in west Oxford, we discovered forty-nine extant letters Baker had sent his friends. Over seven years from 1944, Baker, who by his own admission 'came late to the love of birds', wrote all the letters before he started recording his birdwatching in March 1954. For years, he saw birds 'only as a tremor at the edge of vision', a tremor that evolved into a style of acute observation, perfectly encapsulated by his dictum that the 'hardest thing of all to see is what is really there'.

When Ted and Margaret Dennis welcomed me into their house, I still carried a strong image of Baker as the troubled loner, and was ill-prepared for the warm and mischievous young man they had known. Much later, Ted sent me a photo of a river camping trip he and Baker had made on the Thames in 1951, which shows a smiling Baker hauling back on the oars, his round glasses catching the sun. Ted had no letters from Baker, but he was a link to the group of friends that included John Thurmer and Donald Samuels. They had kept in touch after Baker's death, and I drove to see Don in Kent and John in Exeter in the hope of finding archival material. When I spoke to him on the phone, John couldn't remember keeping anything, but as soon as I visited Don, he handed me a bundle of thirty-three letters – tied up in brown paper, stored in his attic for half a century, it was labelled 'Letters Written to Me, 1944–1948. Consigned to Oblivion, June 27, 1948. R. I. P.' With that news, John was inspired to search his own papers and found sixteen letters, which he generously gave to the growing archive. In *Notes on J. A. Baker,* published in the complete works, I described some of the memories the three friends shared, of Baker's home life, his wayward cricket, his lack of self-pity over the bouts of illness that kept him away from school, and of the adventures they shared. In many ways, it was this cache of letters that, with the binoculars, most inspired. One letter in particular struck me. Written on June 16, 1945, and postmarked two days later, the envelope is addressed to John as 14841727 Sgt. J. Thurmer, and has become known as the 'Roffey letter'. Having long battled with bouts of depression myself, reading a letter addressed from the Roffey Park Rehabilitation Centre with the words 'nervous collapse' and 'it was hell', leading to 'I have begun to feel like my old self', rang unnervingly true. At a time which had seen his home town of Chelmsford badly bombed, and when he was struggling with family tensions and the absence of friends, it was scarcely surprising that Baker, who had just turned nineteen, had suffered a nervous breakdown.

But the letter is full of hope too. Baker mentions that Shelley was born at Field Place on the other side of Horsham from Roffey Park, and writes: 'I have wandered into the fields here in the early morning and heard, as [Shelley] too heard the glorious anthem of the skylark fading away in the heavens.' Baker loved Sussex, where he continued to develop his distinct voice in the many letters he wrote – a prelude to the honed prose that appeared twenty years later. Recovering one's sanity through contact with nature is a familiar pattern, explored in books like Richard Mabey's *Nature Cure*, and more recently, Helen Macdonald's *H is for Hawk*, Katherine Norbury's *The Fish Ladder* and *The Outrun* by Amy Liptrot. On reading *The Fish Ladder*, the comedian Jo Brand described the book as one woman's walk from 'dark into light', and it seems that much writing on nature and landscape, whether declared or implied, deals with the curative power of being outdoors.

In *The Guardian*, George Monbiot takes issue with the language professional conservationists use to describe the 'natural wonders of the world'. For many of us who devote our waking hours to these battles, the continuous drip of familiar use has meant terms such as environment, biodiversity, or reserve are now effectively synonymous with nature, wildlife and place. To refer to a Site of Special Scientific Interest (or 'triple-SI') isn't to decry its value. It is the very opposite, as the word 'special' implies. Monbiot is right when he says that 'those who seek to protect the living planet ... were doubtless inspired to devote their lives to it with the same sense of wonder and reverence.' We were – and reading Baker and other writers has contributed to cultivating that sense of wonder.

For me, the diaries, the letters, the many lessons learned about Baker have set the man in context, and make it clear that he, ahead of his time, belonged to the tribe that champions conservation. Discovering where he went, on foot and on bicycle, was to unravel how he mapped his immediate surroundings for inspiration. It took Baker's diaries to reveal that 'the long ridge' mentioned in *The Peregrine* was Danbury Hill, and that the 'sails beyond land' were plying the Blackwater Estuary. Perhaps it destroyed a little of his mystique, but it has also allowed us to reflect on what the charity Common Ground calls Local Distinctiveness, or the 'extraordinary richness of our everyday surroundings', described so vividly in Baker's texts.

On July 6, 2016, the author and academic, James Canton, hosted a celebration of the Baker archive at the Albert Sloman Library at the University of Essex, and a number of Bakerphiles, including Mark Cocker, Sean Nixon, Ken Worpole and Hetty Saunders, gathered to speak about his legacy. Canton leads the Essex MA programme in Wild Writing, and three of his students, Miranda Cichy, Kirsty Groves and Stephen Rutt, presented their responses to the archive and to aspects of Baker's writing. A few days later,

Melinda Appleby, a landscape writer and researcher, wrote a blog on the event suggesting that we should follow Baker's example. Of course, there are many reasons for doing so, but one links back to an aspect of George Monbiot's challenge that conservationists should 'recruit poets and cognitive linguists and amateur nature lovers to help them find the words for what they cherish.'

In many ways, the like-minded are recruiting themselves, as the growing list of authors, poets, visual artists and musicians who care about conservation join scientists and naturalists. Groups like Common Ground, Dark Mountain and New Networks for Nature, as well as an array of festivals, are creating forums for debate, and forging innovative collaborations. The greatest danger must be division in our own ranks, globally, nationally and locally. Baker cared for his local environment with an absolute passion, responding as Robert Macfarlane argued that we must, with 'fury, burn, scorch and scour in our contemporary nature culture – but also wonder, joy, beauty, grace, play and concentration.'

When Baker was researching an essay for the RSPB's *Birds* written in 1971, *On the Essex Coast*, his last published work, he stumbled on a red-throated diver, 'so matted and bound with oil as to be almost unrecognisable, the mere torso of a bird. It stinks of oil. It is an atrocity, a stumpy victim of our modern barbarity.' His fury is plain, and his warning that 'we must not let its death be soothed away by the lullaby language of indifferent politicians,' leaves a strong sense of an author-activist in the making, whose writing is already crackling and alive with concern, and surely would have continued to be so.

John Fanshawe
NORTH CORNWALL, SEPTEMBER, 2017

JOHN FANSHAWE is an author and environmentalist.He works with BirdLife International, the Cambridge Conservation Initiative, and is a co-founder of New Networks for Nature.

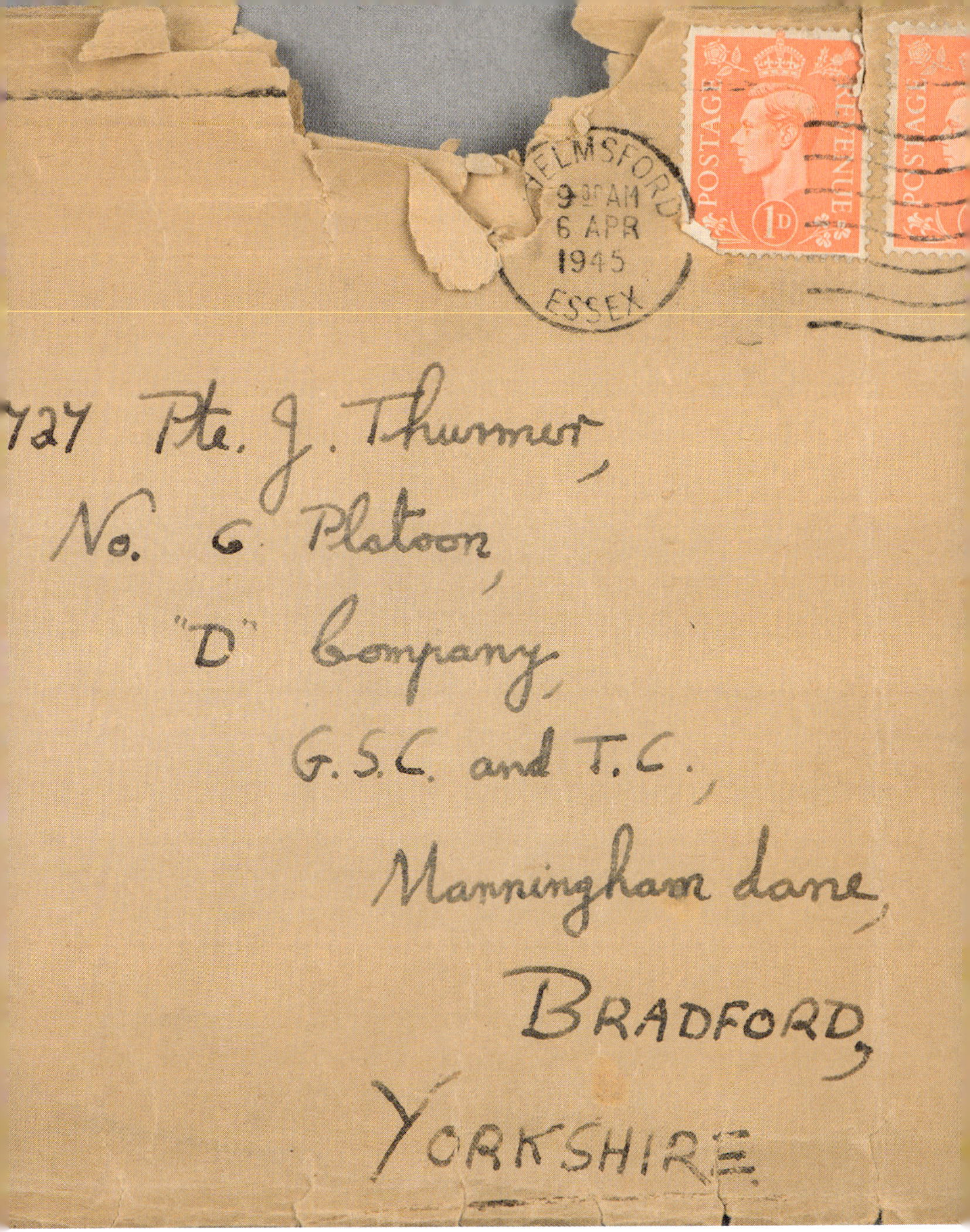

The photographs on the following pages have been selected to reflect the range of the J. A. Baker Archive. In her research for this book, Hetty Saunders documented all the items in the Albert Sloman Library and published A Descriptive Catalogue of the J. A. Baker Archive *with the University of Essex, which is available online.*

...usering as ever ~~though~~ but the thing that most impressed me ...s that, though still inordinately shy he was ~~of~~ much more at h... ...e in ~~a~~ company and less conscious of his imagined deficienc... ...s, you will agree, ~~would~~ so would be a change for the better ...nd I am of the opinion that Army life will ultimately have ... entirely beneficent effect on Buff. ~~from~~

Of Dennis. Dennis was home – to Brentwood, for the purpose ...securing a portion of a flat and moving dependents and furniture ...ereto; and came over on Sunday last to visit 'ego' (Latin ...Virgil informed me, for I or myself). We went for a walk, ...wing the ravages of the fierce west wind and ended up at ...nbury, – as was, of course, our original intention. The countryside ...s indeed beautiful and ~~[illegible]~~ to my mind the environs of ...nbury are not to be bettered for variety of landscape and ...auty of flora etc. We discovered in our peregrination a ...bit caught helplessly in a home-made snare – this rabbit ...nis duly strangled – attempts to release the snare having ...ved fruitless. A rabbit struggles unremittingly in the snare with ... energy born of desperation and, I should imagine is affected by ...similar sensation at being so ~~[illegible]~~ pinioned as humans ...ffering from claustrophobia would experience ~~when~~ if locked in a cupboard ...n taken up by Dennis the rabbit commenced to writhe agitatedly ... as soon as the hand touched the neck it seemed that the ...tched creature resigned itself to death and was paralysed by ... of that ~~•~~ event. Its eyes were bolting and abnormally ...ht and so ~~pang~~ poignant in their utter terror that I could no...

[illegible]

A2-11

20, Finchley Avenue,
Chelmsford.
5 - 4 - 45.

Dear sock,

Good-evening! and, as always greetings!
(to be sung flat by twenty male voices, slightly ineibriated, in Pushtu slang) – "Hear the Mighty Jerry Wilmot
Quick of tongue and deft of tonsil
Scampers through the Baseball fixtures
Gabble, gabble, faster, faster until,
Like a coyote on the prairie

But there, it's a long fellow that has no turning and my ~~inspiration~~ inspiration like the strength of the mighty Kwa-sind, has failed me in my hour of need.

For the extracts from the "Daily Mail" – many thanks – I particularly like the one about the 'Postmistress'. I am returning these as, doubtless, you would like to retain them for future exhibition. For your kind offer of the loan of Joad's Koran – also – thank-you. However my leisure-hours are fully occupied at the moment with ~~voluminous~~ "Music in London (3 Vols.) by Shaw, "In Pursuit of Spring" – by that master of sensitive descriptive prose, – Edward Thomas "Frank Harris" by Hugh Kingsmill, "Dombey and Son", "A Life of "James Elroy Flecker" and the score of Verdi's opera – "Il Trovatore" I also wish to read Shaw's dramatic criticisms in the near future, and to resume my suspended perusal of Shakespeare's

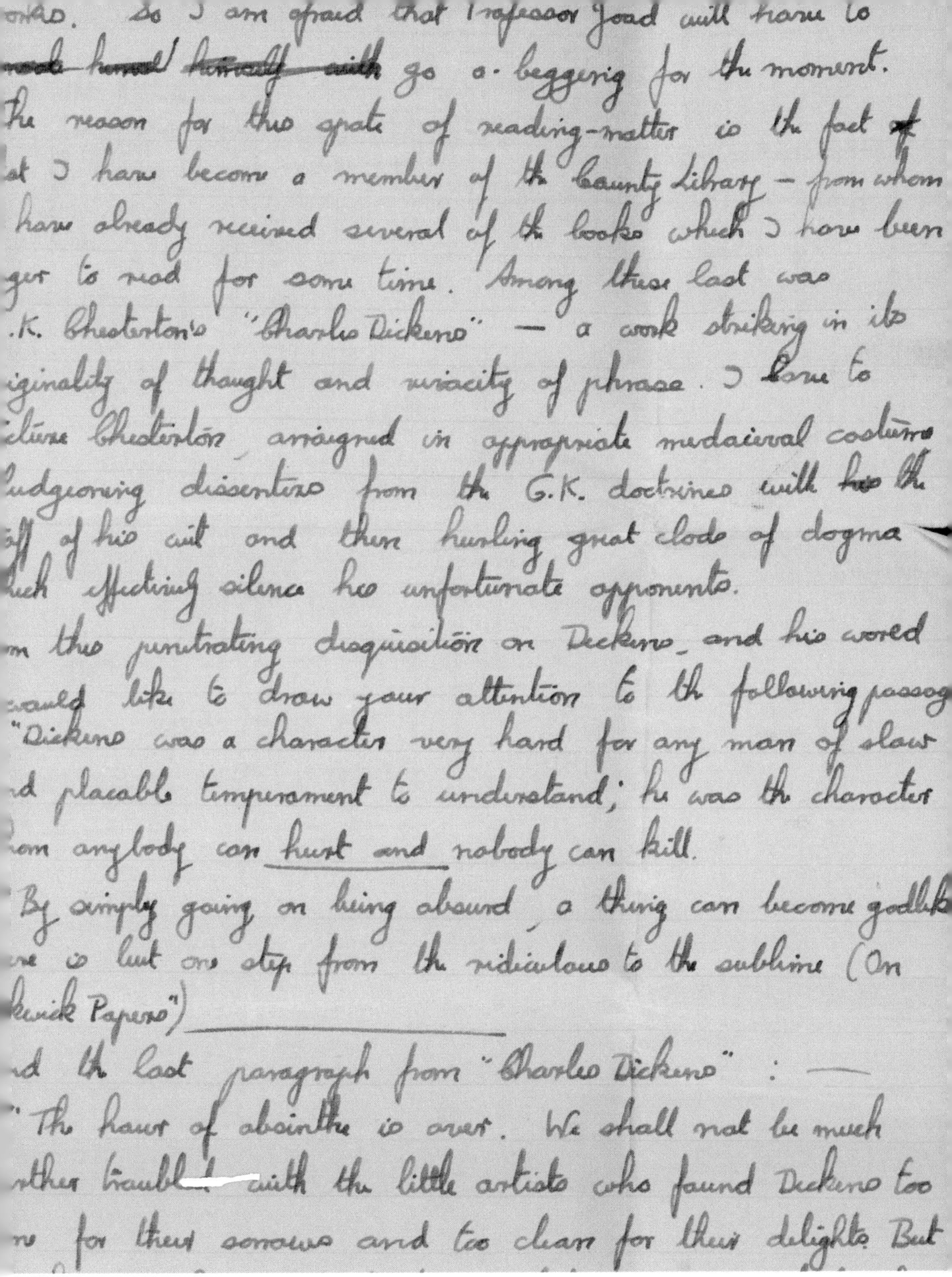

works. So I am afraid that Professor Joad will have to ~~make himself himself with~~ go a-begging for the moment.
The reason for this spate of reading-matter is the fact ~~of~~ that I have become a member of the County Library – from whom I have already received several of the books which I have been eager to read for some time. Among these last was G.K. Chesterton's "Charles Dickens" – a work striking in its originality of thought and vivacity of phrase. I ~~love~~ come to picture Chesterton arrayed in appropriate mediaeval costume bludgeoning dissenters from the G.K. doctrines with ~~his~~ the haft of his wit and then hurling great clods of dogma which effectively silence his unfortunate opponents.
From this penetrating disquisition on Dickens and his world I would like to draw your attention to the following passage:
"Dickens was a character very hard for any man of slow and placable temperament to understand; he was the character whom anybody can hurt and nobody can kill.
By simply going on being absurd a thing can become godlike; there is but one step from the ridiculous to the sublime (On Pickwick Papers")
And the last paragraph from "Charles Dickens": –
"The hour of absinthe is over. We shall not be much further troubled with the little artists who found Dickens too sane for their sorrows and too clean for their delights. But

The letter shown here and on the previous pages is from 'Doughy' Baker to John Thurmer, April 5, 1945, and gives insight into his reading habits.

Roffey Park Re-Habilitation
Centre,

Nr. Horsham,

Sussex.

June 16th, 1945.

Cher ami,

Forgive – if you can find it in your heart so to do – my failure to answer your voluminous tract with my customary alacrity. This omission was occasioned by the fact of my powers of concentration etc. being temporarily undermined by a 'nervous collapse'. On May 9th – I came to the above address for a six weeks sojourn (approx). I had then been from work for three weeks – wallowing in the depths of neurotic depression and instability. It was hell and it ~~is~~ only during the last fortnight or so that I have begun to feel like my old self, or rather – my old self minus that 'nervous intensity' which rendered my happiness so precarious. This trouble had been threatening for a very long time – the immediate factor which hastened its approach being my idolatrous devotion to a certain lady. Years of misery ~~or~~ occasioned by family quarrels and the like, however have been the basic cause of my lack of confidence and introspection. But all that is past and I am confident that I shall leave here purged of my doubts and dreads.

Roffy Park Re-Habilitation Centre is caters for some 100 to 120 patients all suffering from nervous debility in some form. The estate originally belonged to a wealthy shipping magnate and was ~~e~~ established in its present form on June 1st 1944. There are four qualified ~~psy~~ psychiatrists in residence – the Medical

Pages from Baker's letter to John Thurmer sent from Roffey Park Rehabilitation Centre, June 16, 1945.

A1·19

1.

8, Writtle Road
Chelmsford
Essex

Sunday, September 15th.

46

Dear Sam,

This letter is unique. It may remain so – so let us celebrate. I raise my glass to the continued health and well-being of your cadaverous self and say, in all sincerity – "May your braces never dangle". It is just over a week since I was installed at the happy homestead – which means that I have just under a week of this happiness, remaining. (Einstein is my middle name or 'nom d'un chien')

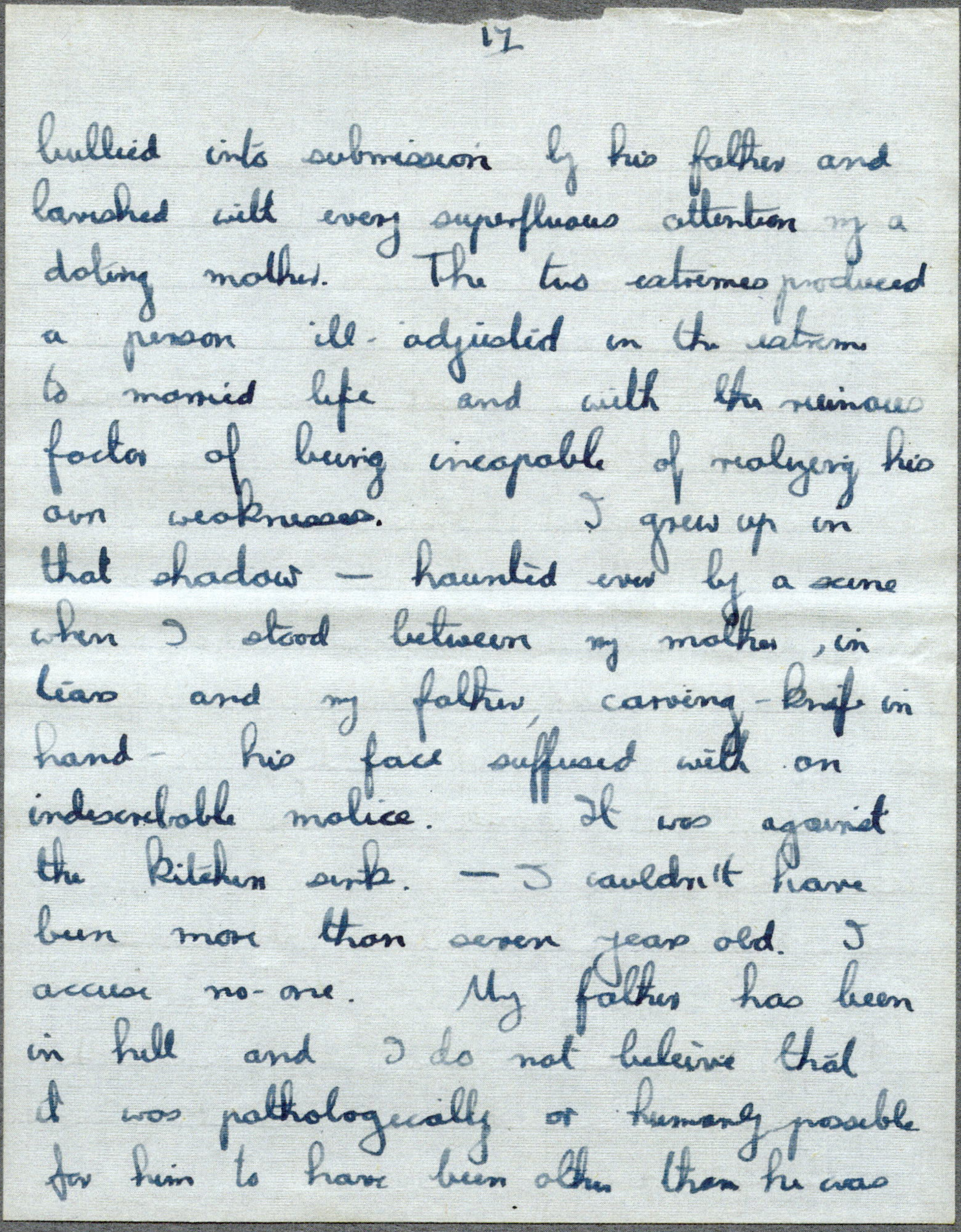

17

bullied into submission by his father and lavished with every superfluous attention by a doting mother. The two extremes produced a person ill-adjusted in the extreme to married life and with the ruinous factor of being incapable of realizing his own weaknesses. I grew up in that shadow – haunted ever by a scene when I stood between my mother, in tears and my father, carving-knife in hand – his face suffused with an indescribable malice. It was against the kitchen sink. – I couldn't have been more than seven years old. I accuse no-one. My father has been in hell and I do not believe that it was pathologically or humanly possible for him to have been other than he was

Pages from a letter from 'Doughy' (J. A. Baker) to 'Sam' (Donald Samuel), written from the Samuel family home on Writtle Road, September 15, 1946.

But, Sam, I had no sense of security, — I had my mother but though we could comfort one another. — it had to be surreptitiously — my father was a jealous man. Everything — yes literally everything had to be hidden from him for fear that he would actively disapprove.

I missed all that you had, and there are things I have seen that you would not believe. O that it should be so. Even now, at twenty, my father has only to reproach me in that all too familiar way, — for me to fly into hysterics and throw the nearest object at his head. It is not so with any one else — but that person who is should be nearest and dearest to me evokes a devil in me.

my poetry.

And so my effusion ends. I thought it would be unique because it would be the only letter I ever wrote at 8 Whittle Rd. I was wrong - it is unique - because it is the only letter I shall ever write about my own soul - about my inmost self.

I'll write about other things - during this coming week, Sam.

Meanwhile - carry on smoking.

I have complete faith in your continued silence on these matters of which I have previously given you only an inkling.

Good luck.

Yours sincerely,

Dougly

I am happy here and looking forward to your return as much as the family.

An

Enlargement

makes your

Snap

into a

Picture

■

Let us
Enlarge your
Best
Negatives

Flash Photography
With Any Camera
At last you can take SNAPS in the home with certainty of success
FLASH pictures taken in the family environment have that extra personal appeal
It's Simple !
It's Inexpensive !
Ask for our advice

Doreen poses while John takes the photograph, 1950s.

A reversal of roles: John is photographed by Doreen.

J. A. Baker (second row, fourth from the left) in an unknown and undated group photo. Most likely the – male – staff at the Automobile Association office where Baker worked.

Baker (centre foreground) enjoying himself at what is likely the Chelmsford Automobile Association's Christmas party, 1950s.

Baker on a river camping trip with friend Ted Dennis in Oxford, 1951.

Bartholomew's
Contour-coloured
World map series
with boundaries
roads and railways
SCANDINAVIA
AND THE BALTIC
Scale 1:2,500,000
Printed and Published
in Great Britain by
JOHN BARTHOLOMEW & SON LTD
EDINBURGH
CLOTH 6s

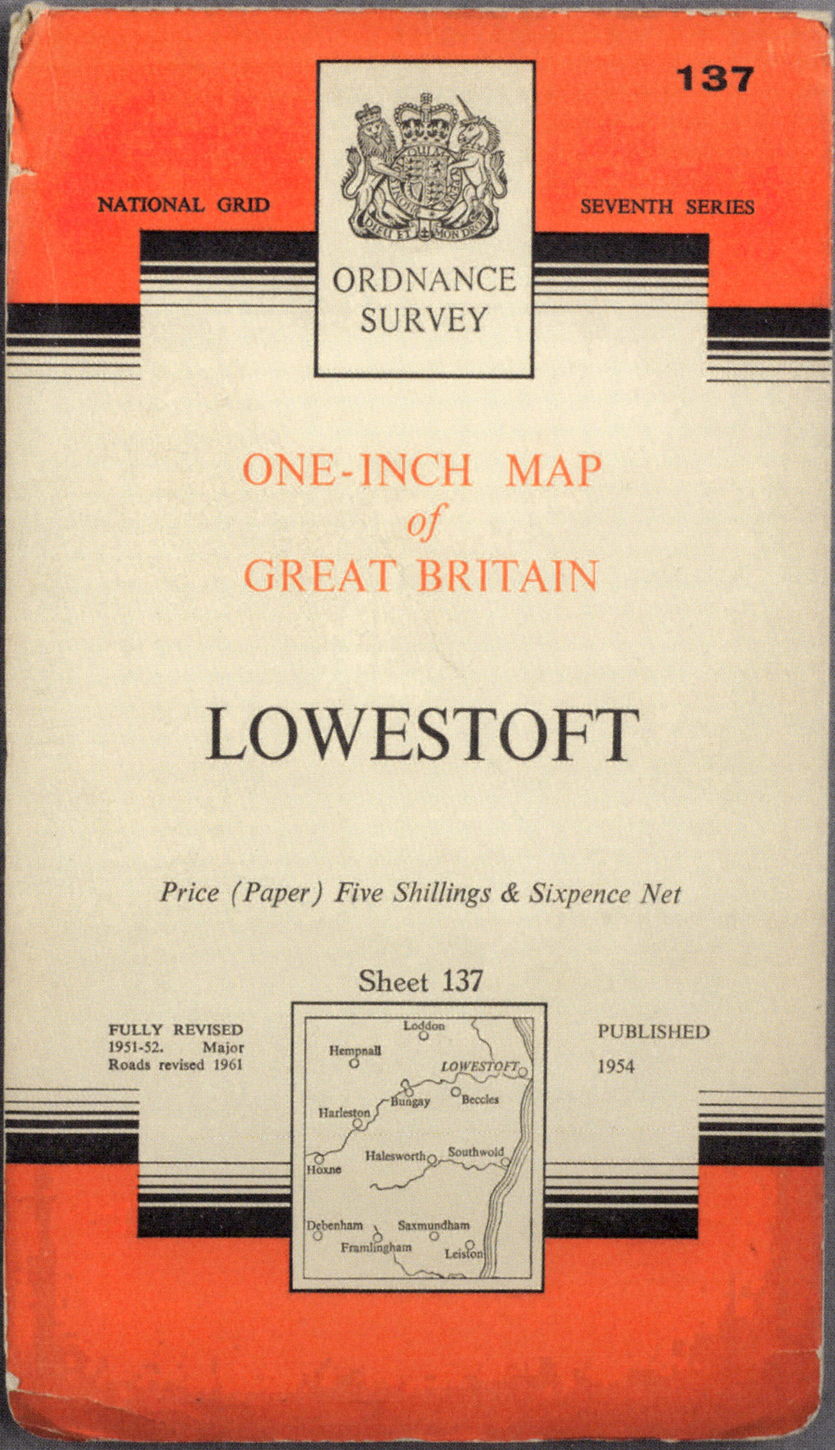
137
NATIONAL GRID
SEVENTH SERIES
ORDNANCE
SURVEY
ONE-INCH MAP
of
GREAT BRITAIN
LOWESTOFT
Price (Paper) Five Shillings & Sixpence Net
Sheet 137
FULLY REVISED
1951-52. Major
Roads revised 1961
PUBLISHED
1954
Loddon
Hempnall
LOWESTOFT
Bungay
Beccles
Harleston
Halesworth
Southwold
Hoxne
Debenham
Saxmundham
Framlingham
Leiston

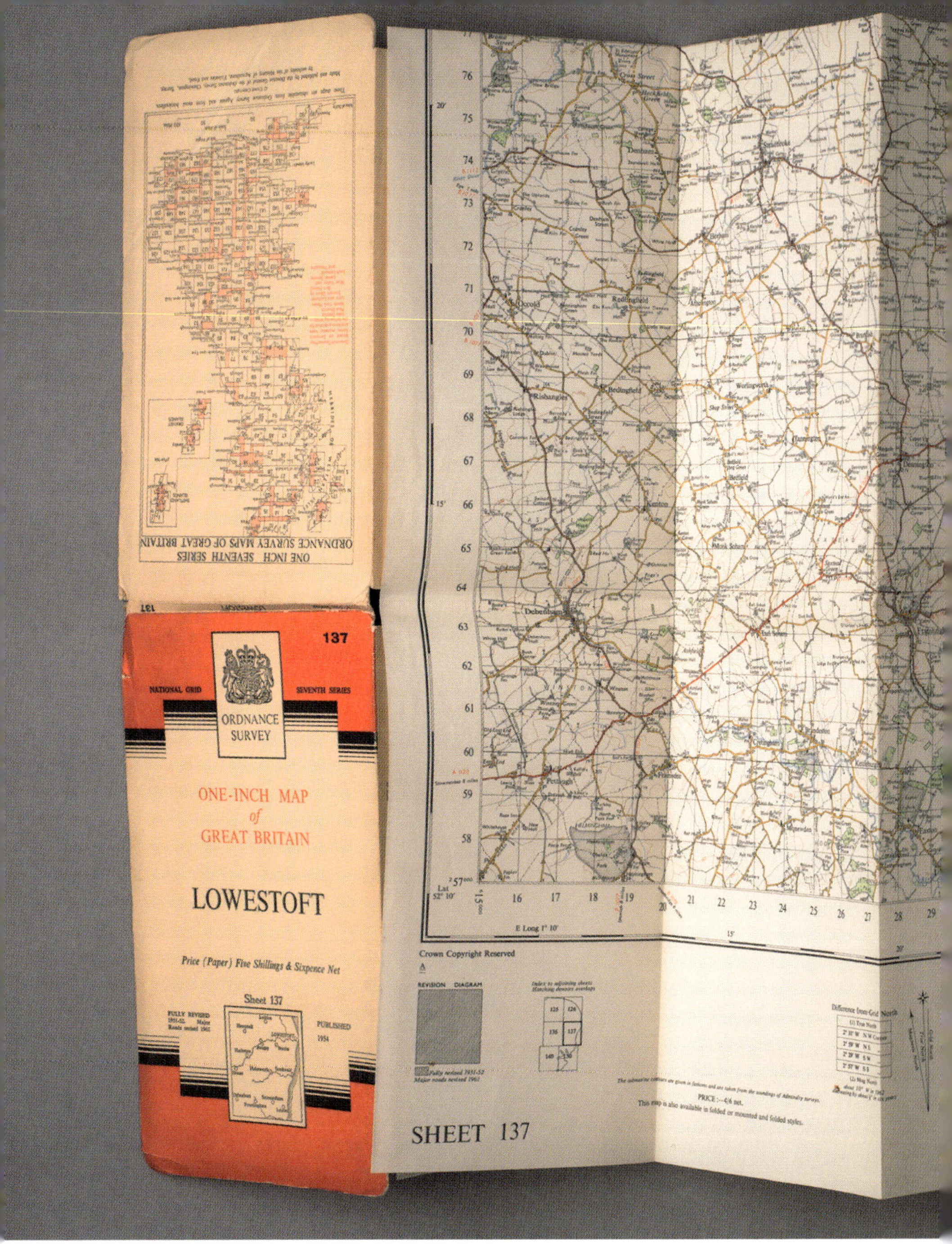

PREVIOUS PAGES: *Baker's map collection includes sheets of Lowestoft (OS, 1962) and Scandinavia and the Baltic (Bartholomew's World Series, 1963). Though Baker almost certainly never travelled abroad, his map of Scandinavia would have given him insight into the summer hunting grounds of many of the migrant peregrines that he saw over-wintering in Essex.*

ABOVE: *Baker's Ordnance Survey map of the Lowestoft region, which covers the Suffolk and Norfolk coasts to the north of Essex (reprinted in 1962).*

WITHAM
LITTLE BRAXTED
Little Waltham
Wickham Bishops
Hatfield Peverel
Broomfield
Boreham
SPRINGFIELD
Langford
CHELMSFORD
CAESAROMAGVS
Little Baddow
Woodham Walter
Great Baddow
Danbury
Sandon
Woodham Mortimer
Galleywood
Bicknacre
Purleigh
Cock Clarks
East Hanningfield
West Hanningfield
Woodham Ferrers
Stow Maries
Cold Norton
Rettendon
South Hanningfield
South Woodham Ferrers
Ramsden Heath
Downham
Hyde Woods
Chelmer & Blackwater Canal

Details from Baker's Ordnance Survey map of Southend-on-Sea in 1957 and 1945 (FOLLOWING PAGE) marked with peregrine sightings. The contours of Danbury Hill are outlined in red ink, and various routes to the east of Chelmsford and around the Blackwater Estuary are also marked.

B. 1026
Hyde Fm.
Prentice Hall Fm.
Spring
Skinners Wick Fm.
Highams Fm.
Tumuli
P
Joyce's Fm.
Lauriston
Red Hill
Decoy Pond
Decoy Pond
Gore Saltings
Goldhanger Creek
The Stumble
Wharf
Osea Island
Osea Fm.
East Point
Pier
Stansgate Abbey
Stansgate Abbey Fm.
Ramsey Marsh
Mundon Stone Point
Steeple Creek
Steeple Wick
Creek

Hall
82
Tollesbury Wick
Marshes
Bohun's Hall
Mell Ho
Decoy Fm
Mill Creek
Pier
Mill Point
RIVER BLACKWATE
Pewet Island
Creek
Bradwell Creek
42
The Stone
St Lawrence Bay
15
16
Inn
Drinkwaters
Barkhams
Bradwell Wick
Bradwell Hall
31
Drinkwaters
16
88
Middle Grove
Beacon Hill
Heron Grove
Rectory
Mott's Fm
31
St Lawrence
Blackbirds
East Hyde

Baker's Harwix Mirakel 8 x 40 binoculars with their worn leather case. The seams of the case have come apart from use and have been repaired with glue and plasters.

Brass and leather-covered telescope (make unknown).

Black alloy telescope (make unknown) with its canvas case.

1955 BIRDS

The Boots Chemists

Scribbling Diary

59th

YEAR OF PUBLICATION

British

Manufacture Throughout

Three days on a page

1955

		15.	45
Goldfinch	||||| |||	8.	64

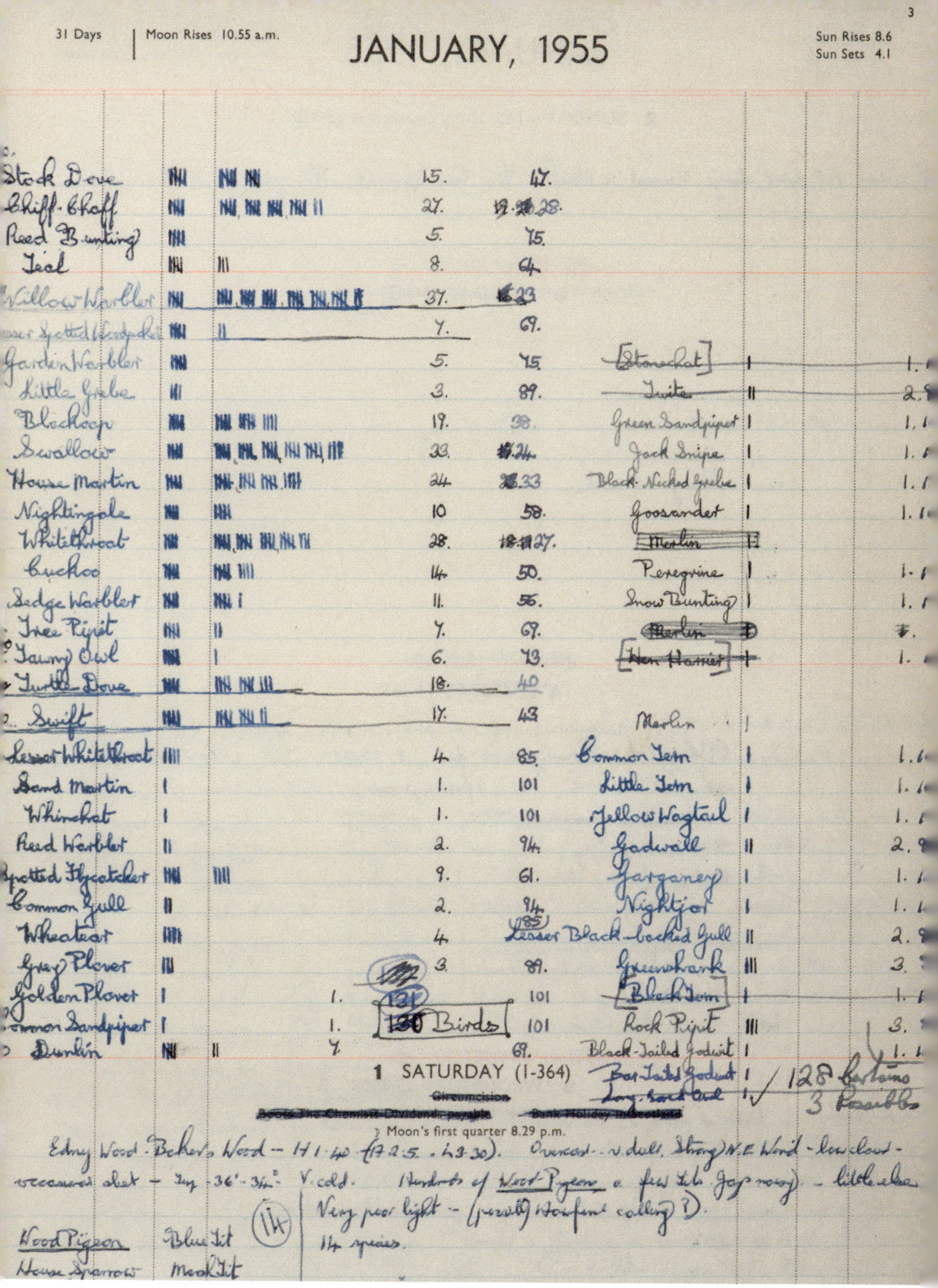

3

31 Days | Moon Rises 10.55 a.m.

JANUARY, 1955

Sun Rises 8.6
Sun Sets 4.1

Stock Dove	15.	47.			
Chiff-Chaff	27.	28.			
Reed Bunting	5.	75.			
Teal	8.	64.			
Willow Warbler	37.	23			
Lesser Spotted Woodpecker	7.	69.			
Garden Warbler	5.	75.	~~[Stonechat]~~	1	1.
Little Grebe	3.	89.	~~Twite~~	2	2.
Blackcap	19.	38.	Green Sandpiper	1	1.
Swallow	33.	24.	Jack Snipe	1	1.
House Martin	24.	33	Black-Necked Grebe	1	1.
Nightingale	10	58.	Goosander	1	1.
Whitethroat	28.	27.	~~Merlin~~		
Cuckoo	14	50.	Peregrine	1	1.
Sedge Warbler	11.	56.	Snow Bunting	1	1.
Tree Pipit	7.	69.	~~Merlin~~		
Tawny Owl	6.	73.	~~[Hen Harrier]~~	1	1.
Turtle Dove	18.	40			
Swift	17.	43	Merlin	1	
Lesser Whitethroat	4	85.	Common Tern	1	1.
Sand Martin	1.	101	Little Tern	1	1.
Whinchat	1.	101	Yellow Wagtail	1	1.
Reed Warbler	2.	94.	Gadwall	2	2.
Spotted Flycatcher	9.	61.	Garganey	1	1.
Common Gull	2.	94.	Nightjar	1	1.
Wheatear	4	(85)	Lesser Black-backed Gull	2	2.
Grey Plover	3.	89.	Greenshank	3	3.
Golden Plover	1.	101	~~[Black Tern]~~	1	1.
Common Sandpiper	1.	101	Rock Pipit	3	3.
Dunlin	7	69.	Black-Tailed Godwit	1	1.
			~~Bar-Tailed Godwit~~	1	
			~~Long-Eared Owl~~	1	

131 / 130 Birds

128 Certains
3 Possibles

1 SATURDAY (1-364)

~~Circumcision~~

☽ Moon's first quarter 8.29 p.m.

Edny Wood – Baker's Wood – 11.40 (7.25 – 4.30). Overcast – v. dull, strong N.E. wind – low cloud – occasional sleet – Temp 36°–34°. V. cold. Hundreds of Wood Pigeon & few tits [?] – little else.

Very poor light – (possibly) Hawfinch calling (?).
14 species.

(14)

Wood Pigeon, Blue Tit, House Sparrow, Marsh Tit

Pages from Baker's birdwatching diary, 1955.

Sun Rises 6.21
Sun Sets 5.59

MARCH, 1955

Moon Rises 11.58 p.m. | 31 Days
Moon Sets 7.37 a.m. | 11th Week

Birds seen — (31 species)

House Sparrow, Tree Sparrow, Yellowhammer, Greenfinch, Chaffinch, Fieldfare, Song Thrush, Mistle Thrush, Redwing, Pied Wagtail, Skylark, Rook, Jay, Magpie, Jackdaw, Starling, Wood Pigeon, Robin, Wren, Hedge Sparrow, Blue Tit, Great Tit, Coal Tit, Long-tailed Tit, Red-legged Partridge, Mute Swan, Lapwing, Black-headed Gull, Herring Gull, Kestrel, Blackbird

13 SUNDAY ~~3rd in Lent (72-293)~~

Temp. – 32°–42°. LH – 9.15 P.M. Jollywood, Stock, Ingatestone, Blackmore, Writtle. AH 1.45 P.M. Bright sunny – warm sun, very in cover, cold N.E. wind – strong.
Heard Stock Dove calling in Oaklands. Mistle Thrushes singing well.
~~14 MONDAY (73-292)~~ Yellowhammer singing well.
Ingatestone sewage farm – very smelly – many Black-headed Gulls. Two Pied Wagtails very dirty. Redwings, Fieldfares, Lapwings. Many Lapwings, Fieldfares everywhere. Redwing on Then slope off Writtle mill, as previous (as Woodpecker) – tame. Heard Hawfinches – bolling Wood. Jays very plentiful in all woodland. Skylarks singing beautifully. Great Tit & Blue Tits singing.
Long-tailed Tit in Birchspring Wood – as before – heard call note.
Kestrel by Ashing Wood. Red-legged Partridge at Jollywood – common Partridges calling.
Portersmarsh Wood – disturbed fox – slunk away – sun very hot on the bracken.

15 TUESDAY (74-291)

Bullfinch in apple tree when I got up – doing nothing – bright red breast & could see plainly without telescope – very red. Chaffinch chases Robin nearly to bottom of Mrs P.'s garden.
Lots – Blackbirds singing – also Song Thrush, Mistle Thrush, Robin.

Birds seen — (30 species)

House Sparrow, Tree Sparrow, Blackbird, Chaffinch, Greenfinch, Hawfinch, Great Tit, Blue Tit, Coal Tit, Marsh Tit, Tree Creeper, ~~Jay~~, Magpie, Rook, Jackdaw, Starling, Wood Pigeon, Wren, Robin, Hedge Sparrow, Moorhen, Skylark, Yellowhammer, Corn Bunting, Black-headed Gull, Herring Gull, Partridge, Mute Swan, ~~Shoveler~~, Woodcock, Mallard

19th Saturday

Temp. – 38°–44°. Sun & cloud – threat of snow V. Strong N.W. wind.
LH. 11 AM. – Sandon – B.F. road – Woodhill – Danbury Pk – Hall Wood & Ruffhams. AH. 2-25 P.M.
Pond nr. Sandon – 6 or so Moorhens very active. Mute Swan a pair on Butts Gn. road. 3+ Tree Creepers at same place in Woodhill as I saw first T.C. last April – very active ~~16 WEDNESDAY (75-290)~~ ~~Moon's last quarter 4.36 p.m.~~ Corn Bunting back at usual territory on main rd. nr. Molrams Lane, – singing. Skylarks also singing well.
By Woodhill – many Rooks & Jackdaws chuckling & circling above the trees. Possibly a Hawfinch calling – (as last week-end). In Danbury Park Marsh Tits calling – jubilant note distinctive – usual places. Coal Tits.
Jay with 'ma-wo' baby call – very strange, sound coming from bushes.
Woodcock rose as I entered park – flew, ascending, until it hovered out of sight over treetops – long brown & fat bird in sunlight & dark trees – blue sky & white cloud. – Lots flushed from bracken near same place – very like an Owl – flight.
Ruffhams Lake – ~~[illegible]~~ put up – quiet quack calling. heavy flight – very black-white appearance from behind. Circled twice before flying off.
Came along to Hall Wood when flock of Chaffinch, Greenfinch & Great

MARCH, 1955

List

House Sparrow	Goldeneye
Tree Sparrow	Pochard
Yellowhammer	Tufted Duck
Corn Bunting	Shelduck
Chaffinch	Wigeon
Goldfinch	Mallard
Bullfinch	Coot
Hawfinch	Moorhen
Pied Wagtail	Snipe
Meadow Pipit	Knot
Linnet	Redshank
Starling	Curlew
Rook	Ringed Plover
Jackdaw	Turnstone
Carrion Crow	Oystercatcher
Jay	Mute Swan
Magpie	Blue Tit
Skylark	Great Tit
Kestrel	Robin
Little Owl	Wren
Short-eared Owl	Hedge Sparrow
Pheasant	Heron
Partridge	Blackbird
Mistle Thrush	Song Thrush
Fieldfare	Black-headed Gull
Herring Gull	Great Black-backed Gull
Great Crested Grebe	Cormorant
Lapwing	Wood Pigeon

(56 species) 17. Thursday

Temp - 36°-46°. V. cold, strong NNW wind. Mainly sunny - increasing cloud & cold. 32° 7.30 P.M. Started from Colchester at 11-10 P.M. for Donyland Woods - Abberton Church - Layer de la Haye - Reservoir - [illegible] - Goldhanger. Left Goldhanger at 6-10 P.M.

Donyland Wood - very nice, but no birds. Nearly peculiar flight of Mistle Thrush suggestive of [illegible] - Nightjar or Owl-like (?) display.

Good view of reservoir from Abberton Church - few birds. Blackheaded Gulls

~~17 THURSDAY (76-289)~~ in flock of dozen or more on a sloping shore

~~St. Patrick's Day~~ ~~Bank Holiday in Northern Ireland and Eire~~ close to Roman River.

Friday Wood - Heathland - Hobby habitat in miniature. Bullfinch flew across open - didn't recognise in unfamiliar flight. Hawfinch in copse - whistling, flew off high in very fast direct line.

Abberton - Pochard - Tufted Duck, many - 1 Shelduck. A number of G.C. Grebes mostly in full breeding plumage - lovely cinnamon & chestnut. Many Gulls - 1 Great Black-back - among the Coot. Many Coot - closely bunched. A number of Wigeon whistling - uneasy. A few Goldeneyes in distance. Cormorants. A Pied Wagtail. A few Mute Swans - far fewer than usual. Disturbed a Pheasant near entrance to sludge field - very alarmed. Kestrel perched on haystack & tree near road. Few Lapwings at reservoir, many elsewhere. Goldfinches singing.

~~18 FRIDAY (77-288)~~ Goldhanger - coast. Many Shelduck & Wigeon - easily put up. Many Curlew - slow flight, with gull-like gliding & wings [illegible] circling to land - also much bubbling calling - obviously breeding practice. More music in their call. Many Redshank. Flock of Ringed Plover - beautiful wheeling and about turning - one Turnstone among them. Also a solitary, probably wounded Ringed Plover. Knot near [illegible] - at edge of tide, with backs to sea - still at high tide, perhaps. Two Oystercatchers - aloof at shingle's end. Meadow Pipit song - when I disturbed it. Many Larks dancing & twittering. Two Snipe towered from fleet right into the setting sun - still zigzagging when passed from sight. Mallard - very fat & handsome. Many Partridge - one had long view of red, fan-shaped tail. Short-eared Owl put up from Wall - near sunset. Looking over shoulder - settled on saltings & slept again. Lovely colouring - and swinging flight. Many Skylarks started singing over wall meadows, towards sunset - ascending vertically.

Corn Bunting singing from gravel near Tolleshunt D'Arcy - full song! Yellowhammer, Blackbirds,

~~19 SATURDAY (78-287)~~ Chaffinches, singing well. Many Fieldfares still. Few Tits mostly. [illegible] after heard. Two Little Owls [illegible] between G. & Maldon. Song Thrush heard. Little Owl calls in its song.

Tits were feeding. Also Blue Tits, & Robins singing in some copse. Finches very active - at times flying off the hedge very much often & flitting back again. Flight seemed singularly silent & soft & [illegible] across [illegible] of flying lines, shadows among the hornbeams. One I glimpsed in [illegible] a Hawfinch, but couldn't find it again - had a clear picture of it however - big, masterful. Marsh Tits were also in the flock, & breeding in some area.

Sun Rises 5.18
Sun Sets 6.46 Gt Woodpecker.

APRIL, 1955

Moon Rises 10.47 p.m. | 30 Days
Moon Sets 6. 9 a.m. | 15th Week

(33 species)

Birds seen	
House Sparrow	Willow Warbler
Tree Sparrow	Chiff Chaff
Rook	Garden Warbler
Jackdaw	Willow Tit
Jay	Blue Tit
Magpie	Great Tit
Starling	Coal Tit
Wood Pigeon	Yellowhammer
Robin	Corn Bunting
Wren	Chaffinch
Hedge Sparrow	Greenfinch
Tree Creeper	Linnet
Nuthatch	Skylark
Great Spotted Woodpecker	
Mistle Thrush	Little Grebe
Song Thrush	Mallard
Blackbird	Moorhen

11 Monday

~~10 SUNDAY—EASTER DAY (100-265)~~

[illegible] sunny – warm – W gale. [illegible] 10.15 Back 2 P.M. [illegible] Walk [illegible] Wood – [illegible]. Beautiful [illegible] – [illegible] Magpie [illegible] [illegible] of woods for [illegible] – [illegible] of feathers very clear.

Greenfinches [illegible] [illegible] green [illegible]. Linnets by stream, with Yellowhammers – some singing – winter plumage. Corn Bunting [illegible] [illegible] Bucks [illegible] – singing. Many Skylarks.

~~11 MONDAY—Bank Holiday (101-264)~~

[illegible] view of Tree Sparrow [illegible] by [illegible] on [illegible] stream – [illegible] brown head. Went up gully to [illegible] Wood – many Robins singing. Two Willow Tits singing [illegible] [illegible] [illegible] each other. Chiff-Chaff. Many Blue Tits. Many Jays & countless Jackdaws in whole area. G S Woodpecker [illegible] – [illegible] [illegible] 'tchik' call – [illegible] [illegible] Hawfinch – [illegible] [illegible] – [illegible] [illegible] little owl's yelp, but [illegible] [illegible] – [illegible] [illegible] [illegible] the Mistle Thrush [illegible] [illegible] flitting about in the gully, looking [illegible] [illegible] slightly [illegible]. [illegible] [illegible] – heard Garden Warbler in [illegible] [illegible] [illegible] – [illegible] [illegible] [illegible], [illegible] [illegible] well, not sustained [illegible] [illegible] [illegible] [illegible]. [illegible] [illegible] [illegible], [illegible] [illegible] [illegible] for [illegible] [illegible] [illegible] – [illegible]. A long song – [illegible] many liquid notes. Clear view of Wren singing [illegible] [illegible] [illegible] Coal Tits in [illegible] [illegible]

Nuthatch calling [illegible] in [illegible] [illegible] – [illegible] Tree Creeper seen – singing [illegible] [illegible]. Green Woodpecker heard [illegible]. Little Grebe in [illegible] [illegible] – diving, splashing, [illegible] [illegible]

~~12 TUESDAY (102-263)~~

[illegible] Mallard [illegible] [illegible] [illegible] [illegible] of Grebe – [illegible] [illegible] [illegible]. Blue Tit. Great Tits. Saw [illegible] [illegible] in wood – Willow Warbler seen [illegible] of stream. [illegible] [illegible] [illegible] [illegible] [illegible] [illegible] song. Skylarks singing [illegible] [illegible] [illegible] [illegible] Robins. Many Wood Pigeons [illegible] [illegible] diving – altogether – a wonderful morning for birds

(22 species)

Birds seen Gt Woodpecker	
House Sparrow	~~Chaffinch~~
Wood Pigeon	Greenfinch
Rook	Yellowhammer
Starling	Corn Bunting
Chaffinch	Linnet
Blackbird	Willow Warbler
Song Thrush	Chiff-Chaff
Mistle Thrush	Blue Tit
Robin	Moorhen
Wren	Skylark
Hedge Sparrow	Jackdaw

13 Wednesday

Wind veering S to E. Warm – sunny day (55) [illegible] [illegible] 48°. Out 5-30 Home 7-P.M. – [illegible] Wood, [illegible] – [illegible] road. Skylarks still singing well up till sunset. Many Wood Pigeons in woods. Green Woodpecker [illegible] [illegible] – heard Gt Woodpecker tick in [illegible] Wood. [illegible] [illegible] Pheasant, Partridge. Saw [illegible] Blackbird [illegible] in Chapel Wood – [illegible] Chaffinch [illegible] [illegible] [illegible] whole – [illegible] [illegible] [illegible] [illegible], Willow Warbler [illegible] Chiff-Chaff singing in territories. Willow Warbler in [illegible]

13 WEDNESDAY (103-262)

[illegible] [illegible] [illegible] [illegible] [illegible] [illegible] – singing [illegible] [illegible] [illegible] [illegible] [illegible] last Spring.

Many Linnets in [illegible] [illegible] – [illegible] to roost in gorse – singing & calling – [illegible] disturbed on [illegible] – [illegible] [illegible] [illegible] ridges. 4-5 singing Song Thrushes between [illegible]. [illegible] [illegible] [illegible] – [illegible] [illegible] [illegible] [illegible] – [illegible] [illegible] [illegible] [illegible] [illegible].

Saw Rook with a [illegible]. [illegible] [illegible] down to [illegible] [illegible] [illegible] in field [illegible]. [illegible] [illegible] – [illegible] [illegible] [illegible] stake.

Clear view of a very pretty Wren at bottom of [illegible] – couldn't get [illegible] enough [illegible] [illegible] [illegible], to [illegible] [illegible]. Many Robins everywhere. 2 singing Corn Buntings near [illegible] [illegible] – [illegible] [illegible] road.

[illegible] Greenfinch is in fine song now – on [illegible] – [illegible] [illegible] near Office – although Mistle Thrushes are silent (or gone). Green Woodpecker calling [illegible] S of Office at 4-30 P.M.

2

(48 species)

House Sparrow	Partridge
Tree Sparrow	Red-legged Partridge
Rook	Lapwing
Carrion Crow	Skylark
Jackdaw	Sparrowhawk
Jay	Little Owl
Magpie	Great Spotted Woodpecker
Wood Pigeon	Green Woodpecker
Stock Dove	Blue Tit
Yellowhammer	Great Tit
Chaffinch	Marsh Tit
Greenfinch	Long-tailed Tit
Mistle Thrush	Swallow
Song Thrush	House Martin
Fieldfare	Starling
Blackbird	Willow Warbler
Moorhen	Chiff-chaff
Coot	Whitethroat
Mallard	Sedge Warbler
Pied Wagtail	Nightingale
Cuckoo	~~Woodcock~~
Wren	Robin
Hedge Sparrow	Mute Swan
Pheasant	Garden Warbler
Coal Tit	

22 Friday – Out at 7 AM. – Orger Park Wood, via Orger, [illegible] Blackmore, [illegible] Whittle, [illegible] Weald Park 8.30 & on to High Woods (2.15). Home at 9 PM. (9.30)
Temp. – 38° · 62° · 48°.
Sun came out at 7 AM. – only slight cloud – warm sunny day – Very [illegible] in afternoon – beautifully fine evening – with lovely grassy smells & fragrance.

Sedge Warbler singing noisily in bushes of [illegible] at Whittle & Swallow at [illegible]. 2 Swallows nr. King Wood. G.S. Woodpecker drumming.
Saw Sparrowhawk flying fairly high & slowly – NE across [illegible] & Fryerns Wood – typical flight.

~~21 THURSDAY (111-254)~~
~~H.M. Queen Elizabeth II born (1926)~~

Skylark didn't start singing till 8.00 or so – in fact it [illegible] singing was very subdued as I set out. Many Willow Warblers singing, few Chiff Chaffs, one or two to a wood. Orger Pk Wood very disappointing – Tree Sparrow, G.S. Woodpecker, many Jays, Song Thrushes, Robins. Just [illegible], Woodfield [illegible] – 2 Whitethroats, singing well & flitting restlessly & several Swallows, 6 or so, in different places. Cuckoo heard, and seen at edge of small wood between Norsted [illegible] & Navestock Side. – flew up from ploughed field – was form of hawk, Wood Pigeon [illegible], but looked Hawk like – couldn't place it at all, until I heard 'cuckoo', then realised. Wings long appear when perched like Falcon. Dark blue & white effect. Took up same perches – [illegible], like a big [illegible] Flycatcher – appeared to have a dark blue & brown (?grey [illegible]), & greyish white head. Heard Lapwing(?) [illegible] near Woodfield – stream.
Weald Park Disappointing – no T. Pipit, Redstart, or Wood Lark. Lovely Blackbird singing in woodland – notes of sweet – sweet, sweet for joy.

22 FRIDAY (112-253)
● New Moon 1.6 p.m.

[illegible] very noisy Jackdaws. G.S. Woodpecker drumming & Green calling – Coal Tits in pines.
Garden Warbler in stream thicket near Doddinghurst – very clear, as usual. Now [illegible] long song. Walking [illegible] Burn Spring, Pease Spring, [illegible] – Stigmans woods – looked for Sparrowhawk's nest but, confusing. (Flushed ~~Sparrowhawk~~ S'Hawk x in Pease's Spring – noisy – [illegible]) little pack of Long-tailed Tits still there – broody chasing. Many Jays – great variety of calls – 100's of Wood Pigeons – still in flocks. Nightingale in [illegible] Spring Wood – 1 or 2 bursts of song (also in King Wood, earlier). Several good views of G.S. Woodpecker in several woods, [illegible] – also good view of Green Woodpecker [illegible] – very [illegible] & silly. Thought I saw gliding Sparrowhawk once or twice but couldn't be sure – a lot of Jackdaws about, as well as Rook – Pigeons, Jays & Magpies. Several Marsh Tits – Blue Tits very common.
View over Fryerns Wood [illegible] – many W. Pigeons gliding into the roost. Also large flock of noisy Fieldfares (also seen earlier by [illegible]). Earlier Flock of Stock Doves nr. Stanford Rivers – several Pied Wagtails nr. Blackmore – brilliant black & white. Little Owl in Weald Park.

~~23 SATURDAY (113-252)~~
~~St. George's Day~~
~~Ramadān (Moslem Month of Abstinence) begins~~

Several singing birds in various places. Lovely Mallard on Weald Park Lake – Wonderful green-blue-black head. Saw a [illegible] Hare nr. Fryerns – mellow & late sun – with two smoothly gliding House Martins circling over the garden – a restful sight epitomising the calm of the evening. Saw Deer by [illegible] Wood – startled – [illegible] the woods – Fallow or Roe(?) – evidently it was a deer I disturbed in [illegible] Wood on Tuesday.

Baker's birdwatching journal, in which he wrote up his outings in more detail, 1954–1955.

1955

(Sa)turday, January 8th Galleywood, Stock, Ingatestone, Mill
11.30 to 4.15. N.E. wind. Cold & dull, 35°–33.5°.
Loud banging in Stock woods found to be (...)
Blue Tits, hammering seeds, or nuts, on trees – (...)
Wood. Hornbeam area; Tits also on ground
Past Pound Wood, I saw a Kestrel perched in a
(t)ree to R. of road, looking hunched and deje(cted)
Not disturbed by uplifted arm, but apparently (...)
(a)nd flew to a tree further along the line.
(I)n flight seemed rather crow-like, probably sug(...)
(t)he lifting of the flexible wing-tips in flight.
(S)tock/Ingatestone road, before Buttsbury, Fieldfares
(t)he field pools on left, just past the farmho(use)
(A)re they thirsty birds? Their 'chak, chak', is (...)
(s)ound. Past Buttsbury, in the floode(d)
(...) before sewage farm, were 14 Moorhens scurr(ying)
(...) busily round the large pool left by the (...)
(S)ome beautifully marked feathers found at (...)
(...)ney Wood, by plough, Writtlepark – ? Pheasants or (...)
(...)den hare, with two primroses, flowering afte(r)
(...) rabbit, with myxamotosis, seen – Writtlepark.
(...) have those feathers now, within reach as (...)
(bu)t not the flowers, though this year's primrose(s)
alive.

Sunday, March 27th Temp. - 47° 43°. V. Strong N.N.E. Cold & cloudy. 11.15 to 2.20. Plenitude of Skylarks at Molrams lane & Waterworks lane junctions, one bird in road, at least five singing, two flocks. A Great Black-backed Gull seen over river valley, from Baddow/Boreham road.
Went up in the birch wood on left of Riffhams Lane; flushed a Woodcock near the top and side of wood. I was very close on it, and heard the harsh call (?), and the tearing sound it made, as it flew off, very fast.
Holt Wood - put off 1 drake and 2 duck Mallard, from Riffhams Lake; they circled round, drake leading, getting higher and higher, as the sun came out. A Great Tit sang "jug, jug".

Saturday, April 2nd

51°-57°-50°. Sunny, cloud increasing. V. Strong S.E/S.W. wind. Fresh, warm in the sun. 10.50 to 5.40. Danbury Pk, common, Bicknacre way to North Fambridge - home via E. Hann. Noted, as before, that in the sun, and if considered without the prejudice of familiarity, House Sparrows look very dashing in spring, mealy-white underparts flash in the sun (M. road Bushey Hill).
Wood Hill House, and lower Danbury Pk, heard Nuthatch giving 'jug, jug' song, rich and loud - restlessly flitting from tree to tree. Another Nuthatch, near the big dead beech at top of park, was carelessly going over the trees whistling ~~four notes~~ over and over - 'p-whit', like a low boy's whistle, loud but

secretive. A Great Tit had a long, and lovely shimmering song. A Chiff-chaff, yellow and 'new-painted' looking, gave a snatch of song.

By Sandon Brook, at the bottom of Danbury Common hill, I stopped by the alders. A Tree Creeper seen on L&R of road, singing very loudly. On R.; a Goldcrest, moving very fast through the trees, calling shrilly; I glimpsed yellow and green wing-bar. Got close to a Green Woodpecker in field below alders, on R., giving a strange 'sotto voce' ~~husky~~ hushed call, as though talking to itself, huskily.

North Fambridge, 1.40 P.M. Going along sea-wall w. bend out, before Hydemarsh, a few Curlew went up from meadow inland of wall, and these were followed by four, what I at first thought to be Curlew, but soon realized were Short-eared Owls. Presumably they had been roosting near the fleet. They flapped, flopped, and glided away in soft and easy flight, soon going down to rest. Then I would come up with them again, and up they would go. I left bike, and walked along sea-wall. Another Owl went up, and passed overhead turning it's big head slowly to look at me over it's shoulder, and then came back again. - still looking down. It's eyes were glaring, hostile - it's face seeming like a mask, overgrown and neglected.

Wednesday, April 18th 5.45 to 7.45 Cold - 43°. Rain ceasing, becoming clear. Brook End to Boreham, - Baddow. A Skylark sang twenty minutes after sunset. I flushed a Redshank near Brook End, and it went calmly away, yodelling.

A Kestrel, or falcon of some sort ?Peregrine, flew to the clump below Boreham House, perhaps to roost. A Mute Swan sat eating grass, by the river - some dropped from its bill, as it opened it in apparent surprise, when I cycled past. I put up a Snipe from the same spot as in March. It flew right away, towering into the sun's setting ball of fire. Mallard flew over, after sunset.

Friday, April 20th About 12.30 A.M., for several minutes - at intervals - ~~It~~ I heard a loud 'frank' call coming from the far side of Oaklands, or, at least, from that direction. It seemed to die away into the distance, and was possibly made by a Heron, passing over.

Saturday, April 21st Dry, strong E. wind. 52°-47°. Sunny, with occasional clouds. Very bright, clear, and cold, very warm in the sun. 2.10 P.M. to 5.10 P.M. To Hanningfield Reservoir, via Galleywood and St. Preston's lane.

As I free-wheeled down the hill, by the racecourse, I had a perfect first view of a Swallow, which flew overhead, across the road from left to right. It flew low, and in bright sunlight I could see the glorious cream of its breast, the deep blue head and back, and the red throat.

SH

Friday, May 13th 1955 62-47°. Dull, damp, W. gale. Birch Spring & Barrow Woods, via Stoneymoor Wood & Morg. 4 more 'Kite Hawk' found. At about sunset, in very dull light, I was standing in the ride, near the edge of Barrow Wo[ods] when a bird flew down the ride, straight into the [tree] where I had previously thought the nest was a Hawk['s]. The flight was fast and quiet, only a slight 'whuff' [of] wings as the bird went past me. It flew straig[ht] to the tree, without any sort of check or perceptible stalli[ng], perching instantaneously, out of sight. It changed [its] perch ~~&~~ and flew off without my seeing it go.
This was probably a Sparrowhawk, nothing else fits t[he] style of flight, the confident hurling of itself at the [tree], folding to a branch so suddenly. The same surp[rise] as one got as a child when the stick thrown up [to] knock the conkers down, ~~stick~~ suddenly lodged [in] the leaves, and was lost, just lost. All there [was] left to do was to walk foolishly away.

[illegible]

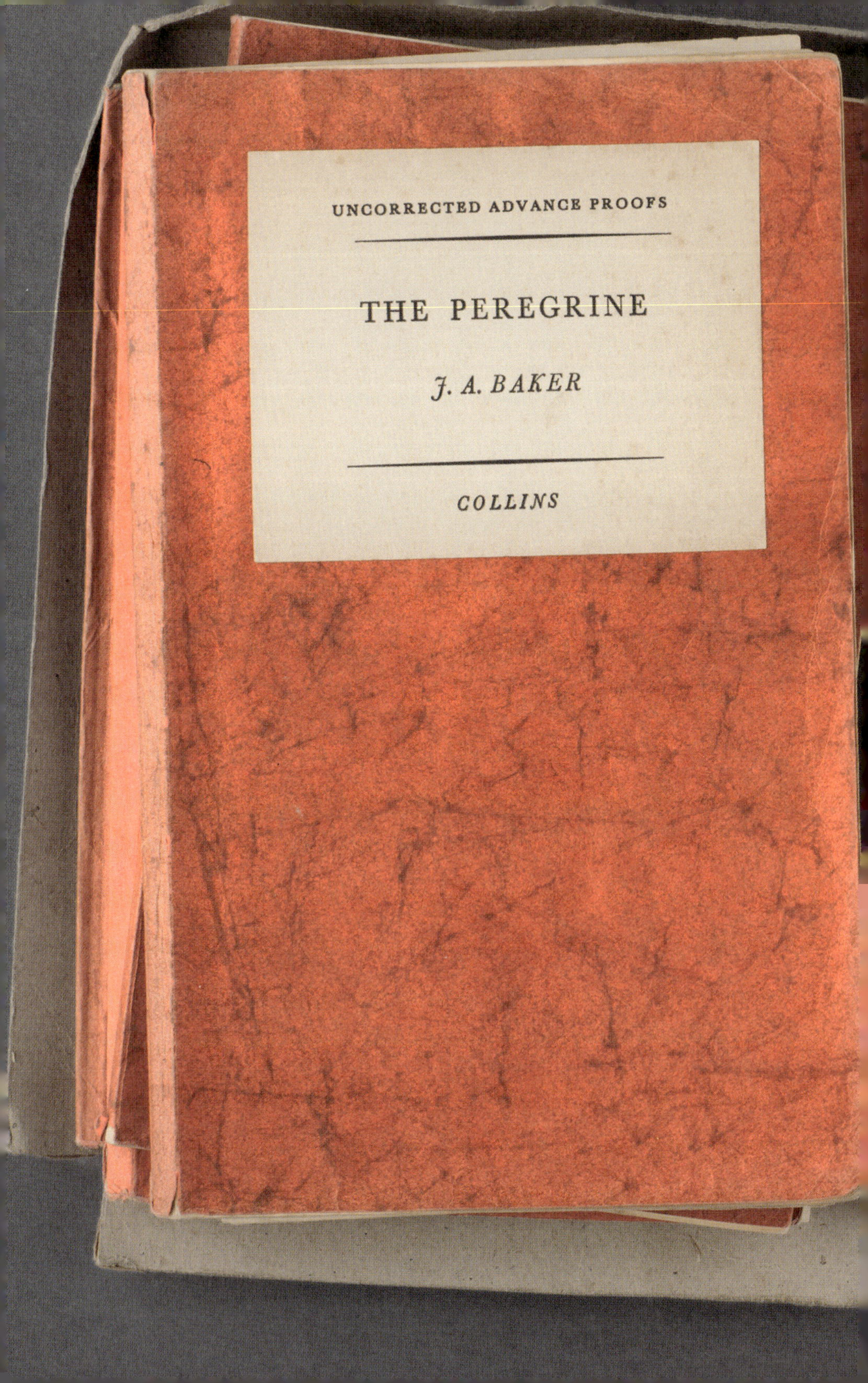
UNCORRECTED ADVANCE PROOFS
THE PEREGRINE
J. A. BAKER
COLLINS

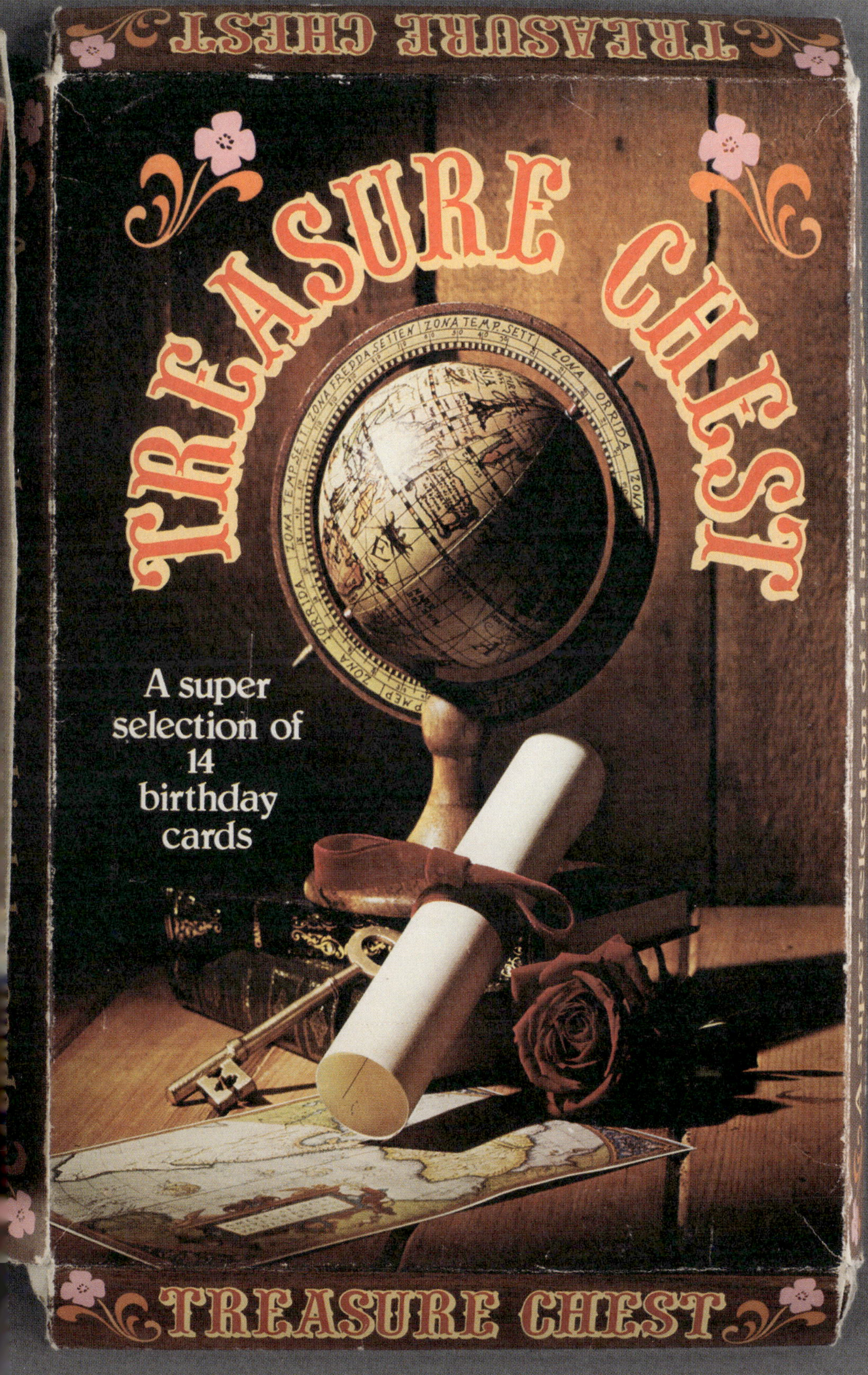
TREASURE CHEST
TREASURE CHEST
A super selection of 14 birthday cards
ZONA TEMP. SETT
ZONA FREDDA SETTEN
ZONA ORRIDA
TREASURE CHEST

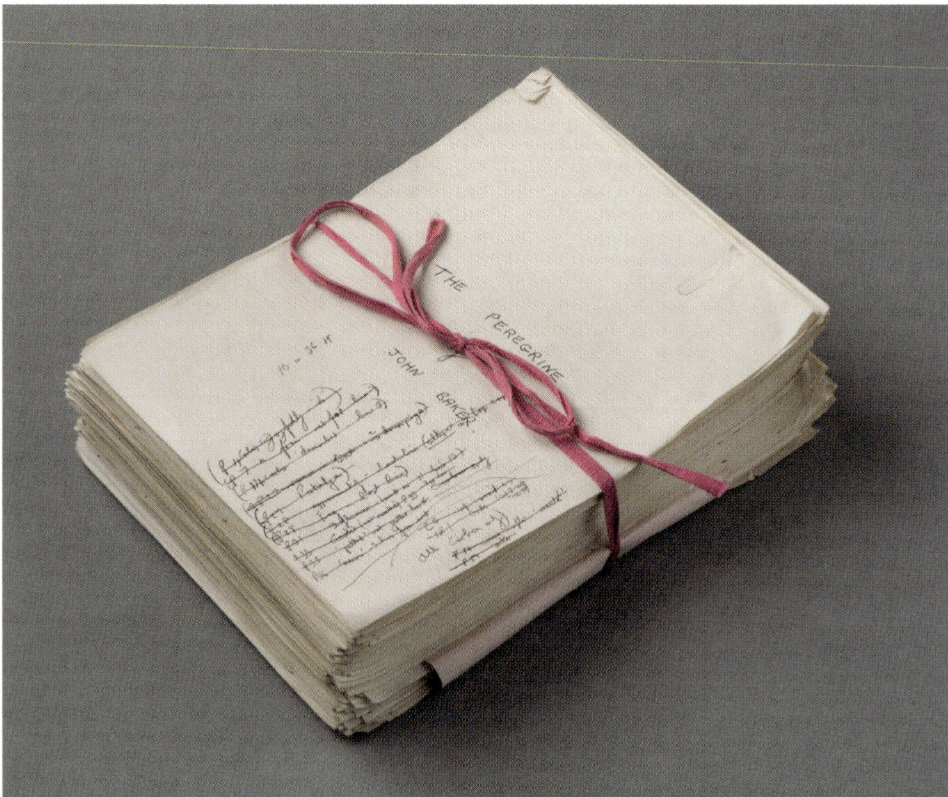

Pages from an early handwritten manuscript of The Peregrine.

The Peregrine (or 'Peregrines')

The hardest thing of all to see is what is (really) there.
Books about birds ~~will~~ ~~you~~ show ~~you~~ pictures of ~~the~~
peregrine, and ~~the~~ (the) text (is) ~~will be~~ full of information,
long and isolated in (or) the gleaming whiteness of the pa
~~peregrine~~ (hawks) ~~stare~~ stares back at you, bold, ~~and~~ statues
~~and~~ brightly coloured. But when you (have) close(d) the book
will never see that (fine) bird again. Compared with
static image you ~~need~~ ~~carry~~ (carry) in your mind, the
reality will ~~it~~ seem ~~dis~~ dull and disappointing. The
bird will never be so large, ~~or~~ so shiny-coloured, it
~~never~~ ~~the~~ It ~~sinks~~ is deep in landscape(s) always
seems always at the point of being lost. Pict
are waxworks beside the (pure) passionate reality of the b

Female peregrines, known as falcons, are between
seventeen and twenty inches long; ~~appro~~ roughly the length
man's arm from elbow to finger tip(s). Males, or
are three ~~or~~ to four inches shorter, fourteen to sixte
long. Weights also vary: falcons from $1\frac{3}{4}$ to $2\frac{1}{2}$ p
males from $1\frac{1}{4}$ to $1\frac{3}{4}$ pounds. Everything about pere
varies: colour, size, weight, personality, style: everything

1

Four miles to the

Introduction

~~The long ridge lies~~ lies across the skyline like a smoke reef (a) of cloud, (four miles to the east of my home)

East of my home the long ridge lies across the skyline like the (low) hull of a submarine. Above it, the sky is bright with reflections of distant water, ~~and there is always a feeling~~ There is (a feeling) of sail beyond land. ~~The trees of the~~ Hill trees mass together ~~like~~ in a dark-spired forest, but when I move towards them they slowly fan apart. The sky descends between, till they are solitary oaks and elms, each with its own wide territory of winter shadow. ~~Perhaps it is the~~ The calmness, the solitude of horizons draws (lures) (on) me towards them, through them, and on to others. They layer (in) the many like strata

From the town, the river flows north-east, bends east round the north side of the ridge, turns south ~~towards~~ to the estuary. The upper valley is a flat, open plain; lower down it is narrow and steep-sided; near the estuary it is again flat and open. The ~~upper~~ plain is like an estuary of land, scattered with island farms. ~~The Woods and the~~ Or woods and orchards on the low gravel hill, its gradual slopes look steep and ridge-like from the valley. The river is small and meandering, slow-flowing; too small for the ten miles long, two miles wide estuary, which was once the mouth of a much larger river, draining most of midland England.

March 2

This was the eighth successive cloudless day, and the burnished blue of the sky shone as though it could never again be hidden. The strong south-east wind was cold, but the sun's warmth made the snow seem utterly vanquished and senile, ~~sending~~ sent it slithering watrily down into the rising land.

Woodpigeons and jackdaws went up from North ~~Wood~~ at midday, and cawing crows flew to their tree-top stations. Chaffinches by the bridge scolded steadily for ten minutes, their monotonous 'Pink Pink' gradually dying away into ~~pale yellow~~ sunlit silence. I saw nothing ~~X~~ ~~so~~ ~~I~~ ~~concluded~~ ~~that~~ Assuming the hawk ~~had~~ to have soared downwind, I ~~and~~ searched ~~it~~ for ~~it~~ him north of the ford, and found him in the dead oak half an hour later.

He flew ~~steeply~~ up into the wind, and began to circle. His wing-beats became shallower, ~~until~~ till of the tips of his wings were faintly fluttering. I thought he would soar, but instead he flew quickly ~~away~~ south-east. The lane that divides North ~~Wood~~ dips and rises through a steep-sided gully, ~~and~~ which is sheltered from the wind. ~~Warm air rises from the whole~~ in ~~When the sun has warmed worn the surface of the lane~~ The peregrine has learnt that warm air rises from the sun-warmed, windless slopes of this lane,

3 Dec 11 (contd)

fly directly overhead. They split up as soon as they saw me, scattering to left or right, like woodpigeons. I ~~have~~ had never seen them do ~~this~~ that before, ~~but~~ Repeated attacks by the peregrine, at morning or evening, have ~~them~~ made them very wild, and suspicious of danger from below.

I followed the peregrine to the east, ~~and while with a thousand~~ fieldfares clacking and whistling above me on their way to roost ~~in bushes~~ by the river. From a small stream I put up a green sandpiper. It ~~went about in the dusk~~, and ~~swayed~~ towered into the dusk, calling, and veering and swaying about like a tipsy snipe. ~~Losing the rich, grating, music of its call~~ its call was a wild, whistling ~~ringing~~ 'Too-loo-weet', indescribably triumphant and forlorn. The peregrine ~~fell~~ stooped as the sandpiper rose, but he missed it by a yard. ~~I think~~ He may have been following me, so that I could flush prey for him. ~~but~~ All the ~~attacks~~ stoops he made today ~~seemed~~ were slow and inaccurate. Perhaps he was not really hungry, ~~yet~~ but compelled by ~~his~~ habit to practise ~~go through the~~ a ritual of hunting and killing.

The sky cleared after sunset, and ~~hundreds of~~ thousands of rooks and

Far above them was a sound like the distant striking of matches.

eye like crimson flame!

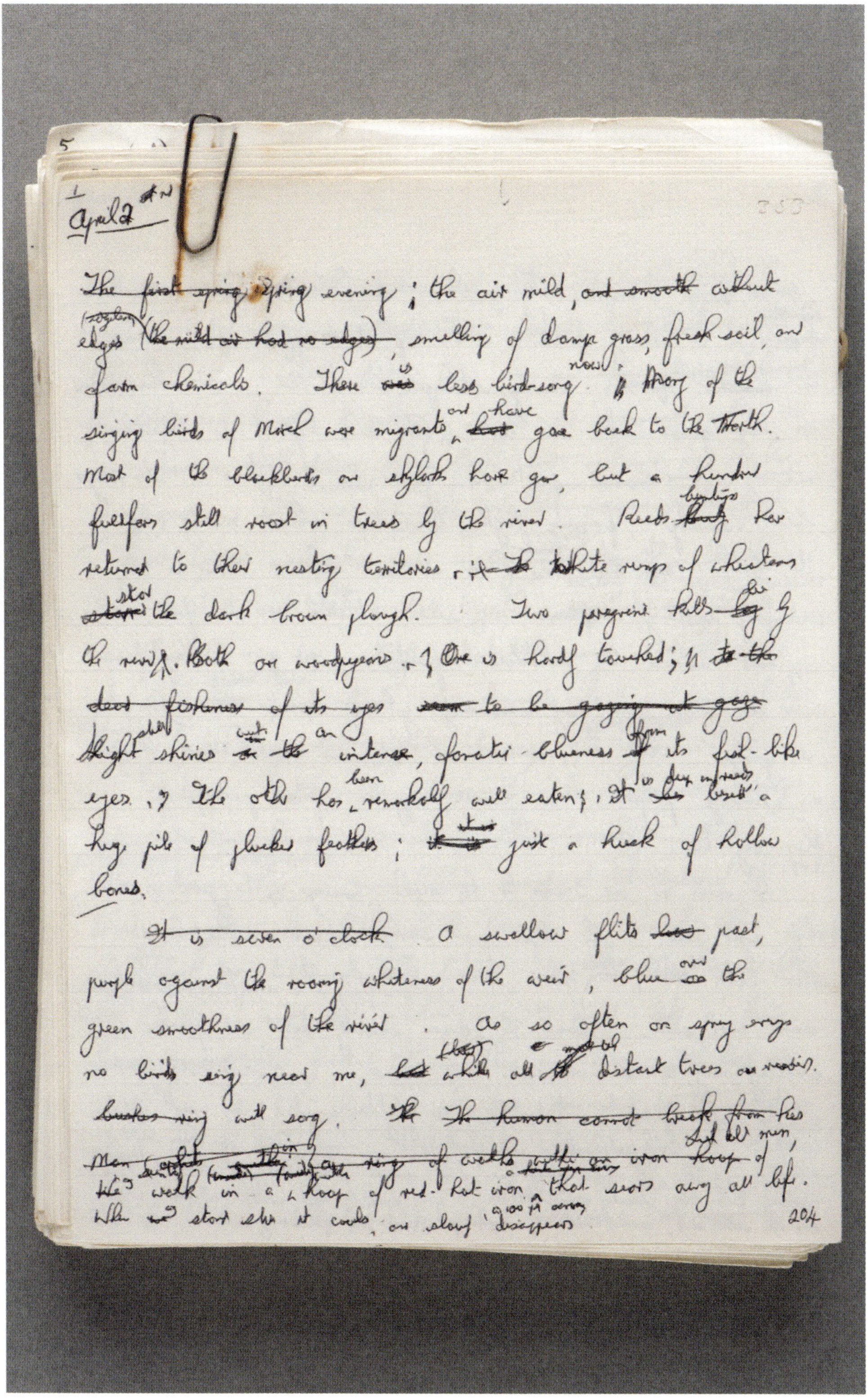
5

1

April 2nd

The first spring evening; the air mild, without edges, smelling of damp grass, fresh soil, and farm chemicals. There is less bird-song now. Many of the singing birds of March were migrants and have gone back to the North. Most of the blackbirds and skylarks have gone, but a hundred fieldfares still roost in trees by the river. Reed buntings have returned to their nesting territories. White rumps of wheatears star the dark brown plough. Two peregrine kills lie by the river. Both are woodpigeons. One is hardly touched; the slight shine of cut on the intense, fanatic blueness from its fish-like eyes. The other has been remarkably well eaten; it is just a huge pile of plucked feathers; just a husk of hollow bones.

A swallow flits past, purple against the roaring whiteness of the weir, blue over the green smoothness of the river. As so often on spring evenings no birds sing near me, while all the distant trees are resonant with song.

like a wreath in a hoop of red-hot iron that sears away all life. When we start she cools, and slowly disappears.

204

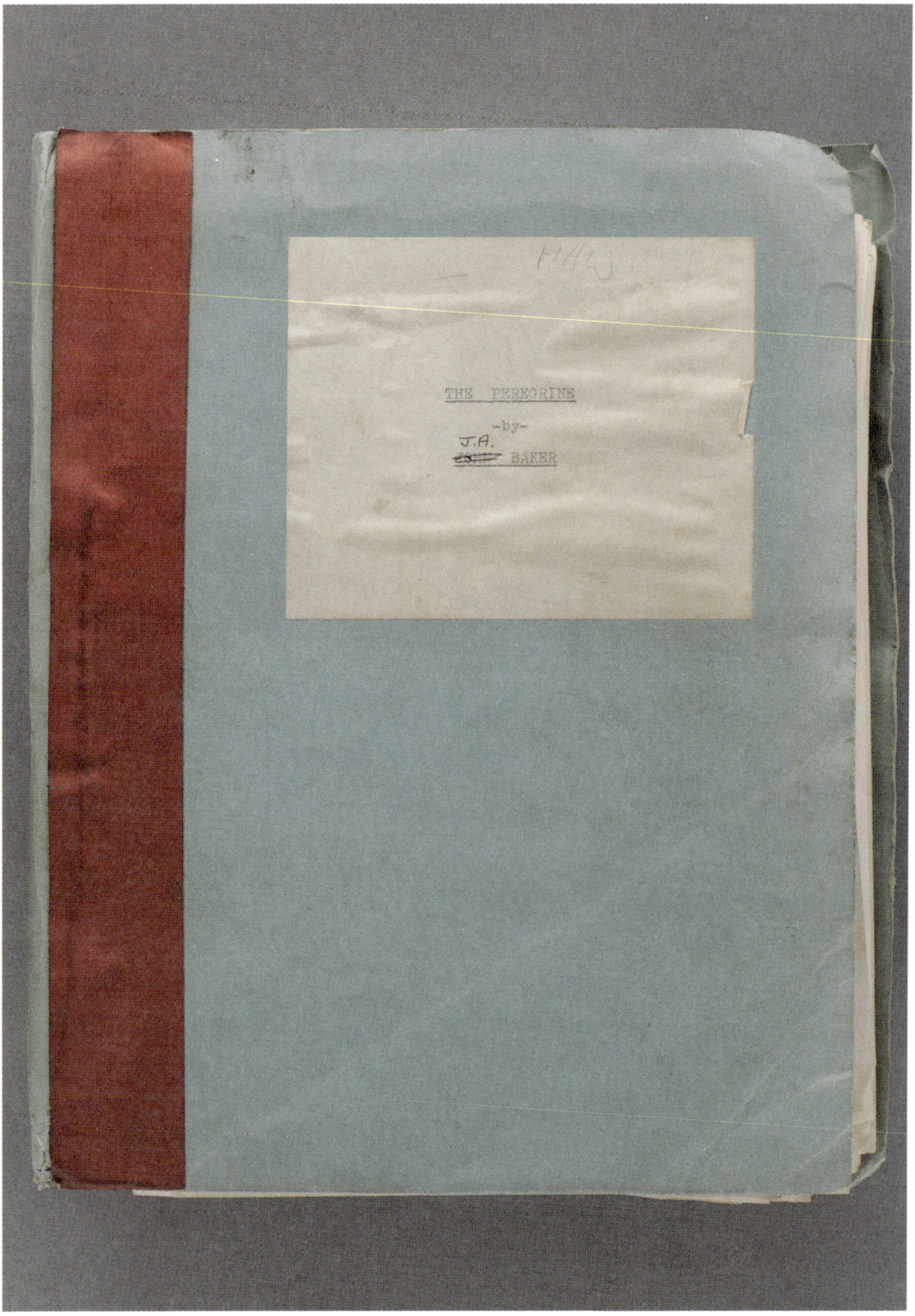

The typed manuscript of The Peregrine *that Baker first sent to Collins, with editorial notes from the publisher (probably Michael Walter).*

single quotes

THE PEREGRINE

-by-

JOHN BAKER

PART 1 — 18 pt ital u + lc. sunk 2

Beginnings — 18 pt ital caps 1½ pt letter #d sunk 5

— sunk 9

East of my home, the long ridge lies across the skyline like the low hull of a submarine. Above it, the eastern sky is bright with reflections of distant water, and there is a feeling of sails beyond land. Hill trees mass together in a dark-spired forest, but when I move towards them they slowly fan apart, the sky descends between, and they are solitary oaks and elms, each with its own wide territory of winter shadow. The calmness, the solitude of horizons lures me towards them, through them, and on to others. They layer the memory like strata.

From the town, the river flows north-east, bends east round the north side of the ridge, turns south to

This is all good, I feel: it's just the lack of a theme + jumping from one subject to another where there is no deliberate splitting up of the book that becomes tiring. As it is now it's presented as a continuum but lacks the real continuity of the Peregrine.

But it's all good material which you could use in another framework.

'Was it real? Was that really a bird?'

The valley filled with the long shadows of the trees. Little owls called in the early dusk the trees had made. The air became very cold. The soft calls of the owls wafted upward like rings of smoking breath.

April 21st.

A dead mole lay on its back in the centre of the ride, as though it had fallen from the sky. Its small slack feet seemed to feel at the air, like hands. It was soft and solid to the touch, the pouchy fur soft as the skin of a peach. There was no mark on it. It lay like a drowned man, rejected into air.

Feathers and bones in a hollow of dry leaves were all that was left of a woodpigeon the sparrowhawk had killed. The feathers were scattered like a nebula. Bloodstained acorns had tumbled from the dead bird's crop. Cupped leaves held water and dark blood. Finding a kill excites; the hawk is near, but unseen; eyes glint in every tree. So must the savage feel, finding the ashes of a fire that is not his.

Standing by the dark sockets of the badgers' sett, I heard the sound of someone walking through dead bracken. But there was no one. The sound came nearer, rising up

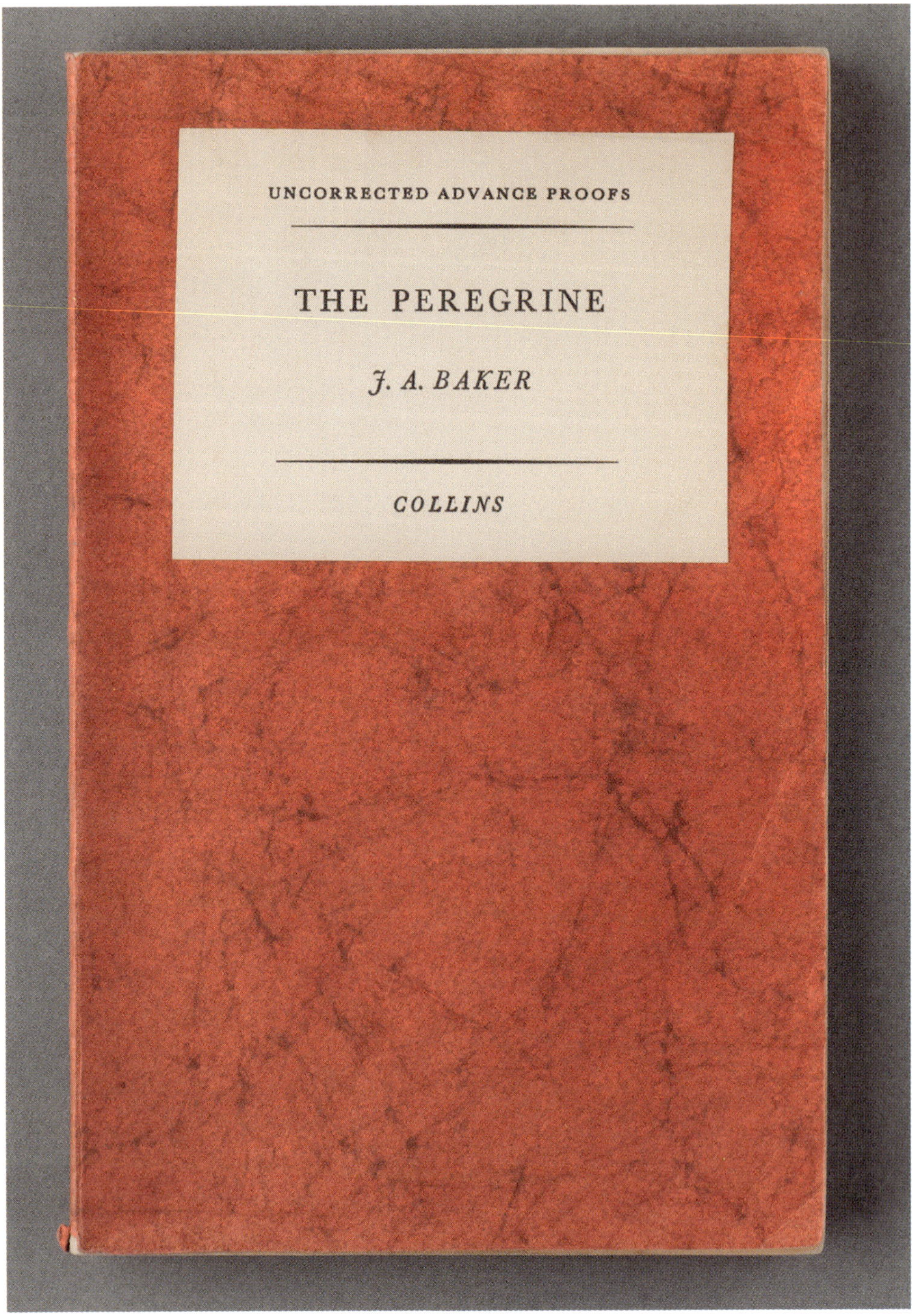

A proof copy of The Peregrine *(1967). Years after publication, Baker annotated his proofs with notes for potential new writing.*

I

BEGINNINGS

East of my home, the long ridge lies across the skyline like the low hull of a submarine. Above it, the eastern sky is bright with reflections of distant water, and there is a feeling of sails beyond land. Hill trees mass together in a dark-spired forest, but when I move towards them they slowly fan apart, the sky descends between, and they are solitary oaks and elms, each with its own wide territory of winter shadow. The calmness, the solitude of horizons lures me towards them, through them, and on to others. They layer the memory like strata.

From the town, the river flows north-east, bends east round the north side of the ridge, turns south to the estuary. The upper valley is a flat open plain, lower down it is narrow and steep-sided, near the estuary it is again flat and open. The plain is like an estuary of land, scattered with island farms. The river flows slowly, meanders; it is too small for the long, wide estuary, which was once the mouth of a much larger river that drained most of middle England.

Detailed descriptions of landscape are tedious. One part of England is superficially so much like another. The differences are subtle, coloured by love. The soil here is clay: boulder clay to the north of the river, London clay to the south. There is gravel on the river terraces, and on the higher ground of the ridge. Once forest, then pasture, the land is now mainly bubbles of his tremulous hollow song. It echoes down to the brook, breaking the frozen surface of the air. I look out at the west's complexity of light. A heron, black against the yellow sky, kinked neck and dagger bill incised, sweeps silently down into the brook's dark gulf. The sky infuses with the afterglow.

Softly through the dusk the peregrine glides, hushing it aside with silent wings. He searches the constellations of small eyes, sees the woodcock's planetary eye look upward from the marsh, shafts back his wings, and plunges to the light. The woodcock rises, twists under the blade of the hawk, and wavers away. He is overtaken, cut down. He drops with a squelching thud. The hawk lands on the softening bird, grips its neck in his bill. I hear the bone snap, like barbed wire cut by pliers. He nudges the dead bird over. Its wings wave, then it lies on its back. I hear the tearing of feathers, the tug of flesh, the crack and snap of gristle. I can see the black blood dripping from the gleam of the hawk's bill. I move out of the dark of the wood into the paler shadows of trees. The hawk hears, looks up. His white-ringed eyes are huge with dusk. I creep nearer, knees soaking in the marshy ground. Thin ice crunches. Frost is forming where the late sun shone. The hawk pulls at his prey, looks up. Four yards separate us, but it is too far, a distance as unspannable as a thousand foot crevasse. I drag like a wounded bird, floundering, sprawled. He watches me, moving his head, looking with each eye in turn. An otter whistles. Something splashes in the cold, piky depth of the brook. The hawk is poised now on the narrow edge between curiosity and fear. What is he thinking? Is he thinking at all? This is new to him. He does not know how I got here. Slowly I mask the pallor of my face. He is not afraid. He is watching the white glitter of my eyes. He cannot understand their staccato flicker. If I could stop them moving he would stay. But I cannot stop them. There is a breath of wings. He has stone, then broke, and flowed away round a bend of the stream.

I avoid humans, but hiding is difficult now the snow has come. A hare dashed away, with its ears laid back, pitifully large and conspicuous. I use what cover I can. It is like living in a foreign city during an insurrection. There is an endless banging of guns and tramping of feet in the snow. One has an unpleasantly hunted feeling. Or is it so unpleasant? I am as solitary now as the hawk I pursue.

January 5th. Broken columns of snow towered over lanes dug from ten-foot drifts. Roads were ridged and fanged with ice, opaque and shiny as frozen rivers. Goldfinches sparkled in snow-lit hedges. Gulls and crows patrolled the white beaches of the fields, looking for stranded corpses. Through mist, under low cloud, hundreds of woodpigeons flew north-east.

A blackbird scolding by the ford at midday was the first bird sound I heard. It stopped when the peregrine flew slowly north into the mist. Near the farm, two thousand wood-pigeons were feeding on brussels sprouts. Three or four birds clung to each stalk, while others fluttered round them or sat in the snow, waiting. The surrounding fields were black with resting pigeons. They hid the snow. Shots were fired, and many birds fell dead. The others roared into the sky. The white sky became black as the black ground whitened. A mile away, the sound of wings was like an aircraft taking off. At a hundred yards, it was unbelievably loud, a landslide of crashing reverberant clangour engulfing the banging of guns and the shouts of men. In woods and orchards there were thousands more of these desperate birds, and vast flocks flew over to the north and north-east, searching for an end to the whiteness below. They go down before the guns, like the cavalry at Balaclava. Rapt in their hunger, they have no guile left. Their bodies

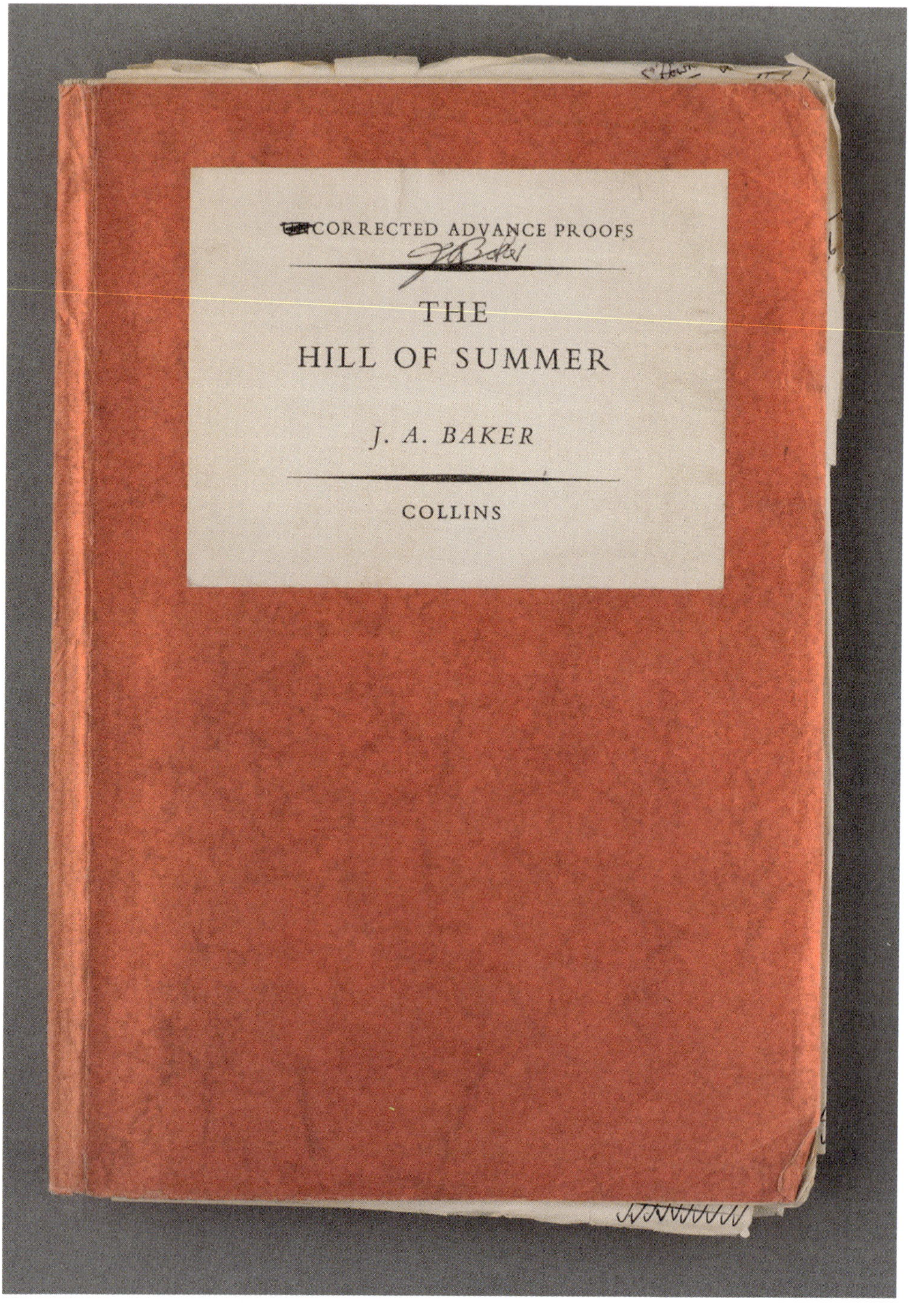

A proof copy of The Hill of Summer *(1969) marked up by Baker.*

— too small, I think.

Contents

2

May: a Storm

The forgotten path is hidden beneath grass and campion and cow parsley. Above it, the hawthorn is warm with the white ash of its blossom. The song of the greenfinches is as slow and sleepy as the languid air, as the warm southern breeze. A cuckoo calls endlessly in the distance, a soft-echoing voice that fades and returns but comes no nearer. These sounds de… the quiet haze of the may.

Under the splinters of the numbed hedge, a whitethro… sings. He creeps among the nettles, furtive, wandering, seen here and there like glimpses of a pouring snake, making the red campion flowers nod and quiver. He will be here throughout the summer, feeding, nesting, singing above his meagre territory, glad of the growth to come, this ragg… mnant of a hedge.

The small woods of the upland plain, wher… remul- once nested, are a brown mist in the summe… h inno- afternoon. The white blossom of an orchard … he arro- flight. It hovers low in the shimmering ha… tree at the edge of a pine wood. Many bird… rising in clearings. Between the trees, the bluebel… old. There lilac smoke that has no definite outline … I enter the

3

May: the Pine Wood

The pine wood hides the sun, like a dark northern god rising in menace above the white road that falls steeply to the west, and the small green hills beyond are receding into a grey autumnal haze. The high town silvers in sunlight, and its sky is barbed with curving swifts. But already the night's simplicity is settling upon the valley. Under the exotic flowering of the early lights, a blue Venetian dusk laps at the windows of the shadowed houses. As I watch, the high town is extinguished, and its shining sky ascends. The stiff-feathered pines shed their darkness into the still air.

A twilight of luminous birches glimmers upon the blackness of the pines. I sink into the mossy summer-woodland smell of the birch leaves. It is a sweet herbivorous breath, like the smell of rain drying away from a hot road. It rises from the wood like a corona of green mist. It is a cave that leads into another world; the subterranean, removed world of the summer night.

A dead mole lies on its back in the path, as though it had fallen from the sky. It is solid and heavy, but the pouchy fur is as soft as the skin of a peach. Its slack feet seem to crumple the air, like small white hands. Its jaws have sagged apart, and a red gape shows between. The teeth are pointed and sharp. There is no pathos in this predatory face. The mouth is held

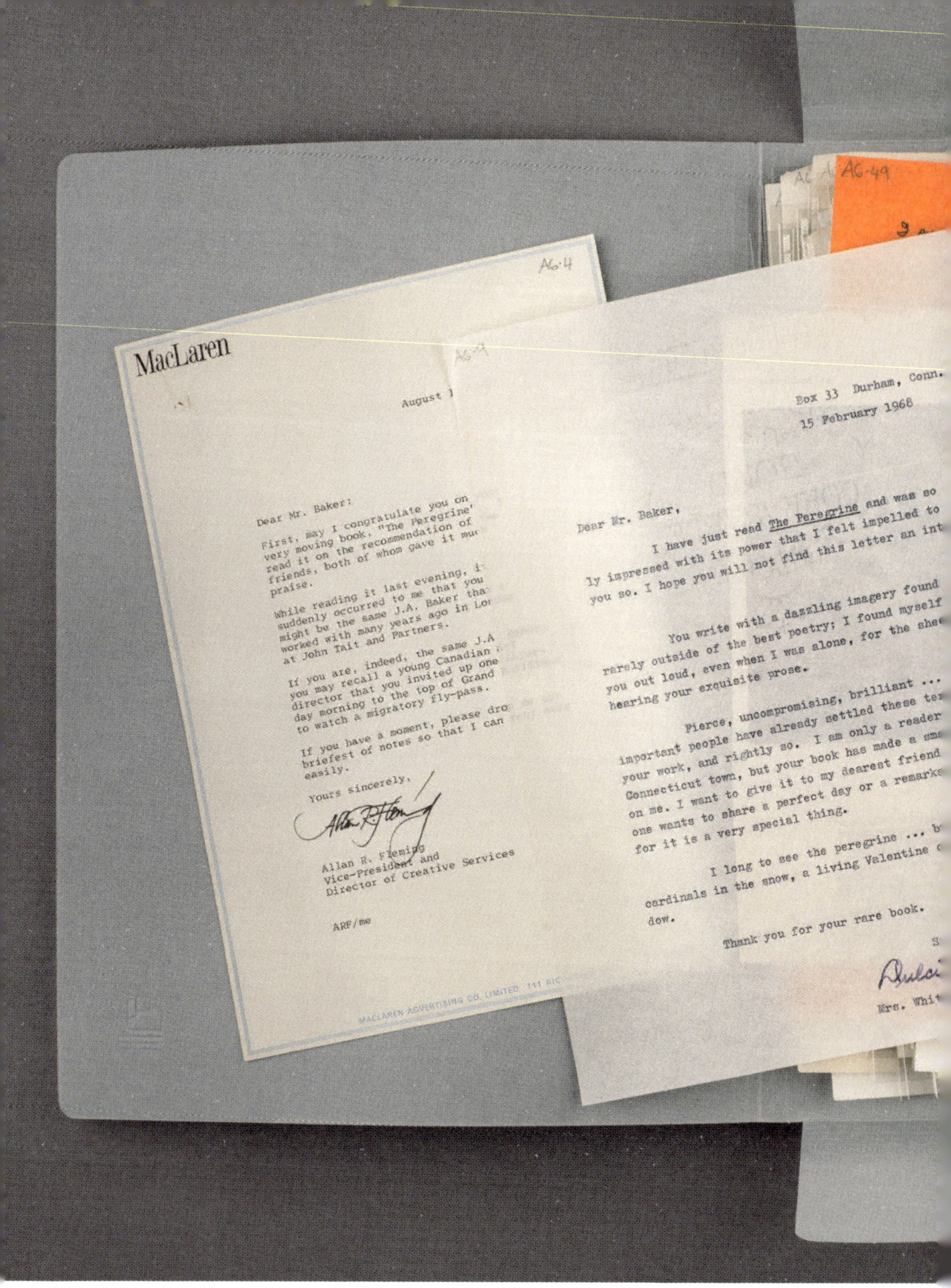

MacLaren

A6·4

August 1

Dear Mr. Baker:

First, may I congratulate you on
very moving book, "The Peregrine"
read it on the recommendation of
friends, both of whom gave it mu
praise.

While reading it last evening, i
suddenly occurred to me that you
might be the same J.A. Baker tha
worked with many years ago in Lo
at John Tait and Partners.

If you are, indeed, the same J.A
you may recall a young Canadian
director that you invited up one
day morning to the top of Grand
to watch a migratory fly-pass.

If you have a moment, please dro
briefest of notes so that I can
easily.

Yours sincerely,

Allan R. Fleming
Vice-President and
Director of Creative Services

ARF/me

MACLAREN ADVERTISING CO. LIMITED 111 RIC

Box 33 Durham, Conn.
15 February 1968

Dear Mr. Baker,

I have just read <u>The Peregrine</u> and was so
ly impressed with its power that I felt impelled to
you so. I hope you will not find this letter an int

You write with a dazzling imagery found
rarely outside of the best poetry; I found myself
you out loud, even when I was alone, for the shee
hearing your exquisite prose.

Fierce, uncompromising, brilliant ...
important people have already settled these te
your work, and rightly so. I am only a reader
Connecticut town, but your book has made a sma
on me. I want to give it to my dearest friend
one wants to share a perfect day or a remark
for it is a very special thing.

I long to see the peregrine ... b
cardinals in the snow, a living Valentine
dow.

Thank you for your rare book.

S

Mrs. Whi

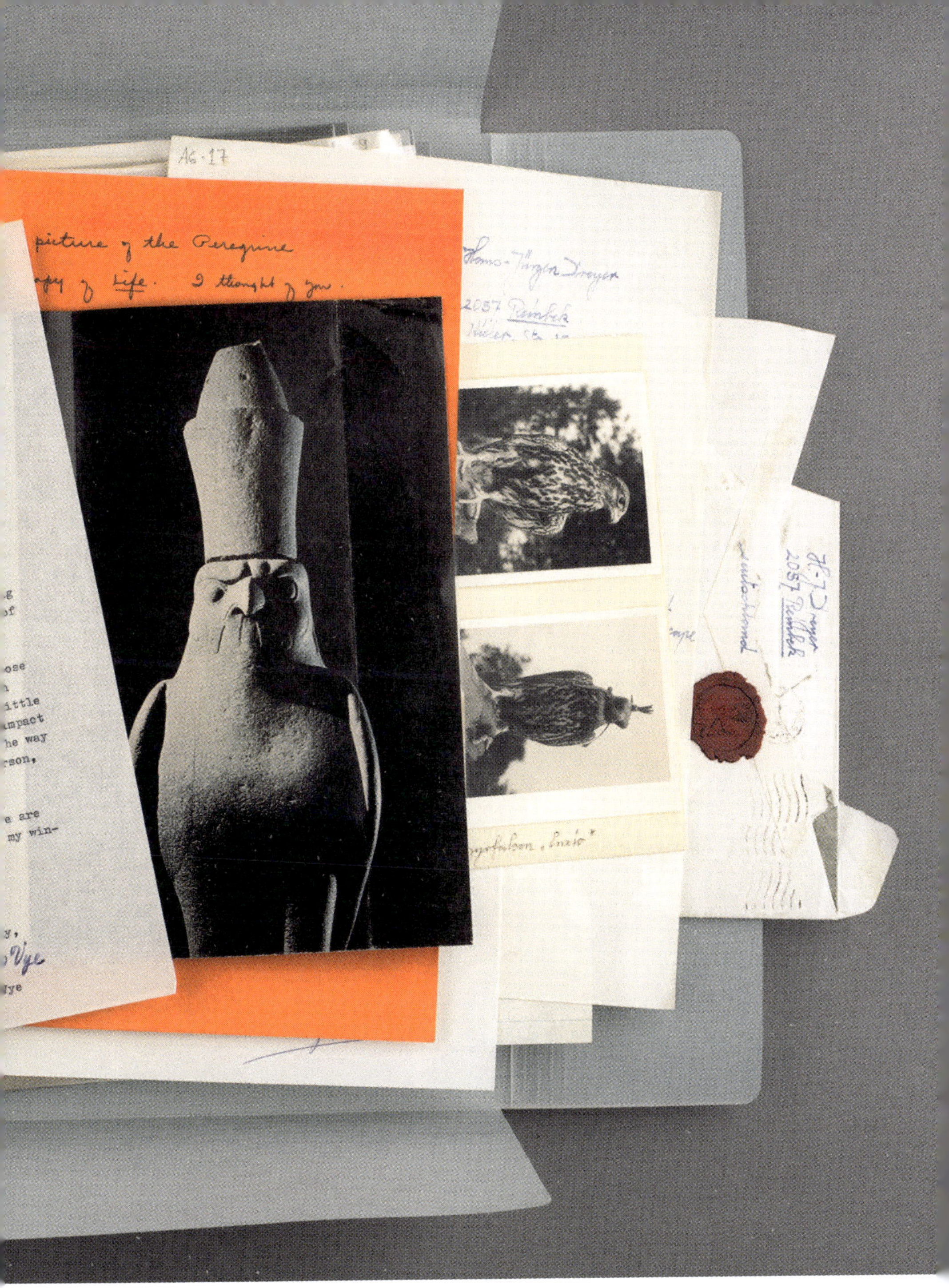

A folder of letters sent to J. A. Baker praising The Peregrine *and* The Hill of Summer.

ONS
ORLD
igby
FEMALE PEREGRINE AT EYRIE (Note separated eggs slightly buried in dust of scrape)

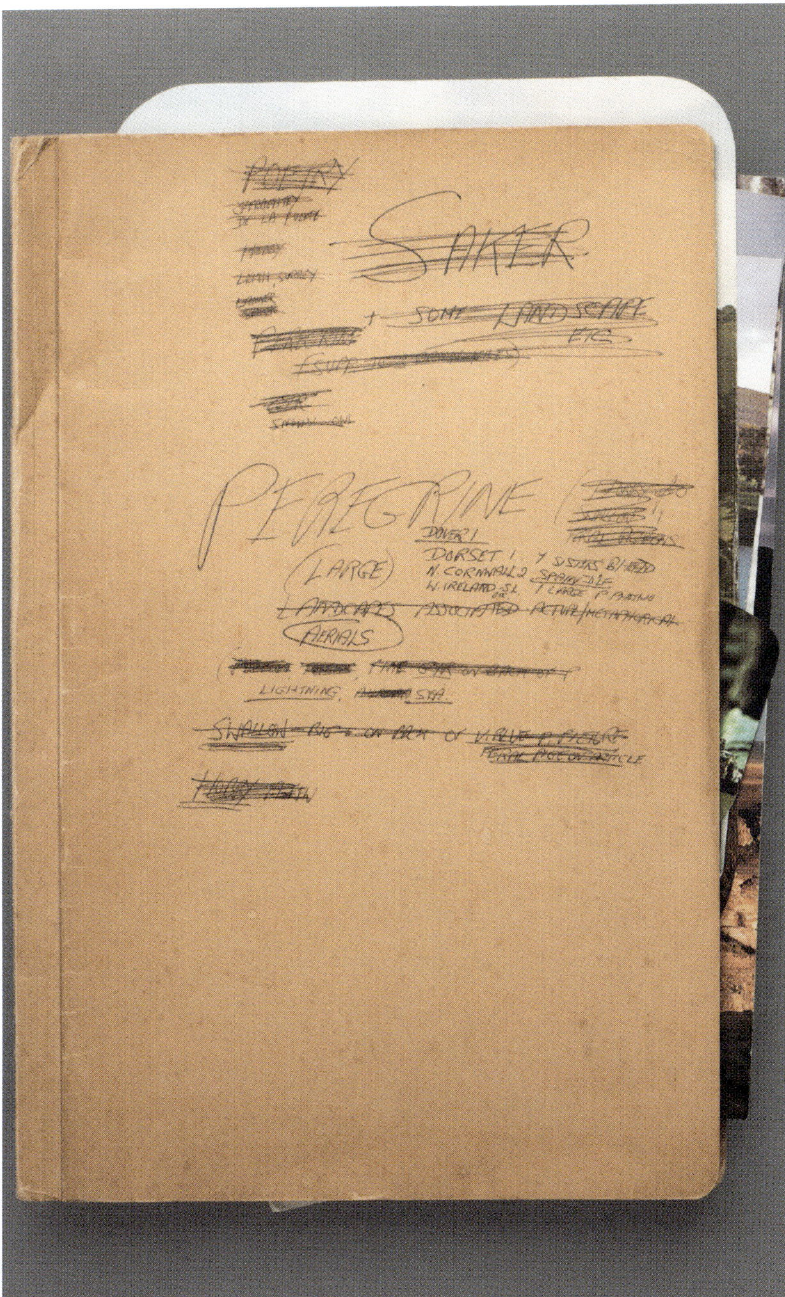

The cardboard folder in which Baker kept his scrapbook of photographs and articles clipped from magazines, collected from the 1970s until his death.

Edney Wood, Writtle, Chelmsford, 2017.

Christopher Matthews

BAKER COUNTRY

CHRISTOPHER MATTHEWS is a photographer living in Chelmsford with an abiding interest in place. His documentary projects are in the collection of Te Papa Tongarewa, the Museum of New Zealand, and since living in the UK he has made work about cultural sites in Israel, the landscapes and architecture of the Cold War, the north Essex landscapes of the painter John Nash, and is currently working on a portfolio of East Anglian photographs by the photojournalist Kurt Hutton. Christopher is also a lecturer at the UCC School of Art, Colchester.

ABOVE: *Baker's Wood, 2017.*

BELOW: *Gore Salting, 2017.*

ABOVE: *River Chelmer, off the A12*, 2017.

BELOW: *Joyce's Bay*, 2017.

ABOVE: *The house in which J. A. Baker grew up on Finchley Avenue, Chelmsford, 2017.*

BELOW: *Woodrolfe Creek beside the Tollesbury Wick Nature Reserve, 2017.*

ABOVE: *Blackwater Estuary, Tollesbury Wick Nature Reserve, 2017.*
BELOW: *River Chelmer at Sanford Mill, Chelmsford, 2017.*

Blake's Wood, Danbury, 2017.

A kill at Grace's Walk, 2017.

The J. A. Baker Archive at the Albert Sloman Library, University of Essex.

SELECT BIBLIOGRAPHY

Aerofilms Ltd, ed. *The Aerofilms Book of Aerial Photographs*. Aerofilms, 1965.

Baker, J. A. *The Peregrine: The Hill of Summer; & Diaries: The Complete Works of J. A. Baker*. London: Collins, 2011.

Blome, Richard. *Hawking: Or, Faulconry*. London: The Cresset Press, 1929.

Callahan, David. *A History of Birdwatching in 100 Objects*. A&C Black, 2014.

Campbell, Bruce, and Elizabeth Lack. *A Dictionary of Birds*. A&C Black, 2013.

Campbell, James. *A Treatise of Modern Faulconry*. Edinburgh: Balfour & Smellie, 1773.

Carlile, Bill. *Pesticide Selectivity, Health and the Environment*. Cambridge University Press, 2006.

Carlson, Douglas. *Roger Tory Peterson: A Biography*. University of Texas, 2012.

Clare, John. *The Later Poems of John Clare 1837–1864: Volume I*. Edited by Eric Robinson and David Powell. Oxford: Oxford University Press, 1984.

Cocker, Mark. *Crow Country*. Random House, 2012.

Cooper, John E. *Birds of Prey: Health and Disease*. John Wiley & Sons, 2008.

Coward, T. A. *Bird Haunts and Nature Memories*. London: Warne, 1922.

Fautley, M. P. B., and J. H. Garon. *Essex Coastline: Then and Now*. Fautley, 2004.

Foster, Charles. *Being a Beast*. Profile Books, 2016.

Hickey, Joseph James. *Peregrine Falcon Populations: Their Biology and Decline*. University of Wisconsin Press, 1969.

Jackson, Mark. *Stress in Post-War Britain*. Routledge, 2016.

Jameson, Conor Mark. *Silent Spring Revisited*. A&C Black, 2013.

Ling, T. M. 'Roffey Park Rehabilitation Centre: An Interesting Social Experiment.' *American Journal of Physical Medicine & Rehabilitation* 26, no. 4 (August 1947): 222.

Ling, T. M., J. A. Purser, and E. W. Rees. 'Incidence And Treatment Of Neurosis In Industry'. *The British Medical Journal* 2, no. 4671 (1950): 159–61.

Ling, T. M., and V. W. Wilson. 'A Survey Of Occupational Problems In A Neurosis Centre'. *The British Medical Journal* 2, no. 4783 (1952): 558–60.

Macfarlane, Robert. *Landmarks*. London: Hamish Hamilton, 2015.

Mackie, Sir Peter Jeffrey. *The Keeper's Book – Sixteenth Edition*. G. T. Foulis, 1924.

Martins, Susanna Wade, and Tom Williamson. *The Countryside of East Anglia: Changing Landscapes, 1870–1950*. Boydell & Brewer Ltd, 2008.

Mellanby, Kenneth. *Pesticides and Pollution*. Fontana New Naturalist. London: Fontana, 1969.

Moss, Stephen. *A Bird in the Bush: A Social History of Birdwatching*. London: Aurum Press Ltd, 2004.

Nicholson, E. M. *The Art of Bird-Watching: A Practical Guide to Field Observation*. London: H. F. & G. Witherby Ltd, 1931.

Ratcliffe, D. A. 'The Status of the Peregrine in Great Britain'. *Bird Study* 10, no. 2 (1963): 56–90.

Ratcliffe, Derek. *The Peregrine Falcon*. A&C Black, 2010.

Rodger, T. F. 'Health In Industry'. Edited by T. M. Ling. *The British Medical Journal* 2, no. 4896 (1954): 1090–91.

Shelley, Percy Bysshe. *The Selected Poetry and Prose of Shelley*. Wordsworth Editions, 1994.

Shrubb, Michael. *Feasting, Fowling and Feathers: A History of the Exploitation of Wild Birds*. A&C Black, 2013.

Sinclair, Iain. *Edge of the Orison: In the Traces of John Clare's 'Journey out of Essex'*. London: Hamish Hamilton, 2005.

Stamp, Sir Dudley. *Nature Conservation in Britain*. Collins, 1970.

Tooth, G. C., and Mary P. Newton. 'Leucotomy in England and Wales 1942–1954'. Reports on Public Health and Medical Subjects. Her Majesty's Stationary Office: Great Britain Ministry of Health, 1961.

Woodford, Michael. *A Manual of Falconry*. London: Black, 1960.

Additional Notes

The scale model of Chelmsford made by the Luftwaffe (mentioned in Chapter Two), found at a German airfield after the end of the Second World War, is on permanent display at Chelmsford Museum.

For details of archive material and further bibliographic information see: Saunders, H. L. A. *A Descriptive Catalogue of the J. A. Baker Archive in The Albert Sloman Library Special Collections at The University of Essex*, 2016. http://libwww.essex.ac.uk/Archives/JABAKERARCHIVE.pdf

INDEX

J. A. Baker at the Blackwater Estuary, 1950s.

ACKNOWLEDGMENTS

At the heart of this project has been the J. A. Baker Archive. Acknowledgments and thanks must be given to the Baker Estate for permission to use material from the archive and to Bernard Coe for the invaluable information that concerned it. Thanks also to the University of Essex, which maintains the Baker Archive, and to those at the Albert Sloman Library Special Collections, especially head librarian Nigel Cochrane.

Thanks are due to those who have been involved with the book's making, editing, and publication: to Adrian and Gracie, for their patience and expertise; to Jo Sweeting for her rapturous art; and to Christopher Matthews for his evocative photography that captures the essence of the Archive and landscapes with such skill.

This couldn't have been written without the encouragement, kindness and generosity of John Fanshawe and Robert Macfarlane, who should both take credit for coming up with the idea in the first place.

I am grateful also to Mark Cocker, James Canton and the others who have in their own work done so much to champion J. A. Baker and his books.

My special thanks to John Saunders.

LITTLE TOLLER WOULD LIKE TO THANK OUR SUPPORTERS:

Geoffrey Aldred, Stephen Ambrose, Mathew Ashby, Rachel Atkinson, Phil Barnard, Emma Barraclough, Peter Bear, Clare Best, Colin Brady, Richard Brett, Sue Brooks, Bob Buhr, Liz Capon, Jennie Condell, Neil Confrey, Simon Costin, Charles Coull, Geoff Cox, Gillian Darley, Ken Davies, Paul Eddy, John Edwards, Nigel Ellis, David Evans, John Fanshawe, Alan Felsenthal, Charles Forsdick, Julian Francis, Jeremy Gibbon, Jonathan Gibbs, Robert Goddard, Scott Grant, Stephen Hackett, Keith Halfacree, Lori Van Handel, Richard Harms, John Harney, Stuart Harrington, Wendy Havelock, Tom Henman, Gill Horitz, Richard Hughes, Carolyn Hupton, Nigel Ince, David Jobbins, Jane Jury, Carolyn Kelly, Paul Knights, Anthony Lacny, Brian Lavelle, Nicholas Lee, Nicky Lee, Patrick Limb, Gillian Longworth, Andy Lovell, Iain MacLeod, Seán Martin, Rachael Moravia, David Menzies, Patricia Millner, Sean Moore, Bruce Munro, Ian Murray, Tim Nunn, James Nuttall, Toby Nuttall, Declan O'Driscoll, John Leigh Pemberton, Claire and John Plass, Wendy Poole, Ahmed Razzaq, Kevin and Tyna Redpath, Andy Roberts, Mark Robinson, Nigel Roby, Holly Richards, Andrew Rickett, Jan Schubert, Richard Scorer, Paul Scully, Doug Simpson, Dickie Straker, David Suff, Andy Tickle, Gregory Thompson, R. E. Thompson, John Urpeth, Jim Urpeth, Sam Ward, Andy Whitfield, Terri White, Sibilla Whitehead, Michael Whitworth, Alan Williams, Gwynedd Williams, Howard Wix, Mark Wormald, Ken Worpole, Debbie Wythe.

THIS BOOK WOULDN'T HAVE HAPPENED WITHOUT YOU!

Wickham Bishops
Great Totham
Little Totham
Hatfield Peverel
Boreham
Langford
Heybridge
MALDON
The Hythe
Northey Island
Little Baddow
Woodham Walter
Danbury
Eves Corner
Runsell Green
Hyde Woods
Woodham Mortimer
HAZELEIGH
Bicknacre
Cock Clarks
Purleigh
Mundon Hill
East Hanningfield
Woodham Ferrers
Stow Maries
Cold Norton
Latchingdon & Snoreham
Rettendon
South Woodham Ferrers
NORTH FAMBRIDGE
RIVER CROUCH
South Fambridge
Hullbridge
Runwell
Battlesbridge
Rawreth
Shotgate
Ashingdon
Hockley
Chelmer & Blackwater Canal
Maldon A D 991